D0203049

MUSIC-MAKING IN NORTH-EAST ENGLAND DURING THE EIGHTEENTH CENTURY

For my father
Charles Edward Williams
(1909-2004)

Music-Making in North-East England during the Eighteenth Century

ROZ SOUTHEY
Roz Southey, University of Newcastle Upon Tyne, UK

ASHGATE

Published by
Ashgate Publishing Limited
Gower House
Croft Road
Aldershot
Hampshire GU11 3HR
England

Ashgate Publishing Company
Suite 420
101 Cherry Street
Burlington, VT 05401-4405
USA

Ashgate website: http://www.ashgate.com

British Library Cataloguing in Publication Data
Southey, Roz
Music-making in north-east England during the eighteenth century
1.Music – Performance – England, North East – History – 18th century 2.Musicians – England, North East – History – 18th century
I.Title
780.7'8'428'09033

Library of Congress Cataloging-in-Publication Data
Southey, Roz, 1952-
Music-making in North-east England during the eighteenth century / Roz Southey.
p. cm.
Includes bibliographical references and index.
ISBN 0-7546-5097-9 (alk. paper)
1. Music–England, North East–18th century–History and criticism.
2. Musicians–England, North East. I. Title.
ML286.3.S68 2006
780.9428'09033—dc22

2005037428

ISBN-13: 978-0-7546-5097-3
ISBN-10: 0-7546-5097-9

Printed and bound in Great Britain by Antony Rowe Ltd, Chippenham, Wiltshire.

Contents

Preface

Only relatively recently has the study of music-making in the 18th century ceased to be centred on London and turned to look out at the English provinces. The work in particular of Jennifer Burchell, in looking at Bath, Oxford, Manchester, Edinburgh and Newcastle, of Susan Wollenberg on activities in Oxford, and of David Griffiths on activities in York have started to illuminate hitherto dark corners, and have given the lie to the old idea that at that period, England had little or no music other than that provided in London for an aristocratic elite, and provided, moreover, by musicians chiefly of foreign origin. Even a casual glance at local newspapers from the period shows that England was full of musicians, teaching, composing and performing in public, and that in many centres, particularly the larger towns and cities, it was possible for a music-lover to attend concerts on a regular basis, and, moreover, to hear in concert-room, theatre and even church, the latest musical works – not very long after many of them had been premiered in London. For the first time, it is beginning to be possible to appreciate the full range of music available to music-lovers of all classes and to re-establish music as an activity not confined solely to a rich elite in the capital.

Most studies, hitherto, however, have tended to look at discrete, relatively small centres – individual towns or cities; this study aims to look at a region – the north-east of England – and to look not only at individual activities but to establish any links that may have existed between centres and between musicians. The north-east in the 18th century is notable for being the home of one of the period's best-known provincial musicians, Charles Avison, whose compositions achieved extensive dissemination and whose book, *An Essay on Musical Expression*, was widely read and commented upon. Avison's prominence at the time and the paucity of research on the other musicians of the area since, has tended to create the impression that he was almost the only musician in the area at this period and certainly the only one worthy of attention. One of the aims of this study, therefore – indeed its chief aim – has been to re-place Avison in his context, to examine the lives and works of other local musicians of the period, and to come to a more balanced view of Avison's importance and significance. In its desire to put into context Avison's writings it may be seen as a complementary volume to the work of Pierre Dubois, in *Charles Avison's Essay on Musical expression with related Writings by William Hayes and Charles Avison*, in which can be found the full texts of all Avison's writings on music.

The term *north-east* would have had little or no meaning to local residents in the 18th century, other than as a vague general geographical expression. The considerable differences in character between such places as the cathedral city of Durham, the trading ports of Newcastle and Sunderland-by-the-Sea, the barracks-dominated town of Tyneside, and rural areas such as Staindrop, Middleton-in-Teesdale and Yarm would certainly have seemed more important and significant than mere geographical juxtaposition. In the absence of any clear historical and geographical borders, therefore, the area covered by this study has been dictated to a large degree by practical considerations. Newcastle, as Charles Avison's base, and Durham, as the home of another large concentration of musicians, form a natural centre, particularly as musicians from these two centres supplied, at various times in the century, music for other towns in the region. Included are all those towns, large and small, that are generally included in the region nowadays: Sunderland, Darlington, Stockton, North and South Shields, Tynemouth and Morpeth; one of the many pleasant surprises associated with this study is the extent to which it has been possible to examine music in such smaller places, particularly towards the end of the century. However, I have not hesitated to venture further afield than the present-day north-east where appropriate information has survived: to York, another very active musical centre during the 18th century; to Hexham and Carlisle, sometimes visited by musicians from Newcastle and Durham; and even to Whitehaven, where the organist was of a north-eastern family and the organ at the parish church was installed by a north-eastern organ-builder.

The unpredictable survival of documentation has of necessity also imposed its own restrictions. A surprisingly large range of documents, frequently previously unexamined in this context, has survived. The most extensive are newspapers which published advertisements for concerts, teaching activities and musical supplies, together with the (all too occasional) reviews, and snippets of biographical information about musicians. A total of five different newspapers were printed in Newcastle from 1711, publishing material that covered activities throughout the region from Berwick in the north to Stockton in the south, from the coast across to Hexham and to the dales in the west. The most comprehensive of these, and the longest-lived, was the *Newcastle Courant*; this has been therefore used as the principal source, with other papers supplying extra or missing data. (Many advertisements appeared in identical form in several papers.)

A wide range of other sources – many of them not primarily musical – allow a surprisingly comprehensive account of activities to be reconstructed. Corporation minutes supply evidence of the appointment and conditions of service of waits and (in Newcastle) of most town organists. Assembly Room minute and account books, and theatre account books provide information on lesser-known musicians, as do parish registers – a number of musicians are known only from the recording of the baptisms or deaths of their children. Ecclesiastical records are informative about church musicians, many of whom also took part in commercial musical activities – particularly significant when dealing with the situation in Durham where the organist and choir of the Cathedral were so influential throughout the century. Diaries and letters supply some of the few first-hand accounts of local concerts and occasionally afford a glimpse of the personalities behind the names. Playbills, in both Newcastle and York, give a glimpse of the musical side of the theatre repertoire and the activities of the most mobile of 18th-century musicians, the professionals of the theatre band. In addition, the discovery of previously unknown handbills – in effect, concert programmes – for Newcastle in the last decade of the century, has allowed the reconstruction of three or four subscription series, and permits conclusions to be drawn about the format, organization and repertoire of the concerts.

Extensive and informative as these sources are, certain problems associated with them cannot be ignored. Not all sources are complete; newspaper coverage for some years in mid-century is erratic and, thanks to the spring-clean of Durham corporation records in the early 19th century, little can be said about the waits in Durham. The nature of the sources themselves can also prove restrictive. Newspapers, particularly in the early part of the century, were more concerned to keep their readers up-to-date with national and international news than to supply information about local events, which the editors may have assumed was already known. Moreover, individual musicians responded in different ways to the idea of publicity – some always advertised their activities, others never. Charles Avison, for instance, never advertised more than time, place and price of his concert series, just before the first concert in October; later in the century, his pupil, Matthias Hawdon, advertised every concert, frequently with a detailed programme. These differences may have owed more to external factors than to personality. Avison's reticence may have been owing to a conviction that his audience knew what to expect; Hawdon's expenditure to an urgent need to attract an audience to a failing enterprise. Ironically, this latter consideration ensures that the musicologist knows far more about struggling series than successful ones. Moreover, advertisements in the papers cannot be taken as a guarantee of accuracy. An advertisement does not prove that a concert took place, or that it took place in the advertised form. Occasional apologies for a cancellation owing to illness suggests that other concerts may also have been put off; some advertisements for Newcastle concerts late in the century conflict with handbills given out on the night.

Bias must also be considered when examining these records. Almost all surviving information about the Gentlemen's Subscription Concert in Durham (1752–60), for instance, emanates from the Dean of Durham Cathedral who was vehemently, and often rudely, opposed to it. The bias towards vocal music and singers means that even such distinguished instrumental visitors as Felice Giardini and Johann Peter Salomon were passed over briefly in reviews while lesser-known vocal soloists are extensively lauded. And in all cases, the compilers of individual sources were not writing for posterity and for future musicologists, and are frequently silent on just the points of most interest; corporation minutes describe the dismissal of waits without explanation, Assembly Room accounts record payments to musicians who are never named, and concert advertisements fail to list programmes or performers. Moreover, written records tend to favour the art-music (the familiarly known 'classical' music) of the middle and upper classes, rather than the music of popular performers – the fiddlers, pipers and singers – of the lower classes.

The extreme dates for this study – 1700 to 1800 – are equally arbitrarily chosen although in practice it is not possible to keep to them; inevitably some explanation of circumstances leading up to 1700 is necessary and the search for consequences of 18th-century actions reaches into the 19th century. All quotations taken from original sources have been used with their original spelling and punctuation, even when highly idiosyncratic; where additions have been necessary to clarify the sense, they are enclosed within square brackets. No attempt has been made to convert financial data – the cost of tickets, salaries and so on – into current monetary values or to suggest equivalent costs but some idea of the price of goods or the value of salaries can been obtained by bearing in mind that the average wage for a labourer in the region at the time was about one shilling a day; the master of the Grammar School in Newcastle received £150 a year from the Corporation – as a clergyman, however, he had (many) other sources of income. In the pre-decimal system of coinage, 12 pence (12d.) made one shilling (1s.); 20 shillings made a pound. A guinea was £1 1s.

Until around the late 1730s, the year began on 25 March, the first three months of the year being considered to belong to what in modern usage would be the previous year. Thus a document dated 20 February 1711 in fact belongs to 20 February 1712. In referring to dates, therefore, I have followed the customary practice of indicating, where necessary, both the written and the actual years, thus: 20 February 1711/12.

I would like to acknowledge the help and advice given by a number of scholars including Ian Biddle, Brian Crosby, Eric Cross, Matthew Gardner, David Griffiths, Simon McVeigh, Magnus Williamson and Susan Wollenberg. In addition, staff at a number of libraries and archives have been unfailingly helpful, amongst them staff at the Central Library, Carlisle; the Central Library, Newcastle upon Tyne; Durham Record Office; the Literary and Philosophical Society, Newcastle upon Tyne; Northumbria Record Office; Tyne and Wear Archives; and York Record Office. The tea and home-made scones at the last were a particularly welcome treat.

And finally my thanks to all my family for their help and encouragement over the years, to my parents, my sisters and brother-in-law, and particularly to my husband, Chris, who has listened to many of the same stories again and again without complaint.

List of Abbreviations

ARA	Accounts of the Assembly Rooms, York
ARM	Minutes of the Assembly Rooms, York
CA	Chapter Archives, Durham Cathedral
CAN	Chamberlains' Accounts, Newcastle Corporation
CAY	Chamberlain's Accounts, York Corporation
CCN	Common Council Minutes, Newcastle Corporation
CP	*Cumberland Pacquet*
DCAB	Dean and Chapter Act Books, Durham Cathedral
DCTA	Treasurer's Account Books, Durham Cathedral
DRO	Durham Record Office
LI	*Leeds Intelligencer*
ML	*Music and Letters*
MT	*Musical Times*
MQ	*Musical Quarterly*
NA	*Newcastle Advertiser*
NARA	Accounts of the Assembly Rooms, Newcastle
NC	*Newcastle Courant*
NCh	*Newcastle Chronicle*
NG	*Newcastle Gazette*
NI	*Newcastle Intelligencer*
NJ	*Newcastle Journal*
NRO	Northumbria Record Office
YC	*York Courant*
YCh	*York Chronicle*
YHB	House Books of York Corporation
YMS	York Musical Society
YRO	York Record Office

Introduction

> Public Music is of Public Utility, not only as it promotes several valuable Branches of Trade, by the frequent Resort of the genteeler People, but as it also keeps alive, and improves the social and benevolent Affections, by the general Intercourse of Friends and Acquaintance, which it occasions.
>
> Charles Avison[1]

The musical history of the north-east in the 18th century has generally been associated with one man – the composer and writer Charles Avison. Much has been written about his works and a little about his life; almost nothing, however, has been done to place him in his historical and social context, or to examine the lives of other musicians working with and around him. As Donne said, no man is an island. It is impossible to assess Avison's work, influence and significance without taking into account the circumstances in which he worked as well as the people who influenced him and who in turn were influenced by him. Was he typical of north-eastern musicians of the day? If he was, in what did that significance subsist?

Avison's life and work were balanced between, on the one hand, his own principles and aesthetic values, cultured in the early years of the century under the influence of Italian composers such as Corelli and Avison's own teacher, Geminiani, and, on the other hand, the prosaic necessity of earning a living in the new commercial circumstances that faced almost all British musicians at this time. Since 1672, a new breed of musician had existed in England; the church and the state – the old principal employers of musicians – had suffered in the religious and political turmoil of the 17th century and no longer had the money to be effective supporters of the arts. The old system of patronage lingered on the continent, most famously exemplified in Haydn's long employment in the Esterházy family, but in England, Handel was more typical of the new breed – relying on his skills as an entrepreneur and promoter, marketing his own music and ensuring that he was aware of fluctuations in public taste, or suffering if he was not. This was the situation in which Avison and other musicians in the north-east found themselves; although many held salaried posts as organists or waits paid by the local corporations, this income was not sufficient to provide a living and other means of support had to be found. In effect, Avison and his contemporaries in the region were freelances, tapping into a multiplicity of income streams.

Such musicians were, to a large extent, at the mercy of their audiences, needing to produce what was in demand – music as a craft rather than as an art. One of the factors that makes Avison significant is his struggle to do just that and yet to retain his musical principles. His principles, for instance, refused to allow him to participate in the establishment of garden concerts in Newcastle – he had previously thrown scorn on the poor quality of music produced at this type of concert – but he clearly saw a demand for music at that time of year and attempted to produce his own series of summer concerts with music he considered more meritorious. Unfortunately, audiences could be fickle. As promoters of the first concerts in London (in the late 17th century) had discovered (and exploited), concert-going was, or could be, closely linked with fashion; fashion demands novelty and change, and constant new attractions. And Avison had, in a sense, two audiences: the generality of music-lovers who hoped for a pleasurable evening's entertainment or some moderate skill in playing harp or harpsichord to show off accomplishments and beguile an idle hour, and the so-called Gentlemen Amateurs, some of whom made serious study of the history and theory of music, and who debated the relative merits and demerits of such issues as simplicity, beauty, virtuosity, expression, and the relationship of music and texts. It was for these latter men (and a very few women) that Avison wrote his *Essay on Musical Expression* – an uneasy attempt to appeal to theorists, aestheticians and performers.

The provinces have generally been seen as remote from the centre – the metropolis of London – constantly behind the times, taking their cue from the capital but in arrears, and never quite attaining the same gloss and sophistication. While there is some truth in this, the real picture is more complex. Even before the improvements in roads and transport of the later 18th century, frequent contact existed between the north-east and the capital. New music, famous soloists and the best productions came north, and swiftly; the latest London hit of 1728, *The Beggar's Opera*, was performed in Newcastle by two separate companies within four months of its London premiere. The north-east was fortunate to be on the main road north from London to Edinburgh – both cities with thriving musical lives – and many famous musicians were only too glad to stop off *en route* to hold concerts and recoup travelling expenses. Nor was the movement one way. Charles Avison spent at least one year of his life in London during his early 20s but he was by no means unusual; it was commonplace for any musician with pretensions to quality to travel south in search of 'improvement' – at Durham Cathedral, for instance, the Dean and Chapter funded such trips for singing men by continuing to pay salaries while singers were away. Some of these musicians stayed in the capital but the majority returned with the latest musical developments and fashions. Throughout his life, Avison was in touch with friends in London; his music and his book were published there and both were well-known throughout England. Other factors provided links with the rest of the country. Prebendaries of Durham Cathedral were pluralists, based generally in the south of England, who brought with them on their brief visits north musical tastes and standards based on the high quality performances they heard in London; the Dean and Chapter trawled southern cathedrals for the best singers. Other musicians travelled considerable distances in search of jobs such as organists' posts and were prepared to travel extensively, once settled, to give concerts and to teach. The north-east was not isolated nor ignorant of trends elsewhere. Indeed, newspapers and diaries show a certain amount of snobbish determination to prove how up-to-date and fashionable the area could be.

Nor was the area isolated from the effects of national and international affairs. War, inflation, depression and difficulties in trade all affected the region and its cultural life, not merely in the expected ways of increasing or decreasing the popularity of public concerts, theatrical events and the like, but also in affecting the kind of music played and composed: patriotic and nationalistic music for instance. But the region was not homogeneous; its different centres had different characters which displayed themselves in their musical activities. Durham was a city of clerics and colliers, and the former were deeply conservative in character, the prebendaries in many cases being scions of noble families. Their passion was for Corelli and Geminiani and, above all, for Handel, whose oratorio texts were capable of so many nationalistic constructions. Handel was never so popular in the commercial setting of Newcastle; in concerts there the demand was constantly for *new* music.

Music therefore – be it in concerts, in theatre or circus, in church or at the impromptu *ad hoc* meetings of the poorer people – cannot stand alone; it cannot be understood without taking into account political, economic, religious and commercial factors. Nor can its history in one century be understood merely by looking at the life and work of one man, however eminent in his time. Music was, and is, infinitely capable of multiple interpretations, of meaning all things to all men, and different things to different men. Avison and his friends, the Gentlemen Amateurs, saw it as an art that could be appreciated by the exercise of good taste, and a science, that was susceptible to rules and accessible to rational understanding. For many others, and for some of the Gentlemen Amateurs too, it was also – or even merely – an entertainment, part of the social scene and a pleasant way of passing time in the company of family or friends, at a public concert or in the privacy of the home. Music could be seen as a tool of social regulation – a way to manipulate sentiment, to be praised as it roused the finer emotions and condemned as it excited the grosser; this was considered of particular relevance to music used as an aid to piety – nothing caused more ire than an organist who over-elaborated music in church rather than subordinating it to devotion. In this context, oratorio performances raised particular controversy: for their theatrical elements, for their audiences' tendency to treat them merely as social occasions and for the lack of reverence with which they were approached. What was to be made of the pleasure gardens which some people (Avison amongst them) considered pandered to the lowest musical tastes? And how tolerable were the irregular lives and uncertain morals of such itinerants as fiddlers and ballad singers?

All these feelings and opinions were exhibited to some extent in the north-east during the 18th century. The meanings given to music, and the emphasis placed on each meaning, differed according to social class, to status, to political circumstances and religious affiliations. Moreover, no neat dividing lines can be drawn; it was perfectly possible, for instance, to see a concert as a tribute to high art and as an entertainment at the same time, to view oratorio as both entertainment and devotion. It is possible, however, to explore these meanings, and the reaction of a range of people to music, in a region where many different kinds of musical activity thrived throughout the century and where a wide range of documentation survives.

Music as entertainment

In 1735, when twelve gentlemen got together to set up a series of concerts in Newcastle, they were said to have the sole object of 'the Entertainment of the Town'.[2] The entertainment, that is, of the better-off portion of the town; the price of 2s. 6d. a night or 10s. 6d. for a full season was always going to exclude large sections of poorer society. This kind of entertainment was for those with the time and money to enjoy it, and those were people who liked to keep up-to-date with fashion. It had always been thus; forty years earlier, the elite of the aristocracy in London had enthusiastically journeyed to Clerkenwell to see and be seen at Thomas Britton's concerts there. And fashion was associated with ephemerality, with all things new, with novelty, change and spectacle. Throughout the century, audiences tended to like performances of which serious musicians and music-lovers like Charles Avison and the vicar of Newcastle, John Brown, tended to be contemptuous or at least scornful. They liked child prodigies who had to sit on their mothers' laps to plonk out simple tunes. They liked 'nimble-finger'd' virtuoso soloists, making 'extravagant Demands for [their] Dexterity that way'.[3] If they were foreigners so much the better; fashion first exalted Italian musicians, then German – British players were never so much in demand. Audiences liked to hear Signor Rossignol warbling bird noises and 'singing' a violin concerto. They liked large-scale performances that made a lot of noise, and turned out for concerts that featured their old favourites or which appealed to their patriotism.

Musicians hoping to promote a profitable entertainment ignored the fashion factor at their peril. It was essential to be acutely aware of what audiences did or did not want; for those who were not alert, or who were out of sympathy with their audiences, bankruptcy could await. Mathias Hawdon, organist of St. Nicholas in Newcastle in the late 1770s and early 1780s, tried to promote the music of Handel's oratorios in the town at a time when elsewhere, in Yorkshire and Durham, it was a surefire winner. Audience reaction in Newcastle was tepid and Hawdon went bankrupt. Now if he had only hired nationally- or internationally-known singers, that might have been different, as the 1791 Musical Festival proved: Madame Mara, Anna Maria Crouch and Michael Kelly – those were performances to turn out for.

And fashion could be fickle. Music as an entertainment was always a vulnerable enterprise. A novelty that was lauded to the heavens one day had inevitably to give way to a new attraction the next, as even Mozart discovered in London. Signor Rossignol, so fated in the 1770s, died in penury in Whitby in 1805.[4] External factors too could play a decisive part. Other entertainments could take precedence; in York in 1749, for instance, the poor support for the subscription series was blamed on a trademen's Assembly that had been newly set up.[5] Inflation, or periods of economic hardship could make people reluctant to spend; national and international affairs could distract would-be audiences. In 1803, a Musical Festival in York was abandoned because its potential audience felt it inappropriate in the face of mounting tension with France; on the other hand, in other circumstances, an appeal to nationalism or patriotism could pull in a large crowd, as Newcastle musicians found out at much the same time.[6]

Entertainment was always a slightly disreputable concept. In a letter written to the *Newcastle Courant* in 1758, Avison was at pains to stress 'the Advantages accruing to Society from the public Use of Music' as if entertainment for entertainment's sake was faintly distasteful.[7] 'Marcellinus', one of Avison's supporters, felt obliged to describe concerts as '*useful* entertainments' [my italics] and the promoter of concerts at Newcastle's Spring Gardens in the 1760s pointed out that they were 'seasonable and rational entertainments'.[8] The result was a division between two types of concerts (although overgeneralizations should not be made and the two types of concerts were often in the hands of the same musicians). Some concerts – benefits and mid-year concerts – stressed the entertainment angle; they aimed for the popular element, trying to attract people who rarely went to concerts and who wanted a light-hearted end to a day spent at the Races or gossiping over the latest cases at the Assizes. The winter subscription series, on the other hand, was more attractive to the serious music lover, who not only wanted to hear good music but also to play in it. In Durham and Newcastle in the first half of the century, wealthy gentlemen set up concert series; although these gentlemen withdrew from active organization very early in Newcastle, they again took over towards the end of the century – throughout the period, they played in the concerts even when professional musicians had the running of them. Balls were often a measure of the intent of a concert; these were 'for the ladies' and had little place at a serious event.[9] Only rarely were subscription concerts followed by a ball – usually after the first or last concert and perhaps at Christmas or New Year or some other significant occasion; almost all benefits towards the end of the century, on the contrary, were followed by a ball.

Not all concerts were open to the public; the Newcastle, Durham and Sunderland Musical Societies seem to have met privately for most of the century and elsewhere diaries record private concerts where commercial considerations were not allowed to intrude. The prebendaries at Durham Cathedral were frequent holders of such concerts, meeting at each other's houses in the College behind the cathedral, or occasionally being more adventurous and holding outdoor concerts. Some of these latter were spectacular enough to be reported in the local press but most were never recorded – a fate that also befell many of the private balls held in the region. Yet, in the Newcastle area at least, these latter were frequent enough to prompt professional musicians to form a Country Dance Band to play at such entertainments. For those willing or eager to dance in public, there were the regular winter dancing assemblies and dancing masters to teach the steps; for those lower down the social scale, such entertainments were even more public and *al fresco*: dancing in the park, or on the lawns of local landowners to celebrate the birth of an heir, or in the streets to mark the withdrawal of the press-gang. The performers at these latter entertainments were the waits, or pipers employed by rich landlords such as the Duke of Northumberland, or wandering fiddlers and ballad singers. For some people, like the engraver, Thomas Bewick, these remained the representatives of the real music of the area, the true musical voice of the north-east. Wealthier men, like Bewick, or the Sharps – archdeacons of Northumberland and prebendaries at Durham Cathedral – appropriated this music, learning how to play the local pipes and taking it out of its natural setting, which they professed to admire, into their drawing rooms.

Elsewhere, for those local citizens with a little money, rather than nothing at all or a great deal, music could be heard at the Spring Gardens (one shilling admission to the gardens and music, with an extra charge for refreshments), at the theatre or even at the circus (cheapest seats one shilling in each case). The theatre was the only place to hear large-scale musical works – ballad operas, and pantomimes – as well as popular and engaging actresses singing folk-songs and the hits from the latest London successes; the circus offered such musical delights as a man playing a violin while standing bareback on two galloping horses. A very long way from Avison's idea of 'the public use of music' as decorous and useful.

Music as art or science

The Gentleman Amateur – the wealthy man with time and money enough to buy a musical instrument and to play on it, or to attend musical events and patronize the musicians – was for many writers the epitome of the true music-lover. William Hayes of Oxford suggested that only such men could bring true impartiality to the study of music; a professional musician must always be presumed to be biased by commercial considerations. The gentlemen, and a few ladies, belonged to the nobility and gentry, to the clergy and professions and – stretching a point perhaps – to the ranks of the wealthier tradesmen. For some of these, music was merely a pleasant diversion. They played musical instruments – though excellence was generally to be avoided as it suggested sustained hard work and effort which was inappropriate to their status as gentlemen; they enjoyed private and even public performance as long as their names were not proclaimed publicly in advertisements or reviews. They hired local musicians to teach their children, encouraging their daughters to practise genteel accomplishments, at least until their marriages. They met with other gentlemen of similar tastes, in Musical Societies and Catch Clubs, combining the enjoyment of music with a little social intercourse out of the reach of business or family distractions. From time to time, they indulged in extravagant gestures – the building of a new theatre in their houses, the private staging of a popular opera in which family members took leading roles, a concert in boats on the river.

But diversion was not the only aim of the musical dilettante. Musical activity, the gentlemen believed, could be an instrument for social good. Charles Avison's letter to the *Newcastle Journal* in November 1758 stressed the social benefits of music; it 'promotes several valuable Branches of Trade' (by encouraging visitors to spend their money in the town); it 'keeps alive, and improves the social and benevolent Affections, by the general Intercourse of Friends and Acquaintances, which it occasions'; it improved the reputation of the town with visitors, by impressing them with 'the Appearance, the Music, the Place, and the Decorum of the Whole'.[10] Avison's patrons seem to have concurred; they financed subscription series as a means of bringing respectable entertainments to the locality and, on a more personal level, they dispensed patronage to the needy – a deserving musician, a sick and needy singer, the widow and children of a deceased performer. They promoted and supported charity concerts particularly in time of war, although the north-east was notable for the infrequency of such concerts compared to other regions. Moreover, music could be regarded as a stalwart supporter of the state; one of the rationales behind the movement for ancient music and the Handel Commemorations in the last quarter of the 18th century was to re-establish the natural order of society, in which the monarchy and aristocracy were the backbone of the country, its true leaders, if only in the matter of musical taste. In the face of the dangerous expression of egalitarian views, as epitomized by that arch-rebel, Thomas Paine, and by the American and French Revolutions, men and women of a conservative cast flocked to support such movements, amongst them, the prebendaries of Durham Cathedral, almost all cadets of noble families, anxious for their position, the survival of their institutions and of society as they perceived it should be. Some prebendaries – the Dolbens, the Sharps – had been supporters of ancient music since the establishment of the Academy of Ancient Music in the 1720s and their tastes found expression in the performance of the orderly music of Corelli and Geminiani in private concerts, the music of Handel in public concerts, and the anthems of Palestrina, Byrd, Croft and Wise in cathedral services.

Music could be viewed, too, as a moral instrument, instructing modern society in 'manners' and the correct values of the virtuous to set against the vain, immoral attractions of 'amusement' and frivolity. John Brown, vicar of Newcastle, produced in 1763 a learned book – *A Dissertation on the Rise, Union, and Power, the Progressions, Separations, and Corruptions of Poetry and Music* – which looked back to an idyllic, if mythical, golden age when music and poetry were locked fast together in the service of a high moral purpose. Brown's version of the origins of music was designed to tie it inextricably with the teaching of moral precepts; he condemned instrumental music because it could not teach these precepts, having no words; he dismissed opera and even oratorio as mere 'amusements' (although he managed to separate the genius Handel from the music he composed, praising the one and condemning the other). How far Brown's views were merely a product of his own moral stance and his depressive and jaundiced nature, or to what extent his views were shared by local gentlemen is not clear, but, after his death in 1766, the book was sufficiently in demand to be reprinted in an altered format with much of the specialized musical material removed for those who had complained they did not understand it.

But Brown was certainly representative of north-eastern gentlemen amateurs in one sense at least; he believed music to be a worthy subject for serious consideration and learned discussion. Well-educated gentlemen in the north-east, friends of Brown and patrons of Avison, discussed what Pliny and Horace had to say about the practice and purpose of music, considered the origins of music, debated whether it was an art or a science, considered the relative merits of vocal and instrumental music, examined the latest ideas on imitation and aesthetics filtering in from the continent and debated whether it was possible to revive the old Greek values of simplicity and morality. And they encouraged Charles Avison to put many of his, and their, ideas into print, to produce *An Essay on Musical Expression*, published in London in 1752, a book which was the first work in

English to attempt an assessment of the aesthetic basis of music. But it is an oddly ambivalent book. Avison's written views were forward-looking and progressive; he described music as an aesthetic art whose virtues could only be assessed by good taste and good judgement. Yet in his private and performing lives, he admired the Baroque music of his teacher Geminiani and *his* teacher, Corelli, and extolled the virtues of Jean-Philippe Rameau, the advocate of music as a science based on natural laws. Interestingly, the one known portrait of Avison, painted around 1751, depicts a figure much more Romantic in style than Baroque; in place of the direct gaze of the well-known portraits of men like Handel, Avison glances off to his left as if he is contemplating both the future and some visionary distance. His clothing is loose with a hint of Byronic carelessness, a sheet of music in his hand emphasizing his musical credentials. Not the man of business, but the man of vision, although how much the pose was the idea of the painter or whether it was on the insistence of the subject cannot be known.

Music as an aid to piety

An anonymous correspondent to the *Newcastle Courant* in October 1792 was of no doubt of the value of music in worship:

> Every organ erected in one of our churches, is a new encouragement to piety, – a new incentive to a purity and fervour of devotion. We are all acquainted with the powerful, the astonishing effects of music; if that divine art is too frequently, and too successfully prostituted to our meaner feelings, let it not be forgotten, that with a fine magic, it awakens and invigorates our noblest sentiments and passions: – it inspires the eloquence of the patriot, and accelerates the *military* defender of his country to the glorious alternative of victory or death. But to none of the best energies of the human mind, to none of our sublimest pursuits, it is more favourable than to RELIGION.
>
> When our church music is well chosen, and well performed, and when it is addressed to souls, who are worthy of that selection and performance, it most forcibly contributes to disengage our thoughts and affections from earth, – to fix them on celestial objects; – to give us, by anticipation, in *some* degree, the enjoyment of heaven. Without music, therefore, we cannot completely obey *one* charming precept in the sacred writings; – we cannot *worship the LORD in the beauty of holiness.*[11]

This was not necessarily a universal belief; some ministers of churches like the Unitarians, for instance, were inclined to think music in church a distraction that diverted attention from the words of the scriptures. In the Anglican Church, however, music was firmly established, from the sung services of the cathedrals to the metrical psalms of the parish churches. Local dignitaries and gentry gave organs to their parish churches; organists and parish clerks bought the new psalm books, set up choirs, and taught new anthems to their congregations; wandering psalm teachers instructed charity and Sunday school children in new tunes. Old practices were debated and discarded; new practices sometimes proved equally contentious.

As a church organist for most of his adult working life, it is hardly surprising that Avison should wholeheartedly support the use of music in worship. He would have agreed with the *Courant*'s anonymous correspondent, taking for granted music's ability to transport the worshipper to 'the regions of Bliss, in an Extacy of divine Praise'.[12] And more important than the fact that music *could* cause religious ecstasy was Avison's belief that indeed it *should*; he stated very firmly of church music that 'Devotion is the original and proper end of it' and that it should act by 'calmly relieving and lifting up the Heart'.[13] For Avison, the only matter of contention was the form that such music should take. He and John Brown condemned many of the practices current in cathedrals and parish churches: they disliked the conservative cast of music in the cathedrals, with its frequent emphasis on the precise rules of counterpoint and they dismissed the ornate settings of church music, believing that the use of too many parts and of complex harmonies obscured the texts and distracted the listener from the meaning of the scriptures. They rejected too the many abuses that had crept into the performance of metrical psalms in parish churches – the 'old way of singing' as it was known.

John Brown turned his critical eye not only on English practices but also on those abroad – predictably, his comments were almost entirely adverse, particularly where Catholic countries were concerned. In Italy, the use of motets had produced 'wild and incoherent Compositions', principally because the words had been subordinated to the music; moreover, as the words were in Latin, they were 'unintelligible to the greatest Part of those that hear them'.[14] These motets, he claimed, were sung by wandering bands of castrati of bad character and unpleasant personal appearance, whose behaviour encouraged gossip about their lives and personal merits, rather than a contemplation of sacred matters.[15] In France, the situation was a little better as the church there had been in dialogue with Protestant Churches and therefore had a better acquaintance with the sacred Scriptures. (The use of Latin texts in France, Brown suggested with magnificent inconsistency, was of merit as it meant that no-one had to listen to the French language which was, according to Brown, 'hoarse, ill-accented, or of ambiguous Accent, void of Harmony and Variety, and incurably discordant'.)[16] In a rare complimentary moment, Brown spoke well of the gravity of the French style of church music, attributing it to the existence of settled and permanent choirs, which were in turn, of course, owing to Protestant influence.

Brown and Avison agreed that there should be a clear division between the type of music suitable for church and that used elsewhere. Avison wrote that 'a well wrought *Allegro*, or any other quick Movement for the Church, cannot, with Propriety, be adapted to theatrical purposes; nor can the *Adagio* of this latter kind, strictly speaking, be introduced into the former'.[17] He distinguished between secular and sacred music not by the tempi, key signatures or time signature, but by the '*Manner* and *Expression*, which stamps the real character of the Piece'. Brown condemned Italian church music precisely because of this confusion of manner with secular music; it was 'infected with the same Puerility of Stile with their Opera Airs'.[18]

Those composers of whom Brown and Avison approved – chiefly Italian composers – understood this separation of sacred and secular, and produced work which could be recommended to the English church musician. Both men admired Palestrina, Brown speaking of his 'Pieces of majestic Gravity', Avison calling him a 'great' composer and 'the Father of Harmony'.[19] (Brown also credited him with persuading the Pope to institute reforms in church music.) Palestrina's music was enjoying renewed popularity in English cathedrals, thanks to the adaptations of Dean Aldrich of Oxford, and several of the Palestrina/Aldrich anthems were in the repertoire of Durham Cathedral choir. Both Avison and Brown also approved of Carissimi, Avison awarding him a status only one place below that of Palestrina. But their greatest respect was reserved for Benedetto Marcello, principally known in England for his settings of psalms. Brown spoke of Marcello in compliments all the more startling because of his usual jaundiced tones; the psalms were 'sublime, tender, graceful, or joyous' and 'clearly excel the vocal Compositions of all his Countrymen, in Variety, Simplicity, and Truth'.[20] Avison was equally enthusiastic: 'like the divine Subject he works upon, he is generally either grand, beautiful, or pathetic; [i.e. full of pathos] and so perfectly free from everything that is low and common, that the judicious hearer is charmed with an endless Variety of new and pleasing Modulation; together with a Design and Expression so finely adapted, that the Sense and Harmony do everywhere coincide'.[21]

So taken was Avison with these works that, in the second edition of his *Essay,* he advertised (at the back of the book) his intention to arrange the psalms for use in the English church, setting the music to an English translation of the words. This project was for Avison in substantial part an exercise in aesthetics, a kind of addendum to the *Essay*, in that it would give concrete examples of the various styles of music – the sublime, the serene, the pastoral, the sorrowful and so on – in practice. 'SEVERAL Specimens in each of these Stiles will be given to shew the Composer's superior Talents in his different Application of expressing the same Passion'.[22] In the end, he seems only to have set one of the psalms, for George III's coronation in 1761, and the project was taken up by his friend John Garth, who produced eight volumes of the psalms between 1757 and 1765. Avison may have had a hand in setting some of the psalms; he wrote a preface in which he referred to the 'authors' in the plural and to '*their* own weak Abilities' [my italics], but Garth's name alone appeared on the title pages of the volumes.

An exercise in aesthetics the setting of Marcello's Psalms may have originally been, but Avison clearly also had a practical purpose, in producing music suitable for worship according to his own, and Brown's, principles. He wrote in the preface of giving precedence to the text, by providing vernacular settings, by keeping the number of parts to a minimum and by removing trivialities from the music. He saw the finished psalms as 'happily calculated for the real Solemnity [of] the *Cathedral Service*', and the subscribers' list for the finished work suggests that others thought so too – the volumes were bought by organists, choirs and functionaries in Durham, Ripon, Winchester, Carlisle, King's College, Cambridge, and Worcester. This appeal to cathedral musicians was important, for Avison saw the cathedral organist as the necessary prime mover in the reform of church music. Unfortunately, his own relations with the only cathedral organist in the area – James Hesletine of Durham – were bad at this period, and it is likely that Hesletine neither shared Avison's views nor was interested in being influenced by him; the music at Durham Cathedral remained backward-looking throughout the century.

But Avison also perceived the Psalms as being 'of singular Use to the *Organists* of *Parochial Churches*'. Many of these, Avison claimed, 'in various Parts of *England* as well as in the Capital, seem rising into Character, and no Doubt with their Abilities, a due Attention to the Style and Harmony of *Marcello* may produce a finer Taste and Method both in their Compositions and *extempore* Performances'.[23] He may have been correct – several organists at such churches in Whitehaven, London, Manchester and Nottingham also subscribed to the Psalms – but it would have been a rare parish church in the north-east with the resources to sing the Marcello Psalms, possibly only Avison and Brown's own St Nicholas in Newcastle. For many parish churches, particularly in country areas, the metrical psalm was the only music heard in service and here too Avison attempted to put principle into practice by producing a small set of psalm tunes to accompany an edition of Isaac Watt's psalms published at the end of the 1750s. In the absence of action from Hesletine at Durham, Avison was attempting to lead the way in what he considered to be a necessary reform of church music.

Music as a spur to nationalism

In early December 1739, Avison performed, in one of his subscription concerts, extracts from Handel's *Saul* and *Acis and Galatea* as well as martial airs by Purcell – 'To Arms' and 'Britons strike home'. The audience was near-ecstatic:

> The Gentlemen and Ladies join'd the Chorus's at the end of each Song; all present saluted the Performers with loud Peals of Glee, acknowledging a general Satisfaction. … The Company stood up all together, and an universal Vivacity was observ'd to fire the whole audience.[24]

Britain spent over half of the 18th century at war with various foreign states, from the War of the Spanish Succession at the beginning of the century, to the French Revolutionary Wars at the end. Occasionally, the wars came nearer home, with two Jacobite rebellions setting one part of the island against the rest; the 1745 rebellion was the only occasion on which the noise of battle came to the north-east, and reports of the arrival of the Jacobite armies in the local papers were remarkably cool although the atmosphere in the area must surely have been otherwise. Certainly, entertainments must have been of only minor interest to north-easterners at the time; Avison's winter subscription series was clearly disrupted, possibly to a large extent – for the only time during his management of the concerts he extended the season with an extra mini-series in the spring, possibly to recoup money lost in the disruption.[25]

Other conflicts must have seemed much more distant, manifested principally in the disruption to local trade, or in the news of bereavements, by announcements of collections for supplies to the army or for charity to the widows and orphans of fighting men, and in the news of the comings and goings of regiments quartered locally. But north-easterners did not remain ignorant of events; local papers such as the *Newcastle Courant* and *Newcastle Journal* carried at least a page and a half of national and international news, and any major military or naval engagements provoked extra coverage accompanied by first-hand accounts of the events and by charts or maps; these newspapers, which gained extra circulation from copies kept in the coffee-houses, ensured that at least the middle and upper classes could have extensive knowledge of what was going on, albeit at some days' or weeks' remove.

Inevitably, in time of war, concert promoters appealed to the patriotism of their audiences – sanctioned perhaps by Avison's counsel that 'by the Musician's Art, we are often carried into the Fury of a Battle'. References to current events, including music with nationalistic connections or a piece written especially for the occasion or, at the very least, a rendition of 'God save the King', might show that the promoter's heart was in the right place (though the fact that promoters gained commercial advantage from the performance of such music need not cast doubt on the sincerity of their own patriotic feelings). Significant royal or political anniversaries were commonly marked with concerts – coronations, anniversaries of coronations, royal birthdays, the anniversary of the Glorious Revolution. In times of national emergency – during the illnesses of George III or on outbreak of war – nationalistic sentiments showed themselves in a rash of performances of 'God save the King' in a variety of contexts – in church, in civic procession, in the theatre, at celebrations, in midnight forays to burn the effigy of Thomas Paine. Military bands marching into the area were eagerly admired and commented upon in newspapers; they were in demand to play interval music at the theatre and to accompany Freemasons' parades. During the French Revolutionary Wars, a strong link between nationalism and music saved music-making in Newcastle from the decline experienced elsewhere; the establishment of a military band attached to the Volunteer Regiment proved a hugely popular nationalistic gesture and a commercial lifesaver for many a local musician.

How then to explain, amongst all this patriotism and xenophobia, the popularity for all things musically foreign? From the popularity of the Italians in the first half of the century, to that of the Germans at the end, the foreign musician in England was almost always at an advantage over the native-born; in its enthusiasm for Italian performers, the York subscription series bankrupted itself hiring the latest Italian performers in the 1740s. This enthusiasm for foreign performers extended itself to foreign music; with the exception of music composed by local musicians, the majority of instrumental works performed in turn-of-the-century subscription series was by foreign composers, though British parochialism showed itself in the choice of vocal music – here audiences and organizers alike preferred British composers, whose words they could understand. Ultimately, perhaps, fashion and novelty – always a preoccupation of the concert-going public in Newcastle at least – won out over nationalism; audiences turned out for the 1791 Newcastle Musical Festival not for Handel's music, riddled as it was with nationalistic associations, but for the big name performers. It was otherwise in Durham where a conservative-minded prebendal body – the bulk of the concert-going public in the city – clung onto Handel's music as a staple of the subscription series, and supported the cause of ancient music with its nationalistic associations and its support of the aristocracy and monarchy. Despite the frequent appearances of the violinist Felice Giardini and his friend, Giovanni Battista Noferi, who played in mid-year concerts in Durham for many years, the concert-going public in Durham seems never to have been as taken with foreign performers in the same way as audiences in York and Newcastle.

Music as a means of making a living

The political turbulence of the mid-17th century cut musicians adrift from their traditional sources of income – church and state. Although the damage caused during the Commonwealth to the cathedral establishments was slowly repaired, and although Charles II expanded again the musical institutions of the court following his restoration in 1660, the security of the old system of patronage was gone for ever. A new spirit of commercialization entered musical life with John Banister's establishment of concerts at his home in White Fryars, set up because Charles employed but did not pay; Banister's idea of charging for admission not only guaranteed musicians an income for their performance on the day, but opened music to a wider section of society and brought the pressures of market forces to the profession. In future, the musician who had been bound only to the tastes of a single patron would need to be alert to a host of factors – the likes and dislikes of a diverse audience or audiences, fluctuations of taste and fashion, shifting political allegiances, variations in the amount of money available and the audiences' choice on what to spend that money. The xenophobia of audiences was a factor in Handel's decision to abandon Italian opera for oratorio; Gay achieved success with political satire, and his many imitators with variations on Gay's success. And, on a smaller scale, in the provinces, musicians were thrown upon their own judgement and market knowledge. Thomas Wright of Newcastle thrived in the 1780s and 1790s on an acute awareness of the tastes of his audiences, offering first large-scale extravagant novelty concerts, with unprecedently large numbers of performers and the latest music from London, and, later, exploiting the nationalistic sentiments aroused by the French Revolutionary Wars. On the contrary, Matthias Hawdon, organist of St Nicholas's Church in Newcastle in the late 1770s and 1780s, misjudged his audiences constantly, charging too high fees, trying to economize but offending his subscribers thereby, promoting extensively the music of Handel to an audience that had only a passing interest in it.

In this new freelance world, success could depend on having a variety of sources of income, perhaps based on a post with a small but regular salary. Teaching, performing, composition and publication could all play a part, though the potential for disaster was always there, even for the best organized and hard working of musicians. For some, financial necessity was either ever-present or ever-threatening; nevertheless, it was possible to be successful, through ability and hard work, and to achieve that desirable objective of being able to describe oneself as a 'gentleman' – one who lived on invested income rather than needing to work for a living. Some might even, like Edward Meredith of Durham Cathedral, achieve 'stardom', although it was the success of a large fish in a small pond;

Meredith's repeated attempts to establish himself in London met with failure. And no matter that Charles Avison, John Garth and Thomas Ebdon of Durham dined with their pupils – there were dozens of others whose relations with their patrons were those of suppliance, visiting houses to flatter the occupants into buying tickets for benefits, or inserting carefully-worded advertisements of grateful thanks into newspapers after a concert. Musicians were, after all (in the view of their patrons) only another kind of tradesman.

II

Charles Avison was baptized on 16 February 1708/09 at St John's Church in Newcastle. Newcastle was at the time a town of around 16,000 inhabitants and was growing rapidly, although its growth was not as pronounced as that of other towns and cities throughout England; by 1801 it had around 33,000 inhabitants, including a large population of Scottish immigrants. Its prosperity was built on coal mining and shipping, and on other industries such as glassworks, but it paid for its prosperity with severe pollution; both Celia Fiennes and Daniel Defoe (visiting the town in 1698 and 1720 respectively) commented on the smell of sulphur and on the smoke both from the coal mines and from the salt works at North Shields. But the coal, and the wealth it generated, also stimulated a demand for services, for banking, shops and markets, and for legal services such as lawyers and assize courts. The provision of those services encouraged an influx of gentry and wealthy landowners from the surrounding countryside, and that in turn created a demand for leisure activities to help beguile a stay in town. Fiennes and Defoe commented on the fine buildings and bridges of Newcastle, on the good shops and markets, the walks and gardens, the Assembly Rooms and even the entertaining spectacle of dissected bodies on show at the Barber Surgeon's Hall. Over the course of the century, better streets, street lighting and other facilities further improved the attractiveness of the town. Travelling theatre companies were quick to take advantage of the opportunities, and local and travelling musicians put on concerts at busy times of year, such as Race and Assize Weeks. The situation was ripe for a competent musician and businessman to exploit.

Charles's father, Richard, probably originated in Yorkshire, where the name of Avison or Aveson is common; the name is not recorded in Newcastle before Richard's arrival. A Richard and Ann Avison – almost certainly Charles's parents – were in London in 1699, when their twin daughters were born; Anne and Elizabeth were baptized at St Martin's in the Fields on 12 December 1699. Richard, like many other provincial musicians, may have been trying to better himself with a stay in the capital. In mid-1702, the couple were in Normanton in Yorkshire where a son, Edward, was baptised and, by the end of that year, Richard was a wait in Newcastle, living in the Nolt Market in the heart of the town and earning from his post £5 per annum. This could not have been sufficient to support a regularly increasing family and Richard probably also taught music. His wife, Ann, may have been organist at Gateshead Church.

Richard died on a visit to Durham in 1721 and was buried in St Oswald's graveyard there, when his fourth-born son, Charles, was only 11 years old. At his death, only four of the couple's 11 children still survived; one died two years later. Edward and Charles, and the eldest of the family – the surviving twin, Anne – remained. Anne's later history is unclear; Edward survived his younger brother by 13 years, not dying until 1783.

It is probable that Charles's early training was at his father's hands and at those of the musical community that surrounded these families. Newcastle had five waits and two organists at the turn of the century, all of whom probably took in private teaching. (Edward was also musical and may have participated in both private and public musical activities in the town as an amateur; he was however apprenticed to a staymaker, in which business he later established himself.)[26] As a wait, Richard's status in the community cannot have been high – the waits in Newcastle at the beginning of the 18th century were criticized on a number of occasions by their employers, the Corporation, as being of a poor quality as a band, and for indulging in malpractice. (There were no specific allegations against Richard.) In view of the low pay for waits and the number of children, the family almost certainly would have been relatively poor. Yet by the prime of his life, Charles was consorting with the principal figures of the Newcastle social world, with respectable clergymen and land-owning gentry and nobility. He was invited to dinner with the prebendaries of Durham Cathedral, many of whom were the younger sons of nobility, and as early as 1761 was describing himself as a 'gentleman' – usually an indication that the individual concerned was living primarily off invested income.[27]

The stages by which this transformation was achieved are not entirely clear. Normally, a boy showing promise and talent might be expected to be apprenticed to an established musician but there is no surviving evidence to suggest this; Richard's early death may have complicated matters.[28] The next certain evidence of Charles's activities is an advertisement for a concert he gave at Hickford's Rooms in London in 1734. By this time he was fully committed to a musical career and was, or had been, studying under the guidance of the Italian composer and violinist, Francisco Geminiani. Charles's visit to London, like his father's, is hardly surprising; such visits were commonly made by musicians in the north-east for what the Dean and Chapter of Durham Cathedral referred to as 'improvement'. It was customary for such trips to be made at the instigation of, or at the expense of, an employer; the Dean and Chapter sent their singing men off to the capital and, later in the century, so did the Corporation of Newcastle. In view of the fact that the waits' posts frequently passed from father to son, it is possible to speculate that Charles may have become a wait and undertaken his trip to London at the expense of the Corporation. Even his youth would not have been a bar to this; York Corporation bestowed the wait's post upon 14-year-old Stephen Bulkeley when his father died, and underwrote his musical education. In the absence of firm evidence, however, the exact circumstances of Charles's visit to London must remain speculation.

In 1735, Charles returned to Newcastle. This was in no way a declaration that he had failed to establish himself in London. For the majority of provincial musicians, a visit to London was not intended to be permanent and relatively few remained in London; Charles may always have intended to return to his native town where competition would be less intense than in the capital. A suggestion that he was offered the post of organist of York Minster at this point is unsubstantiated by any firm evidence. He took up a post of organist of St John's Church (where the new organ was not yet quite ready to play) at a salary of £20 per annum, but moved on within six months, to the better paid post at St Nicholas's church (£40 per annum). He held this latter post until his death in 1770. At the same time as he took up the St Nicholas's post, he became involved in a scheme to set up a winter series of concerts; four years later, he assumed sole charge of the series and maintained control (not without a few upsets and controversies) for 35 years. In addition, he set up a teaching practice and in late 1736 considered himself sufficiently well off to marry; nevertheless in the early years of the marriage, his wife, Catherine, supplemented their income by giving sewing lessons.

The subsequent arrival of nine children (three of whom survived to adulthood) must have added to expenses but there is little evidence to suggest that the Avisons were ever in serious financial difficulties. As early as 1748, Charles was sufficiently well-off to contribute £100 to the refurbishment of the organ at St John's Church, in return for a guarantee of the post, which he put out to deputies, reaping a percentage of the income. He was also able in the same year to lend £70 to a lady of a local gentry family (receiving back 70 guineas to take account of interest).[29] Supporters claimed that he was repeatedly offered well-paid posts outside the town – in Edinburgh and Dublin, for instance – but chose to stay in his home town. (Again, no direct evidence survives to support these claims.) He was on social terms with local notable families such as the Ellisons of Gateshead; one of the women of the family acted as godmother to his daughter, Jane, in 1743.[30]

But the professional musical community in Newcastle and in the north-east was more than just Charles Avison. In Newcastle itself existed a body of professional musicians of varying quality and status, from the waits and organists to the dancing masters and theatre musicians; some of these enjoyed an eminence that threatened Avison's own – when Avison returned from London, in 1735, a much-lauded Swiss violinist was the best known musician in the town. In Durham, a high quality group of musicians were connected with the Cathedral: the organist, James Hesletine, who had once been a chorister of the Chapel Royal, and ten singing men, excellent and excellently trained singers recruited from the best cathedrals in the south. Ties were strong between all these musicians although arguments inevitably sometimes occurred. Avison frequently used singers from the cathedral choir as vocal soloists in his concerts; the cellist, John Garth of Durham (unconnected with the cathedral) was one of Avison's closest friends. Charles's elder brother, Edward, married late in life to a widow of the Kell family, a local family of waits, and Ann, Charles's mother, regularly acted as godmother to the children of other local musicians – the Martins and the Jubbs, also waits. In smaller towns, such as Sunderland, North Shields and Morpeth, waits, organists and dancing masters also plied their trade, and Avison must frequently have seen, if not had extensive connection with, street musicians, fiddlers, pipers and ballad singers.

He also had connections with the wider, national, musical community; his return to the provinces from London did not mean that he cut himself off from national and international developments. He was aware of the work of other contemporary composers and musicians, introducing the town and region to the works of such celebrated contemporary composers as Rameau. He corresponded with friends in London and with well-known philosophers such as John Jortin, a London clergyman. He kept in touch with Geminiani, who visited him in Newcastle in 1769, and was a friend of the noted Italian violinist, Felice Giardini, with whom he collaborated on an oratorio. His own compositions, to judge by their subscription lists, were disseminated throughout the country, being frequently bought by musical societies. His book – *An Essay on Musical Expression* – was widely read and, in some quarters, caused a furore because of its perceived criticism of Handel. Moreover, the wider musical world often came to the north-east. Giardini and other eminent London instrumentalists visited Newcastle and Durham annually, to play in Race and Assize Week concerts; Newcastle, Durham and Sunderland were on the itineraries of touring musicians: the Loves (Sunderland and Newcastle in 1733); the Hungarian clarinettist, Mr Charles (1754 et al); Robert Bromley, a blind child harpist (1761); and, after Avison's death, the musical prodigy, William Crotch (1780) and the bankrupt Charles Dibdin (1799 and 1800). Musicians travelling between Edinburgh and London stopped off to appear in local concerts; thus in 1762 Avison enlisted the aid of the celebrated Signora Cremonini.

Avison appears to have had no reservations in encouraging his two surviving sons to follow him into the music profession. Edward and Charles junior probably acted as their father's deputies as organists of St John's and St Nicholas's and almost certainly also played in the theatre band. But Edward died young, a mere six years after his father, and Charles junior clearly possessed neither the charisma nor the financial acuity of his father; he died in 1795, aged 45, in severe debt. Avison's influence had other more subtle manifestations; one of his former pupils for instance, Matthias Hawdon, succeeded Edward as organist of St Nicholas. But his chief long-term influence may have been baleful for, after his death, musical life in Newcastle fell into a deep trough from which it never fully recovered. The cause of this abrupt decline is difficult to pinpoint – Avison's own popularity must have made him a hard act to follow, and his immediate successors do not appear to have had Avison's rapport with his audience nor his commercial ability. Inflation and war also played their part in lessening the public appetite for public music-making. Not until the mid-1790s, did musical life in Newcastle revive to any great extent. The musician responsible for this rally was Thomas Wright, a violinist, clarinet player and composer, who owned (having probably purchased it from the sale of Charles Avison junior's effects after his death) one of the elder Charles's compositional notebooks. Whether Wright (who almost certainly never knew Charles Avison senior) bought the book out of sentimentality, curiosity, or because he perceived it still to be of practical value is not known.

Notes

[1] *NJ* 4–11November 1758.
[2] *NC* 10 April 1736.
[3] Idem.
[4] *NCh* 20 April 1805.
[5] *YC* 17 January 1749.
[6] Ibid., 22 August 1803.
[7] *NJ* 4–11 November 1758.
[8] Ibid., 10–17 March 1759.
[9] *NC* 1–8 October 1748.
[10] *NJ* 4–11 November 1758.
[11] *NC* 13 October 1792.
[12] Charles Avison, *An Essay on Musical Expression*, 1st edition (London: C. Davis, 1752), 4–5.
[13] Ibid., 74, 78.
[14] John Brown, *A Dissertation on the Rise, Union, and Power, the Progressions, Separations, and Corruptions of Poetry and Music* ... (London: L. Davis, C. Reymers, 1763), 208.
[15] Ibid., 211.
[16] Ibid., 212.
[17] Avison, *Essay*, 105–6.
[18] Brown, *Dissertation*, 210.
[19] Idem; Avison, *Essay*, 48–9.
[20] Avison, *Essay*, 50–52; Brown, *Dissertation*, 210.
[21] Avison, *Essay*, 84–5.
[22] 'Proposals for Publishing by Subscription, Specimens of the various STILES in Musical Expression, selected from the PSALMS of BENEDETTO MARCELLO' in Charles Avison, *An Essay on Musical Expression*, 2nd edition (London: C. Davis, 1753).
[23] Idem.
[24] *NJ* 1 December, *NC* 1 December 1739.
[25] *NC* 19–26 October 1745, 22 February–1 March 1746.
[26] Ibid., 7 May 1737.
[27] DRO D/Br/D948, 11 June 1761: bond between Charles Avison of Newcastle upon Tyne, gentleman, and Henry Ellison of Gateshead Park, Esq.
[28] Norris Lynn Stephens, *Charles Avison: an Eighteenth-century English composer, musician and writer* (PhD Dissertation, University of Pittsburgh, 1968), 3–4.
[29] NRO Carr-Ellison MSS, 855, Box 4.
[30] DRO D/Br/D 939: will of Jane Ellison of Durham City, 9 April 1757.

PART ONE

MUSIC AS ENTERTAINMENT

Chapter 1

Public Concerts

The first known public concerts took place in London in 1672 as the bankruptcy of Charles II's court and the impoverishment of church music caused by the Commonwealth led musicians to look for alternative sources of income. The leader of the King's band, John Banister, opened up a room at his music school in Whitefriars to all comers, charged a shilling for entrance and provided cakes and ale and music for three hours. Three rather shambolic hours by all accounts, as there was no programme-planning or rehearsal and the entertainment was entirely dependent on those musicians who decided to attend.[1] But it was all a great success, nevertheless, and the concerts became part of the fashionable round and were quickly imitated by other promoters, although the social activity may have mattered a great deal more than the music; Sir John Hawkins later remarked of Thomas Britten's concerts in Clerkenwell that 'the house was very old and low built, and in every respect so mean, as to be a fit habitation for only a very poor man. Notwithstanding all, this mansion, despicable as it may seem, attracted to it as polite an audience as ever the opera did'.[2]

The fashion seems to have taken its time to work north. A concert was held in York in 1709 but none are known further north until three years later when unnamed performers put on a concert in Newcastle – no less than 40 years after the first concerts in London.[3] At first sight this delay might seem unsurprising, given the general belief that the provinces have always lingered long behind the metropolis. Yet northerners did not regard themselves as out of touch with the good things of life; Defoe said of York that it was as in touch with the world as was London and remarked upon the abundance of good company, the popularity of the Races and Assemblies, and the attractive public buildings.[4] Durham Cathedral's prebendaries were men who spent most of the year in their southern dioceses and must have brought fashions and information north with them on their yearly visits. The extensive sea-trade of Newcastle, based around coal, inevitably increased the area's contact with other parts of the country, facilitating the movement of ideas as well as commodities. Other fashions were seized upon eagerly; in 1728, for instance, the hit of the London theatre season – *The Beggar's Opera* – reached Newcastle only four months after the first performance in the capital.[5]

The apparent delay in taking up the new entertainment of concerts may in fact be an illusion caused by lack of evidence. The main source of information for concerts in the north-east are local newspapers: the *Newcastle Courant*, which lasted throughout the century, the *Newcastle Journal* (from 1739), the *Newcastle Chronicle* (from 1764) and the *Newcastle Advertiser* (from 1788). Other much shorter-lived journals such as the *Impartial Intelligencer* (1735–7) also carried advertisements for concerts. But the longest-lived of these – the *Newcastle Courant* – was first printed only in 1711 and for a decade or two was much more concerned with national and international events than with local entertainments. Before the papers came on the scene, parish registers and council minutes are the main sources for musical information and these are not likely to carry information on concerts. It seems possible, therefore, that concerts were indeed held in the north-east before 1712; the first advertisements carry no hint that they were talking of something unfamiliar, their wording suggesting that terms of payment and ticket conditions were already known by readers.

In the early years of the century, concerts are only recorded in Newcastle – not until the early 1730s are concerts publicized in Durham and Sunderland, although again the advertisements suggest that they were not new or unfamiliar. Few details survive of any of these events; performers are not named and repertoire is merely hinted at. However, local musicians were clearly deeply involved in concert-promotion, and collaboration between musicians in various centres was already well-established. Two concerts in 1733, for instance, were advertised as being performed by 'a Sett of the finest and best Masters from York, Durham, &c.' and 'by the best Masters in these Parts'.[6] Nor were local musicians the only people to promote concerts; an anonymous 'famous lute-master' came to the town in May 1725, using concerts as an advertisement for his teaching activities and offering to teach ladies and gentlemen to sing, or to play the lute or flute.[7] Charles and Nathaniel Love – apparently from London – gave concerts in Sunderland and Newcastle in 1733.[8] A Claudius Heron, who advertised a concert a year later, in June 1734, was plainly a cellist and may have been related to the prominent local family;[9] however, later in life he was resident in London and it is unclear whether he was a local man who left the area or a London musician touring the north.[10]

The concerts took place in makeshift venues, at the Grammar School on Westgate Road, or at Mrs Benson's Assembly Rooms on the same street – Newcastle in the 18th century never had a purpose built concert hall.[11] The long rooms above taverns such as the Turk's Head in the Bigg Market and the Red Lion in Durham were often used as concert venues later in the century. The entertainment was, however, limited to those who had money and leisure – these concerts were aimed at the richer citizens of the town. The usual early location of the Newcastle concerts on Westgate Road, in the more salubrious, wealthier area of town, well away from the sulphurous stink of the coal-smoke which plagued the lower areas of the town, is indicative of the audience the performers hoped to attract, as is the price of entrance, 2s. 6d. – far more than the average working man could afford.[12] Little is known about the actual mechanics of performance; paintings of concerts elsewhere indicate that the band performed standing (except for harpsichord and cello players), and that the audience could be very close to the performers. Seating was informal and possibly not always comfortable – later in the century, singing men at Durham Cathedral were allowed to take benches from the song school as seating for one of their concerts.[13] The few short reviews of concerts that survive indicate that audiences were often uninhibited in their applause and demands for encores, and that they were known to join in with certain popular airs or to stand up to express their solidarity with the sentiments of patriotic songs.[14] Such audience participation may have been encouraged by the performers, particularly in the rendition of such airs as 'God save the King'. Most frequently, however, the reviews simply note that the music 'met with the greatest approbation'.

The phrase 'a concert of vocal and instrumental music' was generally the accepted description for the evening's entertainment – it was to be used consistently throughout the century. The organizers of the 1712 concert advertised 'A CONSORT of *Instrumental Music; As Opera-Tunes, Italian-Solio's, Sonata's, Overtures,* &c. upon the following Instruments, *viz. Spinett, Trumpet, Hautboy, Violins, Bass-Viols, Bassoon &c.*[15] Heron offered 'a *Concerto* and *Solo* upon the *Violincello*, with select Pieces for *French Horns*, and other Instruments' and the visiting lute master promised that he and his nine-year-old daughter would sing Italian and English opera songs.[16] The child prodigy was to be a frequent feature of concerts in the region, ranging from the daughter of the lute-master through to Master Crotch, the famous organ-player from Norwich, and the musical children of James Bryson, who were exhibited in Newcastle in the 1790s. The visiting lute-master's daughter also appealed to his audiences' love of novelties, another trait that was to be demonstrated frequently throughout the century. In the Loves' case, it was the repertoire that was intended to attract the novelty seekers; they advertised both a Cuckoo Solo and a Quaker's Sermon 'perform'd on a single Violin'.[17] Their programme also included 'several Pieces of Musick Perform'd on the *Trumpet, French-horn, Hautboy* and *German Flutes* taken out of the most celebrated Operas, compos'd by Mr *Handel*'; this seems to have been intended to appeal to the desire of northern concert-goers to keep up-to-date with the latest fashions in London.[18] Concerts, even at this early date, had acquired a meaning other than the purely musical.

All north-eastern concerts in the first 30 years of the century were one-off promotions. Regular subscription series – in which the music-lover paid in advance for a number of concerts – had existed in London since before the turn of the century but it is not clear how quickly this practice travelled into the provinces. A subscription series existed in York from the late 1720s; Newcastle caught up in 1735.[19] In September of that year, an advertisement in the *Newcastle Courant* appealed to 'ALL Gentlemen and Ladies that are willing to Encourage a Subscription now on Foot, for a Concert of Vocal and Instrumental MUSICK, to be held at the Assembly-Room'.[20] Twelve local gentlemen seem to have combined together to promote the series but unfortunately they are nowhere named, although Messrs Brown and Sanderson, watchmakers, from whom tickets were available, may have been amongst their number. The gentlemen may have been members of a musical society that had previously met privately – such societies were frequently involved in the promotion of series and a society certainly existed in Newcastle in the 1740s;[21] they set up a series of 12 concerts, held fortnightly on Thursday nights between October and February, offered concerts three hours long (from 6 to 9 in the evening) and charged half a guinea for the privilege of attending the entire season.[22] The success of the first series led to a second although the price was doubled.[23] A third – at the dearer price – also took place before, abruptly, the gentlemen withdrew and handed over the entire management of the series to the man who was to become Newcastle's most prominent musician over the next 35 years, Charles Avison.[24]

In the early 1780s, Avison had been in London, studying with Geminiani, making his earliest attempts at concert promotion, but by the summer of 1735, if not before, he was back in Newcastle, obtaining his first paid appointment – as organist of St John's with a salary of £20 per annum.[25] Three months later, he was performing in the subscription series.

A dispute at the end of the first series gives an insight into the running of this first series and of Avison's part in it. In April and May 1736, a series of letters were written to the *Newcastle Courant*, making it clear that a violent quarrel had broken out between two participants in the series and that the organizing gentlemen had rapidly polarized into two extremely partisan parties. Our knowledge of the dispute is culled from the violently-phrased and vituperative letters written turn-and-turn about to the *Newcastle Courant* by these two parties and has therefore to be viewed with caution and due allowance for bias, but the basic facts at least are clear.

The first letter to the *Courant* was written by one of Avison's supporters, claiming that Avison (referred to throughout as 'a modest young man') had been ill-treated by a 'peevish and petulant Competitor'.[26] This was a Swiss violinist who evidently led the concert band; he was reputed to be an excellent, even virtuoso, player and was a great favourite with the audiences.[27] *His* supporters, on the other hand, claimed that Avison had taken charge of the concerts to the Swiss's detriment. The original plan had apparently been that the 12 organizing gentlemen should be in charge not only of the financial and administrative affairs of the series but also of the choice of repertoire in each concert; all the performers should then be 'on a level' and would be able to concentrate solely on performing to their best abilities.[28] According to the Swiss's supporters, however, 'the modest young man' (the phrase came to be used in a highly ironic sense) had taken charge and was often capricious. They alleged that he had taken a dislike to the Swiss and frequently changed the music after rehearsal (sometimes as little as two hours before the concert), forcing the Swiss and his supporters to sight-read the new music. Moreover, he had, they claimed, taken physical charge of the instruments and music, refusing to allow the performers to take them home to practise.[29] One man asserted that he had overheard Avison saying that the Swiss would 'dearly repent' his behaviour, a comment that he took to mean Avison had advance knowledge of the letters that would shortly appear in the *Courant*. However, Avison's supporters pointed out that the witness was known to be one of the Swiss's partisans.

Insults flew, with Avison's supporters claiming that the Swiss violinist thought too much of himself because of the acclaim he received from the audience (which was, they claimed, uncritical and naïve); he was also accused of demanding London rates for the concerts – 10s. a night rather than the 5s. he was usually paid. But some serious issues were also debated: was it fair to demand that professional musicians should sight-read or was it a skill all such musicians should possess?

(The supporters of the Swiss claimed that sight-reading was 'a Task unreasonable to be put upon the greatest Performer that ever the World produced'.)[30] Was virtuoso playing admirable or merely 'popular'? Opinions differed and the dispute raged on. Matters were exacerbated when Avison, in search of a new leader to replace the Swiss who had walked out in expectation that the concerts would collapse without him, appointed his 12-year-old apprentice to the position; this was interpreted as an insult to the Swiss's abilities by claiming his job was so simple a child could do it.[31] The dispute resulted in the absurd proposal that a musical duel should be fought between the boy and the Swiss at Mrs Hill's Tavern in the Fleshmarket on Wednesday 19 May. Each would bring a cellist as accompanist and a piece of music, play their own music, then swap and sight-read the other's music. James Hesletine, organist of Durham Cathedral, was to be the judge and the winner would receive twenty guineas.

But there was treachery in the air. When the Swiss and his cellist arrived at the inn, the boy was nowhere to be seen and only a message awaited the Swiss, demanding more concessions. In high dudgeon, the Swiss flounced out of the inn and immediately left Newcastle. Avison's supporters sent the *Newcastle Courant* a vicious mock-obituary – 'a … circumstantial Account of the Death of a little lean cholerick Fidler'.[32]

Avison's unofficial direction of the series during its first three years was soon converted into an official status. The Managers seem to have over-reached themselves with ambitious plans; in a letter written to the *Courant* in 1758, over twenty years later, Avison described what happened.

> When the Concert was first set on Foot, (which was in the Year 1737, and was the first Public Entertainment of Music in the North) it was undertaken by twelve Gentlemen, who procured above One Hundred and Seventy Subscriptions for Twelve Concerts, at Half a Guinea each Ticket …
>
> …The Managers thought of nothing as much as the improvement of the Concert: it was, therefore, determined to encrease the Number of Performers, and, consequently, their Expences; for this reason they proposed the Tickets, for the following Season, at One Guinea each; but this Advance of the Subscription not answering their Account, the Concert, on its first Footing, was given up to my Care alone.[33]

In 1738, therefore, Avison found himself officially in charge of the subscription series. He immediately cut the subscription charge to the original level and moderated some of the Managers' more ambitious plans. At the same time, he instituted the habit of holding mid-year concerts; from 1737, he held a concert for his own benefit in Assize Week; a concert in Race Week is known from 1743.[34] These concerts were held at the busiest times of the year – in June (Race Week) and August (Assize Week) – when the town was flooded with visitors eager for entertainment; they were therefore well-attended and usually profitable. For four years from 1751, Avison also held a mid-year benefit for the Newcastle Infirmary, in the process of building at the time and the subject of much philanthropy; on the whole, however, the practice of holding concerts for charitable causes was never popular in Newcastle, nor in the north-east as a whole.[35]

Avison's subscription and mid-year concerts survived for nearly 35 years although their course was not always smooth. The 170 subscribers dwindled to no more than 110 between 1738 and 1753 but increased in the next four years to 140. In the late 1750s, some dissatisfaction began to be shown with the running of the concerts and there is evidence that Avison himself began to feel insecure. A controversy arose over the cost of the subscription concerts in 1758 and Avison seems to have felt that his direction of the series was being challenged. He complained that subscribers who objected to the cost of the concerts – 13 shillings for the season at this time – had no idea of the expenses involved. 'The contingent Charges can hardly be ascertained; such, I mean, as the purchasing and continually repairing of Instruments; the constant Expence for Music, &c. and the maintaining of Apprentices; all these are chiefly necessary in the Business of Public Concerts'.[36] A supporter wrote that he [Avison] 'has lately been called to account for assuming the sole direction of both the performance and subscription, and thereby giving offence when he intended a service'.[37] Avison seems seriously to have considered resigning all but the musical direction of the series 'rather chusing to assist, than preside, where it was so precarious to please'.[38]

His insecurity seems to have manifested itself in his relations with a newcomer to the town, an 18-year-old Irishman, Charles Claget. Claget arrived in Newcastle in July 1758, opened a dancing school and set himself up as a teacher of both dancing and of music; he put on several concerts and may have been planning to run a subscription series in competition with Avison, although he vehemently denied this.[39] Avison's anxiety may have been increased by the fact that he was himself involved at this time in one of two competing subscription series in Durham; he reacted badly to Claget's activities and there was an acrimonious argument, referred to by Claget as 'an unlucky Difference'.[40] Claget protested his innocence in an advertisement in the *Courant* – Avison seems to have accepted his explanations and the dispute was settled. In any case, Claget's challenge was short-lived; he withdrew after a year and a half, heading north to Edinburgh.[41] An awkward compromise was reached over the ticket prices and the subscription series continued, apparently without further difficulty.

The challenges to Avison were not quite over however and in the 1760s, he came up against a type of musical enterprise that he particularly despised. London had had garden concerts at places such as Vauxhall since the 1730s but the idea came late to the north-east.[42] In the mid–1750s, the citizens of Durham had enjoyed the opportunity to wander in the gardens at Old Durham, a house just outside the city, and concerts were on rare occasions held here, although these were usually private affairs, rather than commercial enterprises.[43] Newcastle got its first taste of the entertainment towards the end of the same decade. An advertisement in the *Newcastle Courant* in June 1760 to mark the festivities in the town celebrating the birthday of the Prince of Wales (very shortly to become George III) offered, amongst other attractions, ' a grand Concert of Musick, at Mr. Callendar's new Ranelaugh Garden'.[44] The reference in the advertisement to this being 'the Opening for the Season' suggests that the gardens had in fact been open in previous years, and this supposition is supported by the fact that since 1757 Avison had been running, in addition to his usual winter subscription series, a summer subscription series, of four concerts held at monthly intervals from May to August.[45] It is possible that this unprecedented departure from his usual routine was a response to the inauguration of a type of entertainment he found particularly obnoxious – he had described such entertainments as containing 'a flood of nonsense' in the form of 'shallow and unconnected Compositions'.[46] But the cost of admission to these summer concerts of Avison's was astonishingly high (half a guinea for four concerts, compared to the same price for 12 winter concerts) and they did not survive long; Avison held the last series in 1759.[47]

If these unsuccessful summer concerts were a riposte to the garden concerts, it must have been galling to see the latter thrive. In the early summer of 1761, profits were sufficient to build a 'Music House' on the site, presumably to accommodate the band, and there was apparently no difficulty in obtaining a large number of subscribers as the gardens opened for the summer on 9 July.[48] The cost of the subscription was half a guinea, as it was to Avison's concerts, but this allowed access to 16 nights' entertainment rather than the 12 Avison offered; individual tickets could be bought at 1s. a night. This low price allowed a wider section of the population access to the entertainment, although the cost was still well beyond the pockets of the average labourer. The Callendar family mentioned in the 1761 advertisement were local seedsmen who used their own nursery gardens on the then edge of the city behind St Andrew's Church for the concerts; maps of the time suggest an irregular triangle of land in the angle of two roads, laid out neatly with flower-beds and with a large building at one corner.[49] In 1763, the gardens were renamed (though still retaining the London allusion) as Spring Gardens.[50]

But the garden concerts were always on an insecure footing financially. A meeting in April 1764 to plan the year's concerts resulted in a single concert held on 21 June and the gardens were then taken over by a local publican, Thomas Moore, proprietor of the Sun Inn – the inn already hosted a 'respectable musical club' whose members included Avison's two sons.[51] Moore opted for the modest total of eight weekly concerts on Wednesday nights and offered the extra attraction of a house in the Gardens to provide tea and coffee; this must have proved reasonably successful as the following year he held another full season on similar terms, adding extra accommodation in case of bad weather.[52] By 1766, however, he was emphasizing the very great cost of his expenses though pledging himself to carry it on 'for the Amusement of Ladies and Gentlemen'. His added plea – 'the Proprietor hopes for Encouragement' was apparently unheeded; when the concerts finished for the season on 10 September, the gardens closed.[53]

When Avison died in 1770, it became clear that it was only his reputation and his personal attractions that had been keeping the winter subscription series in Newcastle afloat. The series was taken over by Avison's elder surviving son, Edward, as were the mid-year concerts, but Edward was probably already suffering the long drawn-out illness that killed him six years later and the sudden power vacuum that clearly existed encouraged a rash of competitors to hold concerts in the city. These concert promoters included actresses from the theatre, visitors to the city, local dancing masters and singing men from Durham Cathedral but, one after another, they held a single concert and withdrew, apparently finding the exercise unprofitable. The only persistent concert-promoter, other than Edward, was Avison's younger son, also Charles. Charles junior held a number of concerts in the town between 1770 and 1774 and the earlier ones at least seem to have been tolerably successful. But in 1774, Avison took the unprecedented step of holding a second concert within a month of the first, suggesting that the earlier concert had been a disaster; a year later, he was off in search of 'improvement', his travels taking him as far as St Petersburg in Russia.[54] In 1775 and 1776, Edward grew increasingly more unwell; he was plainly too ill to continue with the subscription series and concert-life lapsed almost completely – not until after Edward's death in November 1776 and the appointment of a new organist to St Nicholas's church did it pick up again.[55]

Edward's successor, both as organist and as concert promoter, was Matthias Hawdon, one of Avison's old pupils. Hawdon had begun his career in 1751 when Avison recommended him to the post of organist at Holy Trinity, Hull, England's richest parish church. From there, Hawdon had moved, in 1769, to Beverley Minster; in both places he had organized local concerts and had been active in the promotion of oratorios throughout the Lancashire/Yorkshire corridor. By the time he returned to Newcastle in 1776, he was a widower with three sons, the eldest of whom was apprenticed to an uncle, a barber surgeon. The middle son may have become a dancing master – only the youngest, Thomas, followed his father's career.

Hawdon was faced with a concert-life that had ebbed almost to non-existence. Moreover, his arrival (in December 1776), was at an awkward time of year – the subscription series would normally have been in full swing by this time. Edward had arranged nothing and Hawdon contented himself with promoting two or three concerts in early 1777, leaving the organization of a full subscription series until the autumn; when this was advertised, it was on a smaller scale than Avison's old series – six concerts instead of 12, held monthly rather than fortnightly.[56] Hawdon also brought the oratorio to Newcastle for the first time, holding two festivals in 1778 and 1781, using soloists from Durham Cathedral.[57] But support for concerts in Newcastle seems to have evaporated; the blows dealt to it by Avison's death and by the lapse caused by Edward Avison's illness seem to have been nearly fatal. By 1781, Hawdon was bankrupt and, while his own financial mismanagement may have had a large part to play, it is clear that public support for a series was lacking. Hawdon threw large-scale Assize Concerts in the hope of raising money while the town was busy but cut the unprofitable subscription series back to three monthly concerts between January and March. By 1785, he was bitterly announcing his retirement from concert promotion:

> M. HAWDON most respectfully returns thanks to his Friends, who have favoured his endeavours in carrying on, hitherto, the Winter Concerts; it would have given him a particular satisfaction, and have encouraged his future endeavours, had the support been more general, but, as it has not of late been any way adequate to the expence, he sincerely hopes his intention of declining them will give no offence to his Friends, or the town in general.[58]

Hawdon's mismanagement and deteriorating health complicated the situation but his assessment of the lack of interest in concerts in Newcastle at this time seems to have been entirely accurate; an attempt by musicians from Durham to run a subscription series in 1786 was also unprofitable and was never repeated.[59] For the next five years, Newcastle had no subscription series and mid-year concerts were only erratically held. In 1790, Charles Avison junior, newly returned from Russia, attempted with Matthias Hawdon's youngest son, Thomas, to revive the series, but had considerably less success than his father and soon gave it up into the hands of a committee of gentlemen. The Committee did not advertise the series and it was apparently not particularly well-supported. In 1794, another attempt was made to revive it but it seems again to have lapsed until 1798 when yet another series was set up. This time it thrived, owing, at least in part, to external factors, not least a surge of interest in military and patriotic music.[60] A series of 12 concerts were held from November to March each year until 1803; the scheme was very similar to that originally envisaged for the 1735 series with the organization, financial and administrative, in the hands of a number of gentlemen (probably associated with the Musical Society). A President and Vice-President were in charge of each individual concert, the President choosing the repertoire to be performed and the Vice-President keeping order on the night. Unfortunately, the gentlemen were prone to their predecessors' mistakes; indulgence in the hiring of London soloists in the 1802 and 1803 seasons led to expenses beyond the resources of the series to bear. The subscription series entered another lull which lasted to around 1809.

By this time, the link with the organist of St Nicholas's church seems to have been broken; Matthias Hawdon, who died in 1789, had been succeeded by Charles Avison junior who in turn was succeeded in 1795 by a 17-year-old boy, Thomas Thompson. Thompson performed in the subscription series but had no hand in its organization; he did, however, continue to run an Assize Concert in July or August. Moreover, the death of the younger Charles Avison in 1795 also broke the link between music-making in Newcastle and the Avison family; he left only young children who died before making any contribution to musical activity in the area.

Concerts in Durham and elsewhere

The earliest known concert in Durham – a benefit at the Grammar School in 1735 – is at such a late date compared to concerts in Newcastle that it is tempting to believe that a great deal of earlier information has been lost.[61] Likewise, although a winter subscription series is not known in Durham until the 1740–1 season, the wording of the advertisement for the series suggests that this might not have been the first – there is no suggestion of novelty or explanation of ticket conditions.[62] The Durham series throughout the century was in the hands of Cathedral personnel: the Cathedral organist was musical director, the gentlemen of the choir were soloists (both vocal and instrumental) and the clerics were organizers and supporters (although their role is nebulous and ill-defined). From 1740 until 1763, the concerts were under the direction of the organist, James Hesletine, and from

Hesletine's death in 1763, in the hands of his successor, Thomas Ebdon; the series ran from October until January or February, and consisted of six or 12 concerts, generally at fortnightly intervals – as in Newcastle, the cost of subscription was half a guinea. Durham, like Newcastle, also had mid-year Race and Assize Week concerts from at least 1745 but these were run not by the Cathedral personnel, but by the composer and cellist, John Garth.

Garth's promotion of Race Week concerts in Durham in the late 1740s was the first sign of a period of contention in Durham that drew in Charles Avison from Newcastle and caused considerable bad feeling. Garth was probably the son of William Garth of Harperley near Witton le Wear in County Durham and was baptised in the latter place in 1721.[63] Although he was 20 years younger than Charles Avison, the two men were good friends and Garth played in Avison's Newcastle concerts. He seems to have had a wide teaching practice, particularly amongst the gentry and minor nobility of the area, teaching amongst others the children of Lord Barnard (later the Earl of Darlington) at Raby Castle near Staindrop. In 1752, Lord Barnard and other supporters suggested that they would finance a subscription series for Garth in Durham in competition with the Cathedral series, Garth having the musical direction and the profits. There may have been a considerable portion of political intrigue in the offer; Barnard was often on the worst of terms with the Dean of Durham Cathedral, Spencer Cowper, both personally and politically, and may have relished the opportunity to do the Dean a disfavour – the Dean naturally supported the well-established Cathedral series. Garth enlisted the aid of his friend, Charles Avison, and planned a series of fortnightly concerts for the winter of 1752–3, to be held in Durham and in alternate weeks with the series in Newcastle, thus enabling the same personnel to play in both.[64]

The two men could not help but be aware that the new venture would be unwelcome to the Cathedral personnel. They seem to have been on good terms with a number of the Cathedral clerics, frequently dining with them and providing impromptu music afterwards. In addition, Garth was probably organist of Sedgefield, a parish whose living was in the gift of the Bishop of Durham, and may have been organist at the Bishop's Palace in Auckland.[65] James Hesletine, organist of the Cathedral, was also invited to the prebendaries' dinner parties but made a point of refusing to join in the music-making; Spencer Cowper ascribed this to jealousy and said that Hesletine could not tolerate a competitor.[66] The chief object of Hesletine's ire appears to have been Avison, although the only documented contact between the two men – a letter from Avison asking for the loan of one of the choristers for a concert in Newcastle – is written in the most civil and courteous of tones.[67]

By refusing to co-operate with Avison, Hesletine almost single-handedly ensured a decade of discord in Durham as far as concerts were concerned. Cowper wrote to his brother in London that Avison and Garth had on several occasions suggested that the Newcastle and Durham bands should amalgamate to form one large band to play in both centres but that Hesletine had rejected their approaches in no uncertain terms and the quarrel seemed irretrievable.[68] In December 1762, therefore, Avison and Garth held the first of their concerts in competition with the cathedral series.

Spencer Cowper approached the whole affair in a martial spirit from the beginning, rejoicing in his ability to deny the series a vocal soloist (Avison and Garth had attempted to persuade one of the Cathedral choristers to join them).[69] He refused to go to the first concert (as did Hesletine) but sent his wife to the rehearsal and concert to report back. Avison and Garth seem to have tried to avoid the repertoire typically found in Cathedral concerts but their efforts merely aroused the contempt and amusement of Cowper and the Cathedral personnel, as did the small size of the audience and the fact that it was composed principally of women.[70] The performers were good, Cowper wrote in a letter to his brother in London, but he condemned the choice of music as 'wretched'.[71] All in all, the Cathedral personnel were inclined to dismiss the new competition as insignificant; Cowper toyed with the idea of lending Avison and Garth a vocal soloist after all – an offer of dubious generosity, as he reminded his brother that the singer he was considering sang through his nose 'like a penny trumpet'.[72]

Cowper predicted that Garth's series would not last but it seems to have been well-supported; in 1753, and succeeding years, the rivalry between the two groups of musicians also extended into the mid-year with Garth and the Cathedral personnel holding competing Race and Assize Week concerts, often on successive days. The Cathedral personnel opted for novelty in the hope of attracting an audience, offering open-air concerts, while Garth tried to tempt music-lovers with prestigious performers such as the Italian violinist Felice Giardini (a friend of Avison). A further attempt to poach singers from the Cathedral in 1755 only exacerbated tension. Cowper was constantly predicting disaster and was jubilant in 1757 when funds seemed to be particularly low; this was also the period at which Avison faced financial difficulties with the series in Newcastle.[73] But Garth's series staggered on until 1760 when it rather damply fizzled out, apparently unregretted.[74]

Hesletine was dead by this time and his successor, Thomas Ebdon, made conciliatory gestures toward Garth. Although Cowper and Hesletine had combined to keep the quarrel between the principals going throughout the 1750s and 1760s, the argument does not seem to have extended to the other musicians, who seem to have been on good terms. Although the choir's singing men were (according to Cowper) gleeful at the prospect of the series' stillbirth in 1752, many of them were associated with Garth in various other ventures. They performed together on a number of occasions – at a concert held by the Mayor of Durham in November 1754 to celebrate George II's birthday, and at the opening of the new organ in Stockton Parish Church.[75] The annual dinner and pre-series meeting of the subscribers to the Gentlemen's Subscription Series (as Garth's series was known) was held in an inn – the Star and Rummer – run by the singing man Peter Blenkinsop, and no less than nine people connected with the Cathedral subscribed to the eight volumes of Garth's *Psalms of Marcello*, which was published yearly from 1757 and contained a preface by Charles Avison. The subscribers included singing men, clerics, the Bishop, Spencer Cowper and, most surprisingly of all,

James Hesletine.[76] Professional competition went only so far, it seemed – perhaps in the end, all musicians stuck together.

Ebdon and Garth collaborated in the promotion of mid-year concerts until 1772, although Ebdon had sole charge of the winter series. Garth finally withdrew from concert promotion in 1772, concentrating on teaching for the rest of his very long life. Ebdon continued to run the subscription series; occasionally visitors mounted concerts in the city and the principal singing men seem to have held an annual benefit, particularly in the 1790s. But in 1793, Ebdon too abruptly withdrew from concert promotion; a brief attempt by a committee to run another series in 1796 was apparently not successful enough to be repeated.

The smaller towns of the region generally had to wait until the second half of the century for regular concerts, although a lack of evidence may account for some of the apparent sparseness – Sunderland, for instance, probably had concerts from the 1730s although it does not seem to have acquired a series until the early 1770s. Following a special concert to celebrate the opening of St Hild's Chapel in 1769 – a concert in which the choir of Durham Cathedral performed *Messiah* – Thomas Ebdon seems to have seen the opportunity to expand into the town.[77] He established a subscription series of six concerts in 1770 and, from at least 1779 (and possibly earlier), promoted an annual benefit in the town, held on 4 June or the weekday closest to that date to celebrate the King's birthday; these concerts were probably identical to concerts in Durham and involved the same personnel.[78] The Sunderland series continued until 1791 when Ebdon gave up the series, as abruptly as he shortly afterwards gave up the series in Durham.[79] The series was taken up by the local organist, George Goodchild, but lapsed on Goodchild's death two years later.[80] The regular King's birthday concert was kept going by performers from Newcastle and by a new organist for several years more, but a revival of the subscription series in 1794 was not repeated and by 1797 almost all concerts in the town had ceased, apart from rare benefits for charitable purposes.[81]

The demise of these concerts in Sunderland – and those in Durham – is difficult to explain. Ebdon may have wanted to give up concert promotion in favour of teaching; about this time, he turned down election as an alderman in Durham, citing as reason the fact that he was away from home so frequently, suggesting an extensive teaching practice in the country. In addition, performers in both centres were from the Cathedral personnel and the principal performers – favourites who could be counted upon to attract an audience – were ageing; newcomers were not always satisfactory. By the mid–1790s, economic factors and the concerns over the political situation with France were also taking their toll.[82]

Other towns around the area also had concerts – both of a one-off nature and winter subscription series. Darlington had a subscription series for several years during the early 1760s – this was, unusually, a summer series, possibly copying the summer series Avison was promoting at the same time. Subscription series are also known in Morpeth (from at least 1786), Stockton on Tees (from 1785), Hexham (in 1762), and North Shields (1772–82).[83] The last was unusual in being promoted by the landlord of the local inn, in which the concerts were performed; Morpeth's series was run by a Committee of Gentlemen.

Performers

The bands which played in these concerts were probably not large. Reviews which found it worth remarking that the number of performers, both vocal and instrumental, reached 40 or 50 in number, suggest that the usual total was much smaller than this, probably under 20. Avison suggested that 21 was an ideal size for a band – principals plus six first violins, four second violins, four violas and cellos, two double basses and one harpsichord. To have fewer was possible, he said, but having more 'would probably destroy the just Contrast between the *Chorus* and *Solo*'; the use of the word 'probably' suggests that he had no extensive experience of this situation.[84] Avison's band was a string band. At the end of his *Essay on Musical Expression*, he expresses his dissatisfaction at hearing bands of mixed string and wind, pointing out that as the instruments warmed up, the strings went flat and the wind sharpened, to the considerable detriment of tuning;[85] the small amount of evidence available suggests that woodwind and brass players rarely made appearances at Avison's concerts and then only as guests or soloists – the Hungarian French-horn player Mr. Charles played at a subscription concert in 1754, for instance, and military bands occasionally made appearances.[86] This situation prevailed throughout the century; not until the 1790s did Newcastle have a woodwind player amongst its resident musicians and even then the player – clarinettist Thomas Wright – was equally well-known as a violinist and leader of many of the region's bands.

The instrumental performers themselves are frequently difficult to identify. In Durham, the singing men – that is, the adult male singers of the choir – performed as both vocal and instrumental soloists; in the 1780s and 1790s, Thomas Robinson and George Ashton, both singing men, became ubiquitous in concerts throughout the north-east as leader and principal cellist respectively of concert bands. Spencer Cowper, in a letter to his brother in 1753, rejoiced greatly because he had acquired in one and the same person, not only a good singer for the choir, but also a good violinist for the concert.[87] In Newcastle, Avison himself played harpsichord in the band; his opponent, the Swiss violinist, was his first leader. At least one dancing master played in the band supporting the Swiss in the 1736 quarrel and as a result being referred to contemptuously by Avison's supporters as 'Mr. Light-heels'. Other players probably included the five waits.

These professional players probably filled the crucial roles with the band – those of leader, section principals and harpsichordist. The professional musical community was always small, however – rarely reading double figures in Newcastle and in some smaller towns, such as Sunderland, consisting of an organist and a dancing master (who in any case was usually peripatetic). These professionals were augmented, therefore, by the so-called Gentlemen Amateurs, wealthy tradesmen and minor gentry, who had the time and money to study music and to learn to play a musical instrument; when the gentlemen who founded the Newcastle series handed the management over to Avison in 1738, they specifically stated in their advertisement that they intended to continue to 'assist him with their performance'.[88] Later in the century, grateful concert promoters on several occasions expressed their gratitude for this assistance – in 1792, for instance,

Thomas Wright, advertising a King's birthday concert in Sunderland, was careful to note that he had been promised the assistance of all the gentlemen performers of Newcastle as well as Sunderland.[89] Cowper's brother, Earl Cowper, occasionally played with the Durham band when visiting the city and it is likely that other gentlemen also did so; the audience at Garth's first concert in 1752 was small because the 14 gentlemen subscribers almost all played with the band. Rarely are these amateurs named, being usually referred to by such phrases as 'a gentleman of this town' but in one exception, the reviewer of the Durham Musical Festival of 1792, remarking that 'the Band was greatly strengthened by several Gentlemen performers, who politely came forward and gave their assistance', specifically referred to seven gentlemen performers, chiefly clergymen and members of local gentry families. Even more unusually, one of these, the Reverend Mr Nesfield of Chester le Street, played a solo flute concerto – gentlemen performers almost always confined themselves to rank and file roles. The mix of amateur and professional players cannot always have been an easy one, and a professional musician who directed such a band must have exercised a great deal of tact to deal with players who were not only his social superiors but who also probably paid him.

The quality of the bands was extremely variable. In the last section of Avison's *Essay*, one can read the heartfelt weariness of personal experience in this regard. Amongst problem performers, Avison mentions those who hold onto notes too long, who fidget when they are not playing, who play inner parts too loudly and do not listen to the other performers, who ornament the music or play melodies an octave higher than written to show off their own skills, and those who make entries late, producing a ragged effect.[90] In the late 1740s, a local vicar remarked that the Durham band was particularly prone to confusion in the matter of tempi, playing slow passages too quickly and quick passages too slowly.[91] A few years later, the Dean, Spencer Cowper, attempted to obtain a decent violin for the band's leader, who could not afford a good instrument, but had to admit, when the new violin arrived, that it did not have much effect because the leader was unable to produce a good tone.[92] An anonymous writer to the *Cumberland Pacquet*, after attending a concert in Whitehaven in 1786, summed up the trials of listening to such bands.

> IMPROMPTU
> *Addressed to a Friend who had the Misfortune to sit near the* Orchestra *at a late Exhibition.*
>
> FORBEAR Invective – though the Catgut grate,
> And frequent Discords fill thy tortur'd Ear:
> Think how much harder is these Minstrels' Fate,
> Compell'd, sad Penance, both to ACT and HEAR.[93]

Most instrumental soloists came from the ranks of the band but occasionally more famous names would appear. In the 1750s and 1760s, Avison frequently hired the Italian violinist, Felice Giardini – a personal friend – to lead his band in the Race and Assize Week concerts; Giardini would also generally play at Garth's mid-year concerts and then travel south to York for the concerts there.[94] When

Giardini withdrew, he recommended his friend, Giovanni Battista Noferi, leader of the Opera Ballet in London, as his replacement. These were men whose main source of livelihood lay in the capital but who, when the town emptied in summer, made a living by touring the provinces to play in such mid-year concerts. Others like Knerler (briefly leader of the concerts in York in the mid–1740s) and Johann Peter Salomon, the London impresario, called in at Newcastle and Durham briefly *en route* between London and Edinburgh – the city benefited greatly from being on the main road north; well-known players and singers being only too pleased to pause briefly and recoup some travelling expenses. Such notables were widely advertised and clearly added a cachet to local concerts.

Regular vocal soloists were always a problem for Newcastle subscription series. Whereas Durham concerts could use a number of excellent singers from the choir, Newcastle had no church choir of a comparable standard. Avison's first series therefore used a singer from the Cathedral, Thomas Mountier. Mountier, originally from Chichester Cathedral, had been one of the stars of London concerts in the early 1730s and may have been acquainted with Avison in the capital – the two men had come north at much the same time. Mountier sang in concerts in both Newcastle and Durham for several years before succumbing to a liking for drink for which he was eventually dismissed from the Cathedral.[95] Avison also used one of the choristers – Robert Paxton – for a short period in the 1730s and the boy was sufficiently well-known to hold a benefit in Newcastle in 1738.[96] But by the time Garth started his concerts in Durham in 1752, bad relations with the Cathedral had dried up the supply of singers and Cowper's animosity ensured that no singers responded to Avison's overtures. When in 1754 Cowper reported that Avison and Garth had persuaded two of the singing men to help, the situation was quickly returned to normal; within a few months, both the singing men had left the Cathedral – one for London, the other for Edinburgh – and it is probable that Cowper's emnity drove at least one of them from the city.[97] As a result, the early concerts of Garth's Durham series had virtually no vocal items at all and it may be that Avison's Newcastle concerts at this period suffered in much the same way. Avison may have solved the difficulty by hiring actresses from the local theatre company – his sons Edward and Charles certainly did so. But the solution was far from ideal given the temporary nature of the actresses' stay in the city (theatre companies moved around a circuit of towns each year) and the irregular nature of some actresses' lives. Edward Avison suffered at the hands of Miss Alphey (a pupil of the castrato Tenducci), whom he hired as soloist for the 1772 season; three weeks before the season started, Miss Alphey – playing with the theatre company in Carlisle – eloped with one of the actors and sent her regretful apologies for her sudden retirement.[98]

By the time Matthias Hawdon reached Newcastle in 1776, the breach with the musicians at Durham Cathedral had been healed, the principals involved (with the exception of Garth) being all dead. Hawdon heard the Cathedral choir singing at a concert put on by Newcastle Freemasons to celebrate the opening of their hall, and seems immediately to have lost himself in admiration for their singing; he hired one or more of them – and occasionally the entire choir – for all his concerts thereafter. Hawdon's bankruptcy in 1781 and subsequent withdrawal from concert promotion in 1785 left the field open for the Durham musicians in both Newcastle and the north-east generally and they quickly established a dominance in music-making in the region. The principal architect of this supremacy was Edward Meredith, a bass who had first appeared in London in the early 1770s, under the patronage of the Handelian enthusiast, Sir Watkin Williams Wynn; Meredith became a singing man in Durham in 1778 and over the next ten years slowly established himself as a singer in all fields. The undoubted quality of his singing made him the most prominent musician of the 1780s in the region; hardly any concert was held in the north-east without his being present and other singing men rode on the coat-tails of his popularity to the extent that, by 1786, at least the principal players and singers in almost every concert in the north-east were from the Cathedral: Meredith and the alto/tenor William Evance (Meredith's usual singing partner); Thomas Robinson (a violinist and the usual leader of most bands in the north-east at this period); and George Ashton (principal cello).[99] Although Meredith left the region for Liverpool in 1788, north-eastern concert promoters continued to use Evance and the other singing men until the mid–1790s when musical life began to take a down-turn. In Newcastle, the singing men were eventually replaced – though not until 1797 – by Newcastle's first resident singers, two sisters, the Misses Clifford.

But however great the admiration lavished on Meredith, the real praise was reserved for visiting singers, particularly those internationally known. Typical were the sentiments expressed in a poem written by an unknown admirer on hearing at one of Avison's concerts in 1762 the Italian singer, Signora Cremonini.

> When Cremonini sings she thrills my Soul,
> With heavenly Sounds, whose Powers controul
> Each turbulent Passion, and inspires
> My much transported Heart with soft Desires,
> Upon her rosy Lips the Angels dwell;
> Her voice surpass the Notes of Philomel!
> Admiring Cherubs list'ning fly around,
> And strive to catch the music-dying Sound:
> Then mounting up, they spread their Silver Wings,
> To Heav'n they soar and tune the golden Strings;
> Again renew their Songs of endless Love,
> And raise fair Cremonini's Notes above.[100]

For those music-lovers who idolized these national and international stars, the highlight of late 18th-century musical life was a Music Festival held in 1791; organized by the London impresario John Ashley, the travelling oratorio festival had played in Hull the previous year and in York only two weeks before the Newcastle performances. Ashley's singers included the famous German soprano, Gertrude Mara, and the English favourites, Anna Maria Crouch, Samuel Harrison, Michael Kelly and Edward Meredith.[101] Newspaper reviews praised the singers in a melodramatically extravagant style, the *Newcastle Chronicle* commenting that they 'so infinitely surpass every thing we had before heard'.[102] Such praise was not lavished on instrumental players. But there was a downside; when such notables were not present, the music seemed hardly a compensation. A second Newcastle festival in 1796, organized by Edward Meredith and Thomas Thompson, the organist of St Nicholas, attempted to cut costs by hiring soloists from Lancashire and Yorkshire – although the performances were praised and the audiences appreciative, the support was not sufficiently numerous to cover the expenses.[103] In Newcastle, at least, something more than mere good music was required to attract substantial audiences.

Repertoire

Information about the specific pieces of music played at north-eastern concerts is fragmentary. Charles Avison never advertised more than time, place and price of his concerts, and only a few hints about the music performed can be gleaned from newspaper reviews and private diaries. After Avison's death – for a period of two or three years – many advertisements for concerts included a full programme, probably because audiences could not know what to expect from new promoters. Edward Avison's advertisements followed the pattern of his father's, suggesting that he changed very little; Matthias Hawdon's extensive advertising, at least in the first two years after his arrival in the town, suggests that he changed a great deal. By the 1790s, however, the fashion for advertising full programmes had died out almost entirely, possibly on the grounds of expense; fortunately, a large number of programmes from that period (and the early 19th century) were preserved by a Victorian collector and survive in Newcastle's Central Library. From these it is possible to reconstruct almost the entire repertoire played at four seasons of subscription concerts between 1798 and 1803.

In the early part of the century, most surviving information relates to concerts held by visitors to the area, such as the lute-master, and Charles and Nathaniel Love. These suggest that the typical concert was a presentation of a number of short pieces, often with some feature designed to appeal to the audience's love of novelties. Over the century, Newcastle concert-goers heard the new instruments such as the clarinet, the basset horn and the harmonica; they witnessed playing with mutes, medleys of bird-song and singers imitating the sounds of musical instruments. A concert in the 1790s offered the spectacle of two men playing one violin 'both bowing and fingering at the same time'.[104] Of the content of Avison's concerts, little is known. Concerts in 1751 included the music of Rameau – Avison had been given a complete set of the composer's works which he arranged to suit the abilities of his Newcastle band and also took to Garth's concerts in Durham in the following year.[105] Many of Avison's own compositions, including the well-known 1744 set of concertos based on Scarlatti's works, were written for the Newcastle concerts; their concerto grosso style – with relatively simple and easy to play band parts and more difficult solo parts for his professional principals – was ideally suited to his mixed amateur/professional band with its wide range of abilities.[106] In addition, the long lists of good and bad composers in Avison's *Essay* give some hint as to the composers whose works were probably performed at Avison's concerts; it is unlikely that he would have omitted Corelli and Geminiani, for instance, or performed Vivaldi or Porpora.

The staple of Durham concerts was Handel; it was a rare subscription series that did not include a complete, or almost complete, performance of one of his oratorios (usually as first or last concert in the series). Mid-year concerts generally presented the lighter works such as *Acis and Galatea* or *Alexander's Feast*, and in 1769 Thomas Ebdon the organist introduced a performance of Handel's oratorios during Easter Week.[107]

The omission of Handel's music from Garth's subscription series in Durham prompted a caustic comment from Spencer Cowper although Avison and Garth may have been trying to maximize audience appeal by offering music of a very different type to that heard at Cathedral concerts. The conservatively-minded clerical establishment at Durham clung to the old works of Handel and Corelli, and were eager supporters of such organizations as the Concert of Ancient Music in London, which had been set up in 1776 at the beginning of the war with America with the aim of re-establishing the position of the aristocracy as arbiters of good taste, a profoundly political action in troubled times. Likewise, they supported the Handel Commemorations of the later 1780s and early 1790s which were, in origin at least, nationalistic festivals designed to rally patriotic feeling in difficult times.[108] Avison's antipathy towards Handel, on the other hand, based on remarks in the two editions of his *Essay* and much debated at the time, is well-known although greatly overstated; he merely remarked that Handel's greatness had been diluted by commercial demands. Avison's reservations about Handel did not prevent him performing the composer's music both in London and in Newcastle, and he and Cowper may have had more in common than either appreciated as far as musical taste was concerned, particularly in their estimation of modern composers; in the *Essay*, Avison spoke slightingly of modern composers, some of whom Cowper had described as writing 'riff-raff' music.[109] But Handel's music was comparatively little played in Newcastle and the only known complete performance of an oratorio in Newcastle during Avison's lifetime was put on by Durham musicians.[110]

There is irony in the fact that Matthias Hawdon, Avison's former pupil, was the great advocate of Handel's music in Newcastle. Hawdon had lived for 25 years in Yorkshire where the chapel choirs of Lancashire sang oratorio regularly and performances of 100 performers were not unusual; he had lived through a kind of mini-mania for Handel's music that flourished in the area between 1769 and 1772, and had taken part in many oratorio performances across the Lancashire-Yorkshire corridor, from Wakefield and Doncaster to Leeds, York, Sheffield, Birmingham, Manchester and Liverpool. Almost his first act on becoming organist at Beverley Minster in 1769 had been to organize an oratorio festival to celebrate the opening of the new Snetzler organ.[111] Hawdon's promotion of oratorios and of Handel's music in general in Newcastle was extensive but the published programmes for his first two series (indicating his intended repertoire) show that he tended to use Handel's music for the grand gesture and the special occasion. These, and the programmes surviving from the early 1770s, immediately following Avison's death, are the first detailed surviving information on the format and content of local concerts. All but two or three were in two acts or parts; each usually consisted of five items, starting and ending with an instrumental piece for full band and alternating instrumental and vocal items. A mixture of genres were represented – overtures and concertos (both of the concerto grosso type favoured by Avison and of the more modern solo concerto type), symphony and quartets, sonatas and marches. Songs were rarely named, unless they were well-known or a popular folk song. Hawdon played works by a variety of contemporary composers – Giordani, Abel, Fisher and others – and usually ended with one of his own marches. But the sixth and last concert of his series and the two mid-year concerts were very different in style to the earlier concerts; the two-act structure was maintained but the alternation of vocal and instrumental items was often abandoned to allow each half of the concert to end on one of the big choruses from Handel's oratorios. Hawdon clearly expected these big set-pieces to appeal to the large number of people who thronged the town at such periods and who probably rarely, if ever, attended another concert.

Yet something was wrong. Despite Hawdon's expectation that these concerts, and oratorio festivals in 1778 and 1781, would have wide appeal, he still went bankrupt. Were Hawdon's difficulties merely owing to mismanagement? Did the expenses of these large-scale concerts simply exceed income despite the attraction of a large audience, or were audiences disappointingly small? The experience of the 1796 Musical Festival suggest that both factors may have had a part to play but Hawdon may simply have been out of sympathy with Newcastle's real underlying taste. The town's audiences were never particularly attracted by attempts to put on concerts of music by dead composers, however illustrious. The passion for the so-called Ancient Music which flourished in aristocratic circles in London, ironically turning a revolt against fashionable vapidness in music into a new fashion, never caught on in Newcastle; the only attempt to hold a concert of such music in the town came as late as 1798. This concert was not extreme in conception or execution; it featured music by contemporary composers as well as 'ancient music' but the fact that the experiment was never repeated suggests that it was not particularly popular.[112]

For the great love of Newcastle audiences was *new* music. Cowper had used the word contemptuously of the repertoire at the Garth/Avison's concerts in Durham but perhaps Avison was more in sympathy with his audiences than Cowper gave him credit for. An admirer, eulogizing Avison in the *Newcastle Courant* in March 1759, cited as one of his virtues the fact that 'he has supplied our concerts with new music, for more than twenty years' and as the century progressed, the demand for 'new music' was more openly expressed.[113] In the 1790s, concert after concert is advertised with the *new* tag – a new clarinet concerto, a new military sonata, a new favourite song. *Music entirely new*, *music composed entirely for the occasion* – these were phrases evidently guaranteed to appeal to a concert-goer's heart and pocket in late 18th-century Newcastle.

Some caution is necessary here – for these are all phrases taken from advertisements for benefit concerts. Advertisements for the winter subscription series rarely refer to repertoire, and surviving programmes for the winter series held between 1798 and 1803 indicate that Handel, Avison, Geminiani and Corelli were sometimes played; Handel's overtures were particular favourites. Although works by contemporary composers still considerably outnumbered works by those who could be described as 'ancient', the latter still represented a significant proportion of the music played. Two different types of repertoire clearly existed for two different types of musical event. The benefit, often held at busy times of year, was more populist in nature, was more prone to advertising new music and to offering musical novelties such as new instruments or unusual genres, and almost always ended with a ball 'for the ladies'. Subscription series concerts were more serious in tone, they featured a wider range of composers, were almost always regular in format and confined their concessions to fashion to the hiring of up-and-coming female singers from London. They were rarely followed by a ball and then only on special occasions, such as the first and last concerts of a series, or at Christmas or New Year.[114]

Audiences

All this suggests that there were two different types of audience within the town, probably overlapping but nevertheless distinct. One audience was that which attended the mid-year concert and the benefits, including people who rarely went to concerts and who wanted something light-hearted and appealing; the other was composed of music-lovers who turned out every fortnight or month to the subscription concerts and who were prepared to spend more time and effort in listening to music. The first audience regarded music as a fashion item, a novelty, a true entertainment; the latter also regarded it as an art. The former group was clearly larger than the latter; they turned out for their favourites, like Edward Meredith, who was not above treating them to popular folk-songs, or medleys of bird imitations, they loved new music and looked for novelties. Benefits were usually held in the large elegant rooms of the New Assembly Rooms on Westgate Road (built in 1776); subscription series were generally held in the small Old Assembly Rooms in the Turk's Head in the Groat Market.

The identity of individuals in the audiences is extremely difficult to discover. Ticket prices alone confined the audiences to the upper end of the social scale: individual ticket prices ranged from 2s. 6d. at the beginning of the century to 3s. 6d at the end; subscription rates were generally half a guinea but could be as high as a guinea. These may have been much lower than London prices but were nevertheless out of the range of many local people.[115] The attempt by the promoters of the Spring Gardens concerts in the 1760s to bring music to a wider range of people – admission to the gardens was only 1s. each – was met with scorn and dislike by Avison at least; he suggested that the Gardens provided only poor quality music to a naïve and uncritical audience. Even so, one shilling was still beyond a large percentage of the population.

Avison, himself in his letter to the *Courant* in 1758, described his audience as 'people of the genteeler sort'.[116] Members of the nobility were few, although advertisements followed the convention of addressing themselves to the 'Quality and Gentry' and 'to the Nobility'.[117] Rarely did such luminaries attend concerts and most of the few references extant to them come from Durham. Garth's supporters in his Durham subscription series were certainly members of the local gentry and were headed by Lord Barnard (later the Earl of Darlington). Barnard also attended a concert held by Thomas Ebdon in Sunderland in June 1789, which fortunately happened to coincide with a few days' hunting he was taking in the area.[118] Lord Darlington, Lady Warkwork and 'most of the principal gentlemen and ladies in and about Durham' turned out for a concert in that city in 1766 – this was a particularly patriotic occasion, being a concert held in honour of the Queen's birthday; the Duke of Norfolk attended a concert in Newcastle in 1794 when visiting a friend in the town.[119] The prebendaries of Durham were often scions of noble families (Spencer Cowper was himself the second son of an Earl) and, particularly at the mid-year concerts, could produce a prestigious audience. The 1770 Assize Week concert boasted the 'most brilliant company that ever appeared in that place; amongst whom were the Bishops of Durham, Oxford, and Manchester, the two Judges, the Deans of Durham and Winchester, several Members of the House of Commons, and all the Prebendaries that were in Durham'.[120]

The fact that the local press so eagerly reported such eminent audiences reveals how unusual they probably were. The Gentlemen Amateurs named as performing at the Durham Musical Festival were probably more typical; they included members of local gentry families and several local vicars, many of whom travelled into the town from the country to hear the concerts, hence the habit, early in the century, when street lighting was poor or non-existent and robbers plentiful, of holding concerts on nights when there was a full moon. (As late as 1792, subscription series' concerts began at 7 pm to accommodate non-residents who might not wish to linger too late in town after the entertainment.) The advertisements for the 1792–3 series also make it clear that 'Gentlemen of the Navy and Army' attended concerts at this period.[121] The names of the Presidents and Vice-Presidents who ran the subscription series between 1798 and 1803 are preserved on the handbills for the concerts; not all of these can be identified but some like W. R. Callender, a member of the family who had lent their nursery gardens to Spring Gardens, were wealthy tradesmen, others were coal owners, still others members of local gentry families.

But the most detailed evidence comes from a list of subscribers to the Newcastle subscription concerts in 1809; many of the names are familiar from the concert handbills of a decade earlier. The list, which survives in Newcastle's Central Library, has been annotated with the professions of the subscribers. A total of 107 subscribers are listed; by far the majority were male – only four were women. Twenty-seven do not have an occupation added; three others were professional musicians. A wide variety of professions were represented by those who remain: 15 merchants; five manufacturers of various sorts – glass manufacturers, a blue manufacturer, a papermaker; six attorneys; three ironmongers; four bankers; three colliery agents; three booksellers and two mariners. A scattering of other professions: engraver, builder, miniature painter, seedsman, grocer, surgeon, tobacconist, tanner, saddler, slater. The list was overwhelmingly middle-class – only one subscriber, Lady Collingwood, represented the upper classes.

Notes

[1] *Roger North on Music: Being a Selection from his Essays written during the Years, c1695–1728*, ed. J. Wilson (London: Novello, 1959), 302–5, 351–3.
[2] Sir John Hawkins, *A General History of the Science and Practice of Music* (London, 1776), II, 790.
[3] *Daily Courant* 1 August 1709, quoted in M. Tilmouth, 'A Calendar of References to Music in Newspapers published in London and the Provinces (1660–1719)' *RMA Research Chronicle*, No. 1, 1961, 73; *NC* 19–21 May 1712.
[4] Daniel Defoe, *A Tour thro' the Whole Island of Great Britain (1724–6)* (London: Frank Cass, 1968), 638–9, 642.
[5] *NC* 4 May, 15 June 1728.
[6] Ibid., 29 September, 1 December 1733.
[7] Idem.
[8] *NC* 22 May 1725, 10 November 1733.
[9] Ibid., 1 June 1734.
[10] Parish registers of St. James, Westminster, passim.
[11] *NC* 1 December 1733, 1 June 1734.
[12] Ibid., 19–21 May 1712, 1 June 1734.
[13] DCAB, 24 February 1798.
[14] *NJ* 1 December 1739.
[15] *NC* 19–21 May 1712.
[16] Ibid., 22 May 1725, 1 June 1734.
[17] Ibid., 10 November 1733.
[18] Idem.
[19] Account Book of D'Arcy Dawes of York, 1 October 1724.
[20] *NC* 20 September 1735.
[21] *NJ* 4–11 November 1758; J. Burchell, 'Musical Societies in subscription lists: an overlooked resource', *A Handbook for Studies in 18th-Century English Music IX* (Oxford: Burden and Cholij, 1998), 1–75. The York concerts had begun in a similar manner.
[22] *NC* 27 September 1735.
[23] Ibid., 7 August 1736.
[24] Ibid., 29 July 1738.
[25] CCN 13 October 1735.
[26] *NC* 10 April 1736.
[27] At no point is the Swiss named and a search of the *Newcastle Courant* reveals no advertisements for concerts or teaching that might be on his behalf. One of the letters referred to the 'many Years he has lived in the Town' [*NC* 24 April 1736].
[28] *NC* 10 April 1736.
[29] Ibid., 17 April 1736.
[30] Idem.
[31] In an early example of the power of the press, the Swiss violinist claimed that he had been told by one of the organizers of the concerts that if he refused to play, the story – presumably suitably angled – would be in the next week's papers.

[32] *NC* 29 May 1736. 'You must know … (gentle Reader) that he has been observed to waste daily for some Time by-past … he spit nothing but Gall for a Fortnight before he dy'd … He began about half an Hour before he died to rave much, and deliver himself in broken Sentences; He had his big black Fiddle (a bad Omen!) in his Right Hand, and his fiddle-stick in his left, a Plaister of crotchets of his own composing defended his Vitals; … his Agonies seized him, (for you must know he was always a great Enemy to *Time*), he spit, star'd, stank, and dy'd.' If the writer was not simply taking artistic liberties, the Swiss violinist must have been left-handed.

[33] *NJ* 4–11 November 1758. Avison's memory failed him in some respects – the subscription series, as already noted, was begun in 1735. His comment that the series was the first in the north only holds if York is considered not to be in the north.

[34] *NC* 30 July 1737; *NJ* 28 May 1743.

[35] *NC* 17–24 August 1751.

[36] *NJ* 4–11 November 1758. Apprentices, like Avison's 12-year-old apprentice at the time of the dispute with the Swiss violinist, often played in the concert band. Any money they earned would accrue to their Master. See Chapter 9.

[37] *NJ* 10–17 March 1759.

[38] Idem.

[39] *NJ* 29 July-5 August, 9–16 December 1758.

[40] Ibid., 9–16 December 1758.

[41] Claget eventually returned to Ireland where he directed concerts for some years in Dublin, before moving to London. His younger brother, Walter, who spent two or three months with him in Newcastle, became principal cellist at Covent Garden but lived in Newcastle for the last few years of his life, dying in the town in 1797.

[42] Simon McVeigh, *Concert Life in London from Mozart to Haydn* (Cambridge: Cambridge University Press, 1993), 38–44.

[43] *NC* 31 May 1755.

[44] Ibid., 7 June 1760.

[45] *NC* 30 April 1757; *NJ* 21–8 May, 25 June-2 July, 23–30 June 1757.

[46] Avison, *Essay*, 1st edition, 72. Avison may also have had a financial reason for the new concert series; this was the year in which he raised subscription prices for the winter series, provoking much controversy. A series in Durham, organized in part by Avison, was also suffering financial problems at this time and it may be that the financial situation was generally difficult for entertainments at this time.

[47] *NC* 25 March 1758.

[48] Ibid., 4 July, 11 July 1761.

[49] The area survived until well into the 20th century, supplying a large part of the city's water from its springs; it is now built over. The gardens were opposite the present site of the football ground at St James's Park [*NJ* 2–9 April 1763].

[50] *NJ* 2–9 April 1763.

[51] Ibid., 21–8 April, 16, 23, 30 June 1764; E. Mackenzie, *A descriptive and Historical Account of the Town and County of Newcastle upon Tyne, including the Borough of Gateshead* (Newcastle: Mackenzie and Dent, 1827), II, 590; *A Memoir*

of Thomas Bewick by himself, ed. Iain Bain (Oxford: Oxford University Press, 1979), 96.

[52] *NC* 23–30 June 1764. Ibid., 4 May 1765.

[53] *NCh* 10 May 1766; *NC* 5 September 1767.

[54] *NCh* 16 April, 14 May 1744: Avison was at the time organist of St John's Church and obtained permission from his employer, the Corporation, to travel to Russia in April 1776. He twice overstayed the time granted to him and finally resigned the St John's post in September 1777 [CCN 15 April 1776, 27 September 1777].

[55] Edward died in October 1776 [*NC* 19 October 1776]. His successor, Matthias Hawdon, was appointed to St Nicholas in December the same year [*NC* 21 December 1776].

[56] *NC* 8 February, 5 April, 19 July 1777.

[57] William Boyd (collector), *Songs sung at the subscription, and other, concerts in Newcastle upon Tyne, 1790–1883* (programmes), passim; *NC* 17 March 1781.

[58] *NC* 3 December 1785.

[59] Ibid., 10 December 1785, 14 January, 4 February, 4 March 1786.

[60] See Chapter 8.

[61] *NC* 24 May 1735.

[62] Ibid., 20 September 1740.

[63] I am indebted to Dr. Brian Crosby for this information.

[64] *Letters of Spencer Cowper, Dean of Durham, 1746–1774*, ed. Edward Hughes, Surtees Society 165 (Durham/London: Andrews and Co/Bernard Quaritch, 1950), 159, 26 November 1752.

[65] Garth was certainly the Bishop's organist at Auckland Castle in the early 1790s – he was probably only called upon to play once or twice a year when the Bishop was in residence.

[66] D. Burrows and R. Dunhill, *Music and Theatre in Handel's World: The Family Papers of James Harris, 1732–1780* (Oxford: Oxford University Press, 2002), 279, Diary of G.W. Harris, 31 October 1751; Cowper, *Letters*, 159, 26 November 1752.

[67] Gloucester Record Office, D3549, 7/1/3. 'Newcastle, July 19th, 1737. I am to have a Public Concert in the Assize Week, and if I could have the boy Paxton over it would oblige a great many of my Friends. I shou'd have requested the Favour of the Dean, because when I went to serve Mountier, he was so kind as to promise the Gentlemen of our Concert (when they din'd with him) to let me have the Boy once to hear him – but as I knew you have the Care of him, and can favour us at present, I thought it best to apply to you. Your Answer as soon as possible will greatly …' The letter is torn off at this point but part of the signature ('… most Obed^{t} …') can also be read. Mountier was a singing man at the Cathedral who was also vocal soloist at Avison's Newcastle concerts.

[68] Cowper, *Letters*, 159, 26 November 1752.

[69] Idem.

[70] Most of the male subscribers chose to play in the orchestra and transferred the tickets to others within their family. Ticket conditions, however, allowed the transferral only to two women, thus ensuring a predominantly female audience.

[71] Cowper, *Letters*, 161, 10 December 1752.

[72] Idem.
[73] Cowper, *Letters*, 190, 11 September 1757.
[74] For a more detailed discussion of this competition in Durham, see Southey, R., 'Competition and Collaboration: Concert Promotion in Newcastle and Durham, 1752–1772', in *Concert Life in Eighteenth-Century Britain* eds. Wollenberg, S. and McVeigh, S. (Aldershot: Ashgate, 2004), 55–70.
[75] *NC* 9 November 1754; Vestry Books of Stockton Parish Church, 1762–1926.
[76] *The first fifty psalms set to music by Benedetto Marcello ... and adapted to the English version by John Garth* (London: John Johnson, 1757–65), vols. 1–8.
[77] *NCh* 1 April 1769.
[78] Ibid., 9 June 1770.
[79] *NC* 19 February 1791.
[80] *NCh* 11 February 1792.
[81] Ibid., 24 May 1794.
[82] See Chapter 8.
[83] *NC* 31 December 1785, 21 November 1772; *NCh* 5 November 1785; *NJ* 30 October-6 November 1762.
[84] Avison, *Essay*, 1st edition, 113.
[85] Ibid., 114. Avison made an exception for the bassoon, which he felt reinforced the bass line effectively.
[86] *NC* 26 October 1754.
[87] Cowper, *Letters*, 169, 23 October 1753.
[88] *NC* 29 July 1738.
[89] Ibid., 26 May 1792.
[90] Avison, *Essay*, 1st edition, 117–26, passim.
[91] Burrows and Dunhill, *Harris*, 252–3, letter to Elizabeth Harris, 19 November 1748.
[92] Cowper, *Letters*, 157, 3 November 1752, 161, 10 December 1752.
[93] *CP* 12 April 1786.
[94] e.g. *NC 22* July, 29 July 1758.
[95] DCAB, 23 October 1741.
[96] *NC* 29 April 1738. It is this boy to whom Avison refers in his letter to Hesletine in July 1737. See fn 67.
[97] The singing men involved were Cornforth Gelson, the leader of the Cathedral band, and one of the three Paxton brothers, local men who were all in turn choristers at the Cathedral. The younger brother, Stephen, left Durham at this period and was probably the man approached by Avison and Garth; he settled in London. Gelson was dismissed from the Cathedral for fathering an illegitimate child; the child was, however, a year and a half old, and Gelson had been openly paying maintenance for it. It is difficult, therefore, to believe that Cowper and the Cathedral Chapter had been ignorant of the offence or that they did not use it as an excuse to be rid of Gelson.
[98] *NC* 3 October 1772.
[99] Ibid., 23 July 1785.
[100] Ibid., 2 October 1762. Cremonini was fleeing from an uncongenial contract in Edinburgh.

[101] Madame Mara had briefly been the regular subscription series soloist in York in 1763–4, under her maiden name of Miss Schmelling.
[102] *NCh* 3 September 1791.
[103] *NC* 6 August 1796.
[104] Ibid., 16 June 1793.
[105] Ibid., 14–21 September 1751.
[106] For a more detailed examination of this and other similar factors, particularly those that relate to the popularity of Corelli's concertos in Britain, see Hutchings, A. J. B., *The Baroque Concerto* (London: Faber and Faber, 1959), 252–68.
[107] *NC* 18 March 1769, 11 April 1772. Only one programme survives from a Durham concert – a benefit for Noferi in 1773. This is probably not typical of the regular series. All but two of the pieces played were instrumental; composers whose works were performed included Handel, Abel, Bach (J. C.) and Noferi himself [*NC* 31 July 1773].
[108] McVeigh, *Concert Life*, 22–7.
[109] Cowper, *Letters*, 161, 21 November 1746.
[110] *NJ* 27 August–3 September 1763.
[111] Ibid., 25 July 1769.
[112] *NA* 21 April 1798.
[113] *NJ* 10–17 March 1759. The letter was signed *Marcellinus*, which has given rise to suggestions that it was written by John Garth who was at this time in the process of editing and publishing the psalms of Benedetto Marcello. However, the fact that the author refers to the Newcastle concerts as 'our' concerts and dates his letter from Newcastle (Garth lived in Durham) must leave room for doubt.
[114] Hawdon regularly ordered 50 tickets for his Assize Concerts, and for his first two subscription series ordered 200 subscription tickets for the subscribers. It is unlikely that he sold all these; in 1782 he attempted to move the series to smaller (and cheaper) rooms as the number of subscribers was so small [accounts of Thomas Bewick of Newcastle, 13 October 1779, 27 November 1780; *NC* 12 January 1782].
[115] Ironically they were also probably out of range of the pockets of many of the musicians who played in the concerts too; rank and file musicians at a concert in 1802 were paid 3s. 6d. each for a day's playing. See Chapter 9.
[116] *NJ* 4-11 November 1758.
[117] *NG* 20 March 1751.
[118] *NA* 21 February 1789.
[119] *NC* 11 October 1794; *NCh* 25 January 1766.
[120] *NC* 25 August 1770.
[121] Ibid., 24 November 1792.

Chapter 2

Theatre Music

Theatres, theatre companies and personnel

Operas were never presented in the concert room in the north-east; the most the opera-lover could hope for was the inclusion of an overture or two – Handel's opera overtures were particularly popular in the Newcastle subscription series of the late 1790s. Large-scale vocal works were performed only in the theatre. Yet at the beginning of the 18th century, the north-east had no fixed theatre buildings or resident company of players. The old practice of travelling players setting up temporary stages wherever the local authorities allowed still held; in Newcastle, the players performed at the Moothall if the justices permitted, or in the timber yard of a local merchant if they did not. The companies of this period are known only by the names of their managers: Mr Peirson's company (which played in Newcastle in 1716), Mr Orfeur's company (1732),[1] Mr Keregan's company and Mr Herbert's (both playing in Newcastle in May 1728).[2] The actors themselves were called comedians – not a comment on their repertoire but a description derived from the old Italian tradition of the Commedia del Arte.

The first permanent theatre in Newcastle (and probably in the north-east) was the Theatre in the Bigg-Market, set up in 1747, but even this was something of a mirage, being in other circumstances the Long Room on the first floor of the Turk's Head Inn. The room was also used for concerts and for dinners, and the companies – who generally performed on Mondays, Wednesdays and Fridays – may have been forced to set up or strike scenery at short notice. The room, of which no description remains, was almost certainly long and thin, and far from ideal for theatrical performances; it would have produced an intimate atmosphere with the audience close around the actors.

The town's first purpose-built theatre was proposed in 1784 and opened in January 1788; as it was licensed in accordance with the 1737 Theatre Licensing Act, it was known as the Theatre Royal. The street upon which it was built, Moseley Street, was part of an extensive new building programme but was itself substantially altered in the massive rebuilding of the town in the early 19th century at which time the theatre was demolished – the back wall, however, still survives as does the alley, appropriately named Drury Lane, that led to the stage door. Engravings from the period show a classically styled building, with a porch of columns supporting a triangular pediment; inside, the theatre boasted two galleries, and was obviously intended to hold a substantial audience. The *Newcastle Chronicle*, somewhat acerbically, commented that it could accommodate 1,500 people 'should that number propose to try it'.[3] For the most part, they did not, although full houses were occasionally reported towards the end of the century.

Elsewhere in the region, a theatre existed in North Shields from at least 1765 and possibly earlier; the building was described as 'not large [but] allowed to be more commodiously neat than any thing of the kind on this side of London' – possibly a jibe at Newcastle which was still enduring the makeshift pleasures of the Theatre in the Bigg Market.[4] Theatres were also built in Durham (1771 and 1791), South Shields (1791 and 1798), Berwick (1794) and Alnwick (1796).

The companies that used these theatres were peripatetic although all tended to acknowledge one town or city as their base – Peirson, Keregan, Orfeur and Herbert were all based at York. By the time the Theatre in the Bigg Market was established in the 1740s, the regular company visiting Newcastle was Mr Baker's, also from York. This last company appears to have performed in the town with very little competition until the late 1760s; towards the end of this period, the company was joined by a Newcastle-born man, Tate Wilkinson, who later established his own company playing principally in the larger towns in Yorkshire, but who occasionally ventured north to his native town. From the late 1760s, Joseph Austin and Charles Edward Whitlock (brothers-in-law) took over the Bigg Market theatre, with Wilkinson's company now and again putting on a Race or Assize Week season. By this time, a pattern of playing was established similar to that of the concert season: a winter season of three or four months (playing three nights a week) and a Race Week season (in which the company played every night). Between these engagements, the company travelled on a regular circuit which could be extremely far-flung. In some years Austin and Whitlock's circuit included Newcastle, Lancaster, Chester, Warrington, Preston, Whitehaven and Carlisle; after their retirement in the early 1790s, their successor, Stephen Kemble, briefly incorporated Edinburgh and Sheffield in to the circuit before admitting that it was too long.[5]

The North Shields company, run first by Thomas Bates and, from the late 1780s, by Bates's son in law, James Cawdell, had a more circumscribed circuit, touring Durham, Darlington, Stockton, Sunderland, Whitby and Scarborough as well as North and South Shields. In 1799, on the death of Cawdell, Kemble took over this circuit too, dropping the more distant towns on his own circuit and contriving to run simultaneous winter seasons in Newcastle and North Shields, playing in Newcastle on Mondays, Wednesdays and Fridays, and in North Shields on Tuesdays and Thursdays. Travelling even the smaller circuits such as this was not easy; the less well-established members of the company might have to walk much of the way and the return to North Shields from Scarborough was generally by sea, a mode of transport which had its own particular hazards. Cawdell wrote a poignant commentary on the physical hardships of such trips in a bitter poem penned 'in consequence of the Company having been wind-bound, &c. for near a fortnight … ', describing the company as 'exposed i'the open sea/Tossing and turning, sick as sick can be'.[6]

Theatre musicians

The Theatre Licensing Act of 1737 prohibited the performance of the spoken word except in licensed theatres; those companies which did not have a license – all the north-east companies until the 1780s – therefore resorted to a number of strategies in order to stay in business. In London, unlicensed theatres turned to presenting musical entertainments (even in some cases, Italian opera) or developing novelty shows which eventually gave birth to the circus. In the north-east, companies resorted to a transparent ruse – apparently never challenged – which allowed them to continue presenting plays. It was not illegal to act, only to charge for admittance; companies therefore took to advertising 'concerts of music' with a play or two as a 'free' extra. In practice, the music made up a very small proportion of the evening's entertainment but was crucial to maintain the ruse – the musicians attached to the company were therefore a vital piece of camouflage.

Some musicians were a permanent part of the theatre companies, travelling with them from town to town and being paid on the same regular basis as the actors and actresses; most companies, for instance, seem to have employed a violinist as leader of the theatre band. In the 1770s, Austin and Whitlock employed a Christopher Smith in this capacity; Smith eventually married in Whitehaven and settled there, teaching dancing, and playing as leader in various local concerts.[7] Later in the century, the clarinettist and violinist Thomas Wright acted as Kemble's leader in Newcastle, although he probably did not travel extensively with the company. Cawdell's North Shields company employed a Mr Brown from London in the early 1790s; Brown used the company's travels to pursue a little business of his own, opening a 'Musical Warehouse' in each town the company visited, offering a wide range of instruments and music. He produced a catalogue of his stock and operated a trial and exchange scheme for instruments; transporting all his goods (including, at one time, two piano fortes), must have added greatly to the company's logistical problems.[8]

The most detailed information about musicians employed by the theatre companies derives from the account books of Tate Wilkinson. These survive for three years, between October 1781 and October 1784, recording income and expenditure on a daily basis for the Yorkshire towns in which Wilkinson's company played, and probably reflect the practice common amongst other companies in the region. During this period, Wilkinson employed between one and four musicians who travelled with the company. His leader for the last 30 years of the century was a violinist called George French; Wilkinson also employed a cellist on a permanent basis although the musicians filling this post generally stayed only a few months before moving on. By early 1784, Wilkinson had in addition a further two musicians on the payroll – he does not state which instruments these men played. The chief task of men such as Smith, Wright, Brown and French was to lead the band in performance, but French at least was also paid for 'writ^{g}' (by which Wilkinson meant music-copying), for composing additional songs and for providing accompaniments.[9]

The bands over which these men presided were hired locally, in the towns in which the companies played. Wilkinson's accounts reveal how small these theatre bands could be: eight or nine local musicians were generally hired for the York season and four for the Leeds season – elsewhere, the absence of payments suggests that Wilkinson may have managed with his permanent players alone. Trumpeters and drummers were also employed on an occasional basis when required. Local waits, music teachers and the apprentices of more experienced musicians were hired but their quality could vary; Wilkinson on several occasions postponed productions because he felt the band was not sufficiently ready to play the works – in Beverley in July 1771 he commented on a handbill that he 'thought it better to defer a musical Farce the First Night, that the Band may be regularly settled'. From time to time, Wilkinson also hired more prominent local musicians to play particularly taxing parts as in York, where he several times persuaded the Minster organist, John Camidge, the vocal soloists from the subscription series and one or two singing men from the Minster, to appear as soloists. This practice was less frequent further north, although Charles Avison's younger son, Charles Avison junior, performed a solo at the Theatre in the Bigg Market at least once, under the extremely thin but fashionable disguise of an Italian alias, as Carlos Avisonsini, and may have been a regular member of the theatre band.[10]

Where singers were required, Wilkinson used members of the acting company; it was rare, although not unknown, for a performer who was principally a singer rather than an actor to be employed. In the 1770s, however, Wilkinson hired a Mr Raworth, whom he seems to have employed almost exclusively to sing incidental songs or vocal parts. Raworth's acting talents may have been slight – almost a year passed before he was entrusted with speaking parts and his appearances in such roles were always limited. Another singer had earlier found the transition to the theatrical world impossible; Richard Elford, one of the singing men at Durham Cathedral, had attempted in the 1690s to establish himself as an actor in London but had failed, apparently because of his wooden acting skills.[11]

Singing was an accepted part of an actor's required skills and, more particularly, of an actress's. Musical ability was frequently commented upon in newspaper reviews; of Charles Incledon in 1796, the *Newcastle Chronicle* commented that 'his powers of harmony are unparalleled, and the compass and melody of his voice truly enchanting'.[12] Such reviews were almost always uncritical and laudatory although this charity did not usually extend to the instrumental performers. When Mrs Kemble made her debut in Newcastle in 1791 (playing Ophelia in *Hamlet*), the *Chronicle* remarked that 'the style and manner of her singing was so sweetly plaintive and harmonious that the audience … unanimously shed the sympathetic tear'. 'The songs were sung with great taste and sweetness,' the *Chronicle* claimed, 'particularly that in which she had not the competition of the fiddlers to encounter.'[13]

So popular were many of these actress/singers, and so widely acknowledged their musical abilities (as well as their personal charms), that it was a common practice for them to hold benefits, not only in the theatre, but also in the concert room. Some of these benefits were 'by particular Desire', that is, by invitation of local notables. Mrs St Clair of the Newcastle company was invited by the ladies and gentlemen of North Shields to hold a concert there in 1751; she could have accepted in the knowledge that the invitation made probable a substantial audience and therefore substantial profits.[14] Other actresses took a more calculated risk in organizing their own benefits as did Mrs Stamper ('late Signora Mazzanti'), again of the Newcastle company, when in 1759 and 1760 she undertook mini-tours of the region, performing works by Pergolesi, Sassone, Handel and others at concerts in Newcastle, Sunderland and Durham.[15] From these self-promoted concerts, it was only a short step to being asked by promoters such as Charles Avison and his sons to perform in the regular local concerts of Race and Assize Weeks or in the winter subscription series. Actors appeared in north-eastern concerts much less frequently than their female colleagues, perhaps because of the presence of so many excellent male singers at Durham Cathedral; Charles Incledon, however, sang at the Newcastle Musical Festival in 1796 and an actor from Baker's company sang at Spring Gardens concerts in the 1760s.[16] The best of the theatre instrumentalists were also in demand, though to a lesser extent: Smith appeared as leader of concerts in the Whitehaven area; George French led the band in the Hull Musical Festival in 1791 as well as promoting several concerts for his own benefit.[17]

Repertoire

Although the musicians, thanks to the 1737 Licensing Act, had a vital part to play in the north-eastern theatres, their role could range from minimal to substantial. At the least, they would be required to play an overture to allow the audience to settle into their seats, and songs and dances to cover scene changes or the gap between the main play of the night and the afterpiece. As the century progressed, some of these items – originally utilitarian in purpose – took on ever larger proportions: one or more songs would be sung between every act of both plays; extensive dancing might take place on stage between play and farce; violin or clarinet concertos might be played as interludes. Folk songs were popular, favourite songs were frequently taken from other works and inserted into plays regardless of whether they made dramatic sense, local dancing masters performed jigs or minuets by way of advertising their services. Additional songs might be composed to compliment various bodies who might be patronizing the theatre on a particular evening or who had 'bespoke' a performance, as on 29 March 1786, when the then leader of the Newcastle theatre band, Thomas Wright, composed and performed 'The Sons of the Forest' in honour of the Gentlemen of the Forest Hunt who had requested the night's performance and who crowded the theatre.[18] This was one of Wright's most popular songs, being performed several times in both Newcastle and Whitehaven and, probably, in the other towns of the company's circuit.

The interpolated items on the bill for 11 December 1795 were typical of the variety of incidental items that might be performed.

> End of Act 2d, Mr. EDDY, of this Town, will sing a favourite Song (written by Dibdin) called *The Soldier's Adieu.*
> END OF ACT FOURTH
> A NEW BRAVURA SONG (written, composed, and accompanied on the Clarionet, by Mr. WRIGHT) to be sung by Miss BARNETT.

The much-admired Song of *The Lilies of the Valley*, By Mr. EDDY.
The favourite Song of 'Twas within a Mile of Edinburgh', by Mrs KEMBLE.
END OF ACT FIRST OF THE FARCE, The favourite Song of *TIPPY BOB,* To be sung in Character by Mr. EDDY.
To conclude with RULE BRITANNIA, to be choruss'd by the whole Company.

Songs sung *in character* were frequently added to plays in a manner that would have been familiar to Shakespeare and other earlier playwrights. Shakespeare's own plays (usually performed in abbreviated or bowdlerised form – *The Taming of the Shrew*, for instance, became *Catherine and Petrucchio*) were often presented with incidental music provided by well-known composers: in Newcastle, *Macbeth* was virtually inseparable from Purcell's music whose singing witches seem to have been an ever-popular trio; *Romeo and Juliet* used Arne's music of 1750 with an additional solemn dirge (to accompany the funeral procession) by Pasquali. Many additions had a patriotic flavour. On 8 July 1758, an ode was inserted into a tragedy to comment upon 'the late glorious Victory gained by Prince Ferdinand of Brunswick over the French'; other songs and ballads marked the loss of the Privateer *Terrible* (in 1758) and the capture of Guadeloupe (1759), or praised the British Militia (1759), the local Volunteer Corps (the 1790s) and General Wolfe (1760). Numerous renditions of 'Rule Britannia' and 'God save the King' took place in time of war or of George III's illness.

The largest of the interpolations was associated with the third act of the tragedy *Isabella, or the Fatal Marriage* where the marriage of the heroine and her lover Villeroy was marked by an epithalamium. At its simplest, this could consist of a single song (as performed by Baker's company in June 1759);[19] at its most extravagant, (particularly under Kemble in the 1790s), it could consist of an entire concert, with the theatre band on stage as if in the concert room. On 20 February 1792, this concert included an overture, two songs and a glee. The disruption caused by moving the band on and off the stage must have been considerable but the impact on the audience was clearly highly favourable as Kemble staged a similar spectacle for his wife's benefit on 26 December 1794. Instead of an afterpiece, he devoted the second half of the night's performance to a concert on the stage which, he promised, 'will form an exact representation of the *Grand Orchestra in Vauxhall Gardens*'. He decorated the stage with 'variegated lamps' and presented a concert of at least nine items, beginning with an overture and including various airs, comic songs, and glees and catches, as well as a clarinet concerto. Similar mini-concerts could be staged to take advantage of the attractions of celebrities visiting the area as on 12 October 1761, when Robert Bromley, a blind boy who performed on the Welsh harp and who had performed in local concerts, played a series of popular airs. Of rather more dubious quality was Signor Rossignol from Naples, who in February 1776, entertained Newcastle audiences with bird impressions and a violin concerto on a violin without strings – the sound presumably imitated with his voice.[20]

Of even more interest to audiences were the large-scale musical entertainments frequently offered as afterpieces. But these were not the Italian operas beloved of some London audiences earlier in the century; on no occasion were such operas performed in the region and even all-sung operas in English were infrequently presented. North-eastern audiences were almost exclusively regaled with the popular ballad opera which mixed spoken dialogue with popular songs often set to traditional tunes or to tunes 'borrowed' from a variety of composers; *The Beggar's Opera* was the epitome of this type of work but there were many later variants that culminated with the operas of Dibdin and Shield, composed exclusively by those composers. Some of these works travelled north with surprising speed. *The Beggar's Opera* was performed in Newcastle, by two companies at the same time, within four months of its first performance in London; one of the companies featured the original McHeath.[21] Thomas Shaw's *The Island of St. Marguerite* (1789) and Stephen Storace's *No Song, No Supper* (1790) both appeared in Newcastle only a few months after their premieres in London.[22] Few, however, were seized upon with such speed as William Shield's 1791 success, *The Woodman.* Stephen Kemble, knowing the constant popularity of Shield in his native region, moved swiftly to bring the production north. 'We hear,' said the *Newcastle Chronicle*, 'that Mr. Kemble has, at a very considerable expence, purchased the Manuscript of the new comic opera of *The Woodman* and intends to have it performed on the night of his benefit, which we understand will be very soon'; the play was performed ten days later, about three months after its appearance in London.[23]

Despite this predilection for swift presentation of the latest favourites, older operas could remain in the repertoire for a surprisingly long time; as many, like *The Beggar's Opera*, were satires on events current at the time of original composition, the immediate relevance of the plot and nuances of the dialogue must largely have been lost on the later audiences. Odell's satire on Walpole, *The Patron*, for instance, written in 1729, was playing to Newcastle audiences as late as 1764. But Baker's company, who staged this performance, were clearly accustomed to playing an older repertoire than companies later in the century; audiences in mid-century were presented with repertoire that was consistently 30 years out of date – it is not clear whether this was the preference of the audience which the company was forced to indulge, or the preference of the company which the audience was forced to tolerate for want of an alternative. Austin and Whitlock's company in the 1770s and 1780s, and Kemble's in the 1790s, presented a much more up-to-date repertoire. In 1776, Austin and Whitlock's company performed eight different ballad operas, of which six had been composed within the last 15 years; Kemble's company in 1791 performed 15 different operas of which nine had been composed within the previous ten years – the only work which was more than 20 years old was the ever popular *Beggar's Opera.* But some of these performances might be less than accurate – not everyone went as far as Kemble in buying up the manuscript of a work. Published copies of an opera were generally vocal score only; the overture was added in short score with only occasional cues included for orchestral instruments. A full performing score had therefore to be worked up from the vocal score, harmonies had to be filled in and orchestrated, decisions made over such matters as introductions to songs, and the whole adapted to the instrumental resources available to the companies; as a result, provincial audiences may have heard a work substantially different from that heard by their London counterparts. Such tasks were part of the duties of the leaders attached to the theatre companies, men like Smith, Brown and French.

The other substantial musical work heard on the north-eastern stage was the pantomime. This invariably centred around the adventures of Harlequin, was generally played by children (except for the role of Harlequin himself), was all-sung (in Harlequin's case, mimed), and heavily dependent on spectacle and on exciting gymnastic feats by Harlequin for its appeal. The poster for the performance of *The Christmas Tale (or, December, May, June and January)* played at the Theatre Royal, Moseley Street, Newcastle, on 27 December 1793, offered extravagant new scenery including 'a view of superb Ruins in a Country Church-yard, by Moon Light' and 'a beautiful, distant Hilly Country, the Sun Rising, the Shepherds unfolding their Sheep, which are seen dispersing and grazing up and down the hills'. A large bird was to fly around the stage, settling on various parts of the ruins, changing the colour of its plumage three times and at last transforming itself into Harlequin. Some of these effects must have been dangerous, which probably only added to the fun.

In some quarters, the pantomime was considered to cater to the tastes of the lowest and least educated theatre audiences; David Garrick at the Drury Lane Theatre in London, the arbiter of theatrical taste in the capital, refused for a considerable time to stage such entertainments although he eventually yielded to popular pressure. Much more to his taste would have been the many performances in the north-east of *The Ode to Shakespeare* or *The Jubilee*. Following the success of the Shakespeare Jubilee of 1768 in Stratford (which he himself had organized), Garrick wrote *The Jubilee* to allow London theatre goers to see Shakespeare's best-known characters parade across the stage, linked by a thin – indeed, almost non-existent – plot. The *Ode*'s popularity was almost immediate; Tate Wilkinson's company performed this almost endlessly to Yorkshire audiences from 1770 onwards, in a version that required an excellent violinist as leader, a solid continuo player and no less than six singers. Wilkinson hired the best known of local musicians, including John Camidge of York Minster, for the instrumental and vocal roles, and performed the principal speaking part himself. The *Ode* was particularly popular in York and Hull. In Newcastle, Kemble issued posters twice the normal size for his productions of the *Ode* around the region, in order to accommodate all the details of the procession (a procedure he copied for performances of Michael Arne's *Cymon* which also included a long procession). On at least one occasion, Kemble cut the *Ode* down still further to form an interlude, consisting apparently of the procession alone.

Of all these operas, pantomimes and other 'musical entertainments' (a term usually applied to farces with a high proportion of incidental music), only four were not premiered in London. *The Gentle Shepherd* was one, a ballad opera full of traditional Scottish tunes and written by Allan Ramsey; it had been premiered in Edinburgh in 1729, a year before its first London performance. In September and October 1760, a visiting theatre company from Edinburgh gave weekly performances of this work, performing it on nine successive Thursdays without any other supporting works – it is reasonable to suppose that it was popular.[24] The remaining three works not premiered in London were composed by Thomas Wright, Kemble's band leader. In December 1797, the *Newcastle Courant* announced that 'the Admirers of the Drama ... will soon be drawn to our Theatre, by a New Operatical Magnet – the MUSIC by Mr. WRIGHT – the DIALOGUE and SONGS by Mr. Riley, for whose benefit it is preparing'. The opera set scenes from Smollett's novel *Roderick Random*; no details are given in advertisements but it is likely that the two men set the section of the novel in which the hero and his companions pass through Northumberland. The music was 'in Mr. WRIGHT's first stile of excellence' although, as Mr. Riley was ill on the occasion of its first performance, he is unlikely to have done justice to the work.[25] No further performances are known. Wright also composed two pantomimes. *The Frolics of Lilliput*, subtitled *Harlequin's Trip to Brobdignag*, followed tradition in using only children for the principal characters but broke with it in also casting a child as Harlequin; it exploited the contrast in size between adult and child actors by using children for the Lilliputians and adults for Brobdignagians. (The literary allusions of this pantomime and the opera were probably at Wright's instigation; he was known to be widely read.) Special effects included 'Harlequin's Descent from the Moon, on the Top of numerous CLOUDS which will disperse, and leave him on the stage' and, rather mysteriously, 'the famous Animation Scene'. Like the opera, this pantomime seems only to have had one performance. Wright's second pantomime, however, had at least two performances, the second of which was produced at the Theatre Royal on 10 December 1794. It was a less complex affair than *The Frolics of Lilliput*, relying on its setting which was blatantly intended to appeal to local sensibilities. *Harlequin's Rambles thro' Newcastle*, as it was called, displayed 'the following new and elegant Scenery' including 'A Grand View of the SANDHILL, *GATESHEAD CHURCH,* (WITH A PART OF THE TOWN) The SHIPS on the TYNE, *And a beautiful Representation of the intended NEW EXCHANGE*'. Also promised was a view of a glass manufactory, with men at work, and a view of the 'Grand Acqueduct' that was planned to be built over the Tyne to carry the proposed new canal between Newcastle and Carlisle, a structure that was destined never to be built.

The 1737 Licensing Act, whose ban on the spoken word encouraged the performance of Harlequin's capers, also led to a spread in performances of a kind more commonly associated today with the circus. In November 1741, two London companies presenting this kind of spectacle visited the north-east at the same time. Robinson's company played *The Jovial Crew* in Sunderland on 30 November 'with several curious and diverting Entertainments ... particularly that celebrated Performance of roasting a Pig on the Slack Rope, by Mrs Robinson, the like never attempted by any Person in Europe but herself'.[26] The other company, Hallam's, offered audiences 'Dutch and French Rope Dancers, Tumblers, or Balance Masters', a 'famous little boy from Russia' who specialized in 'postures', various songs and comic dances and the Pantomime *Harlequin Hermit, or the Jealous Spaniard*.[27] By the last decade of the century, these theatrical performances had developed into the circus proper, using both human and animal acts in the manner popularized by Astley at the Circus Royal Theatre in London. The circus in

Newcastle – it did not advertise any performances elsewhere in the region – played on the open space of ground known as the Forth, almost certainly in a temporary building, and much of its entertainment had only the most marginal connection with music. One advertisement, for instance, offered that 'Mr. Holland will perform several feats of HORSEMANSHIP, standing on two Horses without holding, and play a SOLO on the VIOLIN, in the same manner as he did at the *Royal Circus*'.[28] But pieces that would not have surprised the audiences at the Theatre Royal in Moseley Street were also staged; in June 1790 the circus presented a musical entertainment 'called the LIFE and DEATH of CAPTAIN COOK. The scenery, machinery, dresses, and decorations all entirely new, and under the direction of Mr. LASSELS from the Theatre-Royal, Drury-lane'.[29] The circus was also the only place where ballet, rather than dancing, was to be seen; later in the same month the Forth Circus presented 'the favourite Ballet called the RURAL LOVERS. Principal Dancers, Mrs. PARKER, and Mr. LASSELLS'.[30]

Audiences

An anonymous hand (Kemble's?) has scribbled on many of the surviving playbills from the Moseley Street Theatre-Royal, indicating the takings from each performance or at least the state of the house – 'very thin … boxes full… moderate house' and so on. Tickets cost one shilling for the gallery, two for the pit and three for the boxes; in 1793 and 1794, a full house could therefore expect to yield around £112 in ticket money or, if only full-price tickets were sold, £125. (Late arrivals could obtain half-price tickets except on nights which boasted a special attraction such as a famous performer or expensive special scenery.) In the early 1790s, a good house was one where £70 or £80 was taken on the door, an indifferent house yielded £30 to £40, and a thin house as little as £9 or £10. Inflation and worries over the worsening political situation seem to have taken their toll and the takings decreased considerably over the next few years. By 1795, £20 or £30 was the average take on most nights, several nights yielded only £3 to £4, and £70 was reached only once. Even Mrs Siddons, visiting in January 1795, attracted only a small house and takings of £50 for her benefit; after expenses and Kemble's share of the profits were deducted, her take-away would have been much lower. In late 1794, after a series of very thin houses, Kemble printed on a playbill, with heavy sarcasm: 'Mr. Kemble returns thanks to the Public, for the very liberal Encouragement conferred on the Theatre this season'.

As both spoken plays and musical items were generally performed on the same night, it is difficult to distinguish their relative popularity. Occasionally, however, owing to the presence of particular performers, only musical entertainments were staged; thus in Assize Week 1794, Kemble hired Anna Maria Crouch and Michael Kelly – both known as much for their singing as for their acting – and staged a week of comic operas to exploit their talents. Financially, the week was not a huge success; *The Duenna, Lionel and Clarissa, Inkle and Yarico and The Beggar's Opera*, amongst others, played to only moderate houses, the average takings being around £30 a night and the separate benefits for the two principals attracting only around £60 each. But this was much the same pattern as for the rest of the year; it is likely that external factors such as the weather, financial factors and other attractions in the town could influence the size of the audience more than the repertoire performed.

The identity of that audience is almost impossible to assess. The differing prices for seats allowed for an audience comprising all social classes, from the rougher elements in the gallery to the gentry in the boxes. Several rows of seats in the pit were often reserved for any group that bespoke a performance; at various times these included the Gentlemen of the Forest Hunt and of the Shakespeare Club, the commander and officers of various regiments, the militia and the Volunteer Corps, individual baronets, and local notable women such as the Mayor's wife.[31] At North Shields, South Shields and Durham, the building of new theatres was greeted with extravagant enthusiasm by unlikely sections of the community as in 1797, when a vicar at North Shields was moved to deliver an impromptu 'friendly and impressive' speech on the laying of the foundation stone of the new theatre and the gentlemen present drank copiously to the success of the undertaking'.[32] The Freemasons were often active supporters of theatrical occasions; the foundation stone of the 1791 Durham theatre was laid 'with great masonic eclat' by the deputy grand master for the county after a procession with banners and music and before a special celebratory dinner.[33] Similar ceremonies marked the opening of the South Shields theatre in 1798 and may have been largely owing to James Cawdell's extensive freemason connections.[34]

What attracted these audiences, according to some theatre company managers, were the moral lessons to be drawn from the plays presented. In the 1760s, Mr. Baker's company in Newcastle regularly pointed out the morals of their dramatic tales. 'The design is plainly to guard Mankind from the Dangers which wait upon Bigotry and Superstition,' they explained of the play *Mahomet* in July 1760; a few weeks later, they quoted Smollett's favourable and even sycophantic view of Mary Queen of Scots ('endowed with such Fortitude as no Adversity could discompose') to advertise *The Albion Queens*.[35] When Congreve's play *Love for Love* was performed in 1760, Baker stressed that although the author's wit (and the decidedly 'inattentive' morals of the court that the author frequented) had occasionally misled him into writing lines that would have been better left unpenned, Mr. Digges, the manager of the Theatre Royal in Edinburgh, had 'very judiciously expunged all the passages objected to'.[36] This type of sentiment was echoed in 1765, at the opening of the North Shields theatre, when a prologue written by local poet, John Cunningham, was performed. The actor speaking the prologue in the character of a sailor (an occupation many of the audience must have shared) told of his visit to the London theatres with his girlfriend, Sal. After getting in a gibe at the musicians and 'their damned Sonatas', Cunningham wrote, with dubious rhyme:

> [Sal] loves your plays, she understands their meanings,
> She calls them MORAL RULES made entertaining.[37]

Cunningham's tongue was, of course, firmly in his cheek; it is difficult to judge whether Baker was sincere or merely trying to add an extra layer of respectability to an entertainment and a profession that was often criticized for its loose morals. Kemble rarely felt the need to play the same card, although at Christmas 1792, he staged *George Barnwell*, an instructive tale of a London apprentice gone to the bad, particularly to attract the nervous parent who was hesitating over whether to allow their children a seasonal trip to the theatre. 'It is a moral and a proper Play for this Season of the Year,' Kemble wrote on his playbill; it was his intention, he claimed, to make the theatre 'instructive by the Introduction of Moral and Historical Amusement'. The takings for the night are not recorded but another performance of the play two years later brought in only £3, representing a house of between 60 people at the most and 20 at the least – hardly noticeable in a theatre that could hold 1,500 people.

For, despite the pious protestations of the managers, what theatre-goers clearly wanted was entertainment, as witnessed by the popularity of half-price tickets. Many people came only for the afterpiece, the portion of the evening most likely to contain a musical entertainment, an opera or a musical farce, and no moral arguments were ever raised to justify these pieces. Unfortunately, the urge for entertainment was sometimes greater than the enthusiasm for the pieces played, as Tate Wilkinson found to his cost, at least once; any kind of entertainment would do, on- or off-stage, provided by the theatre company or by the audience. In May 1791, Wilkinson staged a benefit for the theatre doorkeeper, putting on as afterpiece, Stephen Storace's musical entertainment *No Song No Supper*. Tickets were sold at cheap rates ('as plenty, and as cheap as herrings are ... in Yarmouth on a plentiful Season', according to Wilkinson) and attracted a large but rowdy audience; the people in the gallery drank steadily all evening although they were good-humoured and appreciative, particularly of a young actress/singer in the afterpiece, Miss Reynolds.[38] Trouble started when, towards the end of the piece, the crowd demanded an encore of one of Miss Reynolds's songs, a request refused by Wilkinson on the grounds that it would entail a ludicrous repetition of certain plot elements. The audience took charge, creating its own entertainment, hurling candlesticks and other debris onto the stage, insulting Wilkinson, the actors and the band, and finally forcing the encore and an apology from the stage, from all the actors, from Wilkinson and from the leader of the band, George French (whose offence had been to go home thinking the performance was over). But this was no mindless exercise of mob power by the lower classes; the gentlemen in the boxes egged on the gallery, swore violently at Wilkinson and even tried to set fire to the scenery.[39] Cunningham's Sal had put it succinctly: moral tales were all very well but 'we've come to see what pastime you can show us'.

Notes

[1] For detailed histories of the region's theatres, see Harold Oswald, *The Theatres Royal in Newcastle upon Tyne: desultory notes relating to the drama and its homes in that place* (Newcastle: Northumberland Press, 1936); K. E. Robinson, 'Stephen Kemble's Management of the Theatre Royal, Newcastle upon Tyne', in *Essays on the Eighteenth Century English Stage*, eds. Kenneth Richards and Peter Thomson, Proceedings of a symposium sponsored by the Manchester University Department of Drama (London: Methuen, 1972), 137–48.
[2] *NC* 25 May, 15 June 1728.
[3] *NCh* 26 January 1788.
[4] Ibid., 5 October 1765.
[5] Brother-in-law of Whitlock and brother of the famous actor, John Philip Kemble.
[6] J. Cawdell, *The Miscellaneous Poems of James Cawdell, Comedian* (Sunderland: for the author, 1785), 69–73.
[7] *NC* 1 May 1779.
[8] *NA* 20 March 1790.
[9] Tate Wilkinson, *Nett Receipts of the Theatres Royal, York and of Leeds, Halifax, Wakefield, Doncaster and Hull*, passim.
[10] *NC* 25 March 1780.
[11] DCAB 18 February 1698/9.
[12] *NCh* 23 July 1796.
[13] Ibid., 22 January 1791.
[14] *NG* 20 March 1751.
[15] *NC* 3 November 1759, 11, 25 October 1760.
[16] *NCh* 23 July 1796, 10 May 1766.
[17] *NC* 12 April 1791.
[18] Playbill, 29 March 1786. Unless otherwise stated, details of repertoire for the Newcastle Company are taken from playbills held in Newcastle Central Library and details for the York Company from playbills held in York Minster Library.
[19] *NC* 14 June 1759.
[20] Ibid., 10 October 1761, 17 February 1776.
[21] Ibid., 25 May, 15 June 1728.
[22] Ibid., 5 February 1791.
[23] *NCh* 14 May 1791.
[24] *NC* 27 September 1760. The same company had also performed the work in Newcastle several times the previous year.
[25] *NA* 2 December 1797.
[26] *NC* 28 November 1741.
[27] Idem.
[28] *NC* 9 January 1790. The Royal Circus was Astley's venue.
[29] *NCh* 12 June 1790.
[30] Ibid., 19 June 1790.
[31] Such bespoke nights were no guarantee of a good audience; Kemble took only £34 for an evening bespoken by the Gentlemen of the Shakespeare Club on 15

December 1994, despite putting on *The Merchant of Venice*, an interlude (*The Triumph of Genius*) taken from Garrick's Jubilee, and Shield's popular comic opera, *Rosina*.
[32] *NC* 17 June 1797.
[33] Ibid., 2 July 1791.
[34] *NCh* 6 January 1798.
[35] *NC* 5 July, 12 July 1760.
[36] Ibid., 12 April 1776.
[37] *NCh* 5 October 1765.
[38] The account of this evening is taken from Tate Wilkinson's memoirs, *The Wandering Patentee*; *or, a History of the Yorkshire Theatres from 1770 to the Present Time* (York: for the author, 1795), 220–25.
[39] Ibid., 220.

Chapter 3

Popular Entertainments

The price of tickets for concerts – rising from 2s. 6d. at the beginning of the century to 3s. 6d. at the end – was much too expensive for the average man in the street. Even the shilling entry to Newcastle's Spring Gardens or to the cheapest seats in the theatre could represent a day's wage or more to a labourer. Moreover, these were the sort of people Avison and his patrons did not wish to see at concerts. Public music-making was for 'the genteeler People';[1] one of the objections to pleasure gardens was precisely that the low entrance charge attracted undesirable elements, and Tate Wilkinson in York bitterly lamented the rowdiness of the mob that crowded into the theatre gallery when extra-cheap seats were offered on benefit nights.[2] But even these cheapest seats were too expensive for many. For the men and women of the poorest strata of north-eastern society, musical entertainment was limited to what came free on the streets or in the taverns, and what they could provide for themselves.

The musicians who provided for these labouring people were itinerant fiddlers, pipers and ballad singers, and waits who might be seen from time to time accompanying civic processions or crying the hours. But these are musicians about whom very little information survives. Parish registers are often the only source, giving glimpses of their private lives, recording the births and deaths of their children and wives, and detailing their own deaths. From such registers come the names of the only identifiable north-eastern ballad-singers, Jane Mackinhem (Mackinnon?), who was buried in St Oswald's churchyard, Durham, in April 1761, David Hull (active in Newcastle in 1707–8) and Thomas Kidd who died in Newcastle in 1733. Fiddlers are more frequently recorded: Mark Henderson was buried at All Saints, Newcastle in 1702; Mark Chamers' daughter was baptised at St Andrew's, Newcastle, in 1711; William Murray's daughter was baptised at St Nicholas, Newcastle, in 1715; John Dickenson was buried at All Saints in 1763. Several generations of the Smith family in Durham – Elias, Nathan and John – are known almost exclusively from local registers.[3] Such men travelled to fairs and weddings, and frequented streets and taverns, playing anywhere a few pennies might be earned. Elections could be profitable occasions; the *Newcastle Advertiser* recorded in 1796 the death of Thomas Bolt, 'the lame fidler', at Melmerby in Cumberland, stating that he was 'the only musician employed by the late Mr Curwen and Sir Henry Fletcher, during the long contested election in 1768'.[4] In the north-east, pipers were often employed in a similar capacity.

The living was a hard one. Extensive travelling brought its own dangers – the *Newcastle Courant* reported the case of Thomas Potts of Gateshead whose fiddle and rosin box were found floating in a pond on Gateshead Fell, suggesting that he had fallen in and drowned.[5] Moreover, many people in the higher strata of society regarded itinerant musicians as automatically suspect, labelling them as rogues and vagabonds and subjecting them to the penalties associated by law with that status. Any person found outside the boundaries of their lawful parish of settlement without a sufficient source of income might be removed in case they became a charge upon local resources; thus in 1778 Nathan Smith of Durham, his wife and two children were removed from the township of Elvet where they were living on the verge of poverty, and returned to their home parish of Little St Mary (St Mary the Less, in the shadow of the Cathedral), a matter of approximately a mile.[6] References to fiddlers and pipers in local newspapers are always tinged with this shade of respectable disapproval; the *Newcastle Advertiser*'s report on an inquest held in 1792 on 'a lame lad called Drummond, a fiddler, belonging to South Biddick', while not making any overt comments, managed to suggest the just rewards of a misspent life. Drummond, according to the *Advertiser*, had called at a public house in Chester-le-Street 'much in liquor' and had been 'treated by a company with gin; when, in a little time, he drank thirteen glasses, and dropt down dead'. The jury's verdict was that he had been 'suffocated by liquor'.[7]

In view of the hostility that they faced from many sections of society and of the extreme difficulty in making a living, it is unsurprising that many of these men turned to crime. The *Newcastle Chronicle* reported the case of John Forster, a fiddler from Brampton in Cumberland, who was arrested in October 1770 for stealing 'a silver cup in the house of Jos. Smith … which belonged to the church, was of curious imboss'd work, and of great value'. The cup was found in Forster's possession, defaced and crushed.[8] The best-known of these men – the piper, James Allan – lived constantly on the edge of criminal society. Born in 1734 near Rothbury in Northumberland, Allan roamed the border country in Northumberland, Cumberland and the south of Scotland, travelling as far as Dublin and London. For a short period, he was piper to the Duke and Duchess of Northumberland at Alnwick Castle and eventually ended his career as a wait in North Shields. But his criminal career was easily as spectacular; it began in childhood with petty thieving and expanded as he grew older, to include horse and sheep stealing. He several times joined the army and several times deserted, and finally came to grief in 1803 when he was sentenced to death for theft of a horse. The sentence was commuted to imprisonment and he died in Durham jail in 1810. In the 19th century his flamboyant life made him a folk-hero and the subject of a popular tract (from which these details are largely taken); his exploits may have been exaggerated and romanticized, but it is likely that many itinerant fiddlers and pipers lived lives that were in essence very similar.[9]

Waits

Some pipers and fiddlers nevertheless contrived to be tolerably respectable and to make a steady if not prosperous living; Robert Turnbull, a fiddler from North Shields, had sufficient property of value to make a will shortly before his early death in 1761.[10] Some musicians had a second occupation – Matthew Kell, a fiddler from Hexham, was a cordwainer, from a family of cordwainers.[11] In many cases, an overlap clearly existed between such men and the waits who were employed by the civic authorities in almost every town, large or small, in the region, to add a little life and excitement to civic processions and other ceremonial occasions, as well as to rouse the town and call the hours. In 1766, the York Corporation Minutes recorded the duties of the waits there in detail:

> You shall be obedient to the Lord Mayor or his Deputy … and shall attend and play upon such Musical Instruments as you are best Masters of in all Service of the Corporation when required by him or his Deputy. – You shall attend the Sheriffs of this City in their public Cavalcade to Read the proclamation over about Martinmas as also each Sheriff on the day he makes an Entertainment for the Lord Mayor and Aldermen for which Service you shall receive from each Sheriff one Guinea but if the Sheriffs … require your further attendance for the Entertainment of their friends … then you shall be paid as such Service may deserve. – You shall call the City from the first Monday after Martinmas to the end of ffebruary that is every Monday, Wednesday and ffriday in the Morning, (ffast Days and Christmas Week excepted).[12]

Much the same duties were performed by waits throughout the region; in addition, they were available for hire by other bodies, often, as has already been noted, playing in local concerts or in theatre bands. Private individuals too sometimes hired them; when David Home, a native of Berwick, decided to make a lively occasion of his last night at home before going off to join the Lifeguards in January 1755, he gathered together 'the whole Corporation, Mayor, and Aldermen of Norton … with a great many of the other country Villages round, and the whole Set and Train of Musicianers belonging to the said Corporation' and, according to the *Newcastle Courant*, spent the night 'in the utmost Jovelty, Mirth, Pleasure, and Satisfaction imaginable'.[13] Newcastle, Durham and York each had five waits throughout the century (or, in the case of Newcastle, until 1793, when the office was abolished); Sunderland and Berwick had three each and other smaller towns one or two. In the north-east, at least at the beginning of the century, these men were usually not full-time professional musicians, but men of another profession – innkeepers, shoemakers, house carpenters – who used their post as a wait to augment their income. Their abilities as musicians were variable but their customary pride in the post was often evidenced by their describing themselves in parish registers as *wait* in preference to any other occupational title.

In Durham very little is known of the waits, thanks to a 19th-century spring-clean by the local Corporation which saw many of the older records destroyed. Only a few scattered references to waits remain in Mayors' Accounts and in such records as the Grassmen's Accounts of the parish of St Giles just outside the city, which detail payments to drummers, fiddlers and waits for beating the parish bounds.[14] The only waits whose names survive from the early part of the century are both singing men from the Cathedral – Abraham Taylor and Peter Blenkinsop – but both were persuaded by the Dean and Chapter to give up their waits' posts; the Dean and Chapter apparently believed the waits' activities distracted from the two men's performance of the singing man's duties. (They did not, however, attempt to persuade Blenkinsop to give up his management of an inn, an occupation in which he continued until his death over 50 years later.)[15] Later in the century, the Mayor's Accounts refer to two other waits, Peter Bone and Philip Young, but nothing more is known of either man.[16]

The waits in Newcastle are better documented. In addition to an annual salary of £5, they received from their employers, Newcastle Corporation, a new cloak every year, an entitlement that from 1705 was commuted to a money payment (£1 each) two years out of three.[17] It was this band that Charles Avison's father, Richard, joined in 1702, shortly after his arrival in the town, remaining in post until his death in 1721. It was common practice for several members of one family to be waits or for the post to be passed from father to son – the Kells (who may have been related to the Hexham Kells) were associated with the post in Newcastle for over half a century, from Henry Kell, a house carpenter, who was given money by Newcastle Corporation to buy musical instruments for the waits in 1702, to Simpson Kell (possibly his grandson) who was appointed wait in mid-century and held the post until his death in 1763.[18] (A widow of the family married Edward, Charles Avison's brother, in 1759.)[19] But, as with their itinerant counterparts, the waits' status was not high, and their reputation in the town was poor on both musical and moral grounds. A number of problems in 1705 suggests that some waits were too ill (possibly too elderly) to work and that performance quality was low; the Corporation therefore appointed a new wait, John Jubb, 'to make them a better company and a good concert of music'.[20] But Jubb was probably ineffectual – at the time of his death in 1711, the Corporation was still complaining of 'divers irregular practices committed and done … to the great prejudice of the company of waites of this town'.[21] The only named offender was Robert Martin whose two sons, William and John, were also waits. Despite the Corporation's apparent anxiety to do something about these 'irregular practices', however, Martin was not removed from his post and was still drawing his salary shortly before his death in 1737.[22]

Low remuneration may have been a factor in these problems, encouraging waits, even with other sources of income at their disposal, to abuse their positions; this was certainly the case in York where waits were on several occasions accused of demanding gratuities to which they were not entitled. York, like Newcastle and Durham, had five waits, with an additional three employed by the township of Skeldergate, south of the river Ouse; substantial differences exist, however, between the standing of the waits in York and those elsewhere in the region. A dispute over the status of one of the waits' assistants, Joseph Shaw, in 1693, was not over the behaviour of the musicians – although it led to their temporary discharge – but over the fact that Shaw was not a freeman of the city.[23] In no other centre in the north were waits required to be freemen, and the stipulation suggests a social standing rather higher than was usual for waits. This was emphasized by an unusual method of payment; although, like the Newcastle waits, they were allowed a regular livery (granted once every six years and described in 1736 as being made of fine scarlet cloth, with buttons and trimmings, and silver lace to ornament the hats), their regular annual salary was extremely low, fluctuating considerably at the beginning of the century but settling in 1719/20 at £5 per annum, to be divided equally between the five waits.[24] This small payment seems to have been a retainer rather than a salary, ensuring the availability of the waits on official occasions that might clash with other attractions; Corporation Accounts and Minutes record the payment of extra sums for playing at such events as the Mayor's swearing-in days and the annual Sheriffs' Feasts, and the waits were also required to play at local dances and assemblies particularly after the opening of the New Assembly Rooms in the early 1730s. The payments for these events could be substantial; each wait received 15 shillings per day for the six days of Race Week, which sum obliged them to play at the dancing assemblies each night and at a varying number of morning concerts.[25] The income from this week alone could almost equal the entire yearly salary of the Newcastle waits.

As a result of these factors, waits in York were professional musicians from the beginning of the century and possibly before, rather than the part-time musicians of other occupations common elsewhere in the north-east, the standard of their playing was probably better than elsewhere and their organization was regarded as exemplary. A note in the minutes of the York Assembly Rooms in 1764 indicates that, when the Managers of the Rooms decided to reorganize and improve the concert band, they used the conditions under which the waits operated as a blueprint. In conjunction with the Directors of the Musick Assembly (who ran the concerts) they agreed that: 'we will employ at the Assembly Rooms, such a band of Musick as they [the Music Assembly Directors] shall appoint; and as an Encouragement to get a good Band we will allow them 40^{s} a year each, wch is the same Salary the City Waits has & as good a livery besides the usual Salary'.[26] This plan, however, foundered on the lukewarm response of Mr Baker, the theatre manager (who was expected to join the scheme), who 'being asked if he would encourage this new Band, he gave for answer, he wou'd at the same price he now pays'.[27] Two years later, the waits came to grief, being accused of 'ill-behaviour'; the exact offence is not specified although earlier complaints suggest that the musicians may have been illegally passing the hat round during their performances to gain extra income. All the waits were dismissed and a new set appointed; only one wait regained his position.[28]

As the century wore on, the professionalization of the post spread also to Newcastle. Possibly the earliest professional musician in Newcastle to hold the post of wait was Solomon Strolger, who in 1725 was appointed both wait and organist at All Saints, Newcastle. By the 1760s and 1770s, most of the waits were full-time musicians – men like John Ross, later organist at Aberdeen – and in the 1780s, the waits were all musicians of some prominence, though not of the first rank of musicians in the town: William Grey, who occasionally acted as principal cellist in local concerts; John Aldridge, also organist of the town's Catholic chapel; William Wright, younger brother of Thomas and a music-seller and music-publisher; John Peacock, performer on the Northumbrian pipes and teacher; and John Thompson, a former chorister at Durham Cathedral, a singer, violinist and music-teacher. Thompson was the only one of these men who derived income from a non-musical source – he owned a breeches shop which provided much of his income; this, however, was evidently delegated to assistants as he devoted himself to music teaching and performance. But increasing economic pressures, in part at least owing to inflation caused by the political uncertainties in Europe, led

Newcastle Corporation to cut back on expenditure in the 1790s; the waits' posts were deemed no longer essential and the position was abolished. Elsewhere, however, the waits continued to serve until well into the 19th century.

Middle-class appropriation of popular culture

If little information survives about the musicians who provided music for the poorer sections of the community, and less on the nature of the entertainments they provided, other than hints and suggestions, many of the songs and tunes they must have sung and played still survive and remain popular today. In the 18th century, despite the contempt of wealthier members of society for the musicians themselves, these songs were increasingly admired and enjoyed. Charles Avison's notebooks, for instance, contain a few hastily noted traditional tunes although these seem to have been written in by a different hand on a few leftover staves – possibly added by one of Avison's sons at a latter date or even by a later owner of the book, Thomas Wright. The century saw an increasing interest in collecting and preserving such songs, an interest that tied in with the Enlightenment urge to rediscover the past and a more idyllic golden age. Some exploited this interest; the famous Ossian forgeries were readily accepted as genuine examples of old songs by many people including John Brown, Vicar of Newcastle, who took Ossian's existence as proven and lavished praise on the songs and on other compositions of the ancient Irish and British bards. He considered that they had an ideal moral tone and lamented that 'the natural Flame of savage Music and Poetry is now almost entirely quenched in the several Parts of this Island'.[29]

Towards the end of the century, collections of northern songs began to be collected and published by local antiquarians, albeit without tunes. Amongst the earliest of these collections were Joseph Ritson's who published *The Bishopric Garland* (published in 1784) and a companion volume, *The Northumberland Garland* (1793).[30] Ritson, a Stockton-born man, was scrupulous in his collection of songs, and his sense of wonder at such antiquity is evident even in the brief notes he adds to his verses: 'near 400 years old', he notes of 'The Battle of Otterburn'. But Ritson's collections included not only old songs but also modern verses by men such as the actor/writer, John Cunningham; *The Bishoprick Garland*, in particular was weighed towards the contemporary rather than the historical and Ritson's later collections such as *The Newcastle Songster* (later taken over by its publisher, David Bass) include songs by Shield and Dibdin, and other popular songs heard at the theatre.

The publication of traditional tunes had to wait until the very early years of the 19th century and the engraver, Thomas Bewick, may have been at least partially instrumental in their appearance. Perhaps because of his relatively humble origins, Bewick much preferred fiddlers and their music to the music he heard in the more genteel circumstances of the concert-room. His original employer, Ralph Beilby, belonged to the Music Society at the Sun Inn in Newcastle; Bewick frequently took messages to him there and was usually invited to remain. He did not enjoy the concerts there or the music he heard at the theatre; he castigated trained singers whom he found unmusical and praised Scottish songs sung simply in good time and tune. He was on good terms with a number of performers: with William Lamshaw, another of the Duke of Northumberland's pipers; with Lamshaw's pupil, William Cant; with John Macdonald and John Frazier, both fiddle players for Newcastle dancing masters.[31] But above all, he was friendly with the wait, John Peacock, one of the best-known players of the Northumberland pipes in the area. In his *Memoir*, Bewick relates how he was anxious to make sure that the old tunes and instruments should not die out, and encouraged Peacock to pass on the art, leading the way by hiring Peacock to teach his son Robert.[32] Peacock is generally credited with adding an extra five keys to the instrument and in 1801 compiled a book of tunes – mainly traditional – published by William Wright. It is unclear to what extent Bewick and Peacock's efforts led to an increased interest in the instrument but some evidence survives to suggest that it had a presence in some middle-and upper-class households; the Sharp family (prebendaries of Durham Cathedral), for instance, possessed a set of pipes.[33]

The Sharps also owned a Welsh harp, a number of whose practitioners visited the north-east during the century. Newcastle newspapers record the visits of three of these men. A Mr Parry included the region in a tour of the country during 1741 and 1742, travelling from Bristol to Yorkshire and thence to Newcastle, playing at both public and private functions. In Newcastle and Durham in April 1741, he played a mixture of Italian and Scots tunes on the treble harp and his reception was sufficiently enthusiastic to encourage him to return in October of the same year; a less than cordial reception on that later visit may have been the result of personal animosity directed towards him by local musicians – no reason for this animosity is known.[34] Another Welsh harper, Evan Evans, visited Newcastle in October 1777 and again six months later during Race Week but no details remain of his performance or repertoire.[35] However, a programme was published in the *Newcastle Chronicle* for a concert given by a Mr Lloyd in April 1774; Lloyd proposed to play a mixture of traditional (or mock-traditional), and art works that was probably characteristic of the repertoire of these harpers; he performed 'The Lass of Paty's Mill', 'The Highland Laddie' and 'Lovely Nancy', all with variations (presumably of his own composing) to lengthen the work and sustain interest, and framed the two acts of his concert with works more familiar in a concert setting: Handel's 'Water-piece', the overture to *Rodelinda*, 'part of the eleventh Solo of Corelli' and 'the Fifth of Vi Valdo' (no doubt a local editor's rendition of Vivaldi).[36]

Surviving concert programmes record no occasion on which traditional instruments such as the Northumbrian pipes were used in the regular subscription and mid-year concerts in the north-east, although Peacock's membership of at least one military band in 1790s Newcastle, may have meant that the pipes were heard in benefit concerts at that time. But even in the regular concerts, traditional tunes were widely used, either in their own right or incorporated into more extended works; the popularity of Allan Ramsay's comic opera *The Gentle Shepherd* was largely owing to its use of such well-known tunes and airs.[37] 'The Braes of Balendine' was performed in Charles Avison junior's concert of 18 April 1771; later concerts occasionally included Scots songs and Edward Meredith was lauded for his performance of such songs.[38] Traditional songs appeared even more frequently in theatre programmes as music between the acts; Mrs Kemble's performance of 'Within a Mile of Edinburgh' on 16 December 1794 was sufficiently popular to be repeated at least twice on later occasions.[39]

Even more popular was the practice of introducing popular tunes into solo instrumental works as the theme of a last movement rondo. Not only traditional tunes were used for this purpose – Thomas Thompson's piano sonatas during the French Revolutionary Wars included rondos built around 'Rule Britannia' and 'God save the King'. Thomas Wright's clarinet concertos frequently incorporated Scottish tunes –at various times, he composed rondos using 'Lewis Gordon', 'The Highland Laddie' and 'The Corn Riggs', and the *Newcastle Advertiser*, reviewing his benefit concert on March 1791, remarked that 'Mr. Wright ... whose abilities on the clarinet are well-known, has never displayed greater taste and execution, than in the pleasing simple Scotch air which terminated his concerto'.[40] Wright occasionally used European folk songs in a similar manner, inserting a Swiss tune, 'Ranz des Vaches', in a piece for military instruments in 1797. John Brown had commented on this tune and its significance in his *Dissertation*; Wright plagiarized his book to provide an explanatory note in his advertisement. 'This Air is so generally beloved among the Swiss, that it is forbidden to be played in their Troops on Pain of Death, because it makes those that hear it burst into Tears, desert, or die – so great a Desire does it excite in them of returning to their Country.'[41] Even where traditional songs were not directly quoted, their influence made itself felt; Wright's *Six Songs*, almost all of which had been originally written for performance in the theatre, before their publication around 1788, included four songs that might easily have been mistaken for traditional songs and featured the distinctive Scotch snap extensively.

Dancing, dancing assemblies and dancing masters

Peacock's collection of traditional tunes, intended as it clearly was for domestic use (being advertised for playing not only on the pipes, but also on flute or violin), must have been propped on the music-stand in many a drawing room to accompany an informal family dance. Dancing – in public assemblies and at private parties – had throughout the century attracted many people who were unlikely to find themselves in a concert room, although many of these were almost certainly people of the 'genteeler sort', rather than of the poorer classes. However, impromptu dances – often open-air – were frequent occurrences amongst the poorer classes in Newcastle to celebrate such events as the Coronation of George III in 1761 and its many anniversaries, as well as more immediately important happenings such as the withdrawal of the press gang; the 'venue' for these events was often the open expanses of the Sandhill near to the Quayside. In 1750, at Dilston Park, near Hexham, a genteel barbecue at which local ladies and gentlemen dined off roast hog to the music of an excellent band, was ended when the guests found the evening growing too cold and retreated to the warmth of their homes, at which point the labouring classes, made of sterner stuff, moved in: 'after the Gentry had withdrawn,' the *Newcastle Journal* commented, 'the Populace occupied their Places, and concluded the Evening with great Mirth and Jollity'.[42] More formal events also took place on at least one occasion; in June 1770, a competition for dancers was advertised in the *Newcastle Courant*, the event to take place on an especially erected open-air stage on the East Ballast Hills down the river from Newcastle, at the Low Glasshouses. The first prize, which was to go to the dancer 'that moves with the most graceful Attitude', consisted of 'a Holland-smock and Tucker, with narrow blue Silk-rose-knot Ribbons on each Sleeve'; the second prize was 'a genteel A-la-mode Cap and Blue Ribbons'. Men and boys could also run races to win a hat with a red cockade; teams for these races represented different public houses. After a cold supper at some of the public houses, the evening was to end with general dancing and some gentlemen had arranged a concert in a private house. (The organizers guaranteed that only the best dyes had been used for the prize ribbons: 'no other colours will appear … than true blue and good reds'.)[43]

The dancing assembly that was a staple of the winter's entertainments in almost all north-eastern towns attracted a richer clientele. Even smaller places such as Tynemouth, South Shields and Hexham boasted at least a monthly assembly; in larger towns such as Newcastle, the assemblies were weekly and run on a subscription basis in much the same way as the concert series. In York, in 1749, an anonymous writer to the *York Courant* blamed the establishment of a 'tradesman's assembly' for a decline in the popularity of the winter subscription series which he clearly regarded as a superior entertainment, not least because it brought the gentry and nobility into town with a considerable amount of money to spend. His reasons for suggesting that the assembly adversely affected the concert series are not clear but his general point was that such assemblies were in any case injurious to society. 'Has not this *Tradesman's Assembly*, a direct Tendency to make them neglect their *Business*? Does it not promote the destructive Vice of *Gaming*? Does it not create an Emulation in *Dress* and other *extravagant Expences*, to the Prejudice of *most* Families, and in the Ruin of *Many*? Does it not tend to raise, in the Minds of young *Persons* a Taste of *high Life, beyond their Circumstances*?'[44]

In Newcastle and elsewhere, these entertainments were arranged to avoid clashes with concert and theatre nights; in view of the small number of musicians available, most of whom played at all venues and events, this may have been principally a practical measure. In Race Weeks, dancing assemblies were arranged so that music-lovers could go on to the assembly afterwards; in York for many years, Race Week concerts were held in the mornings to avoid a clash with the evening assemblies. So-called Assembly Rooms existed in many towns, although in smaller places such as Darlington and Sunderland they were often merely the long-rooms of public houses. In York and Newcastle, however, large, elegant rooms were built especially for the dancing assemblies (and for the card assemblies also held weekly); York's stylish New Assembly Rooms on Blake Street date from 1730, Newcastle's on Westgate Road from 1776. (The latter replaced the old Assembly Rooms in the Groat Market, probably in the Turk's Head Inn and an even older set of rooms elsewhere on Westgate Road.) Although these Assembly Rooms were also used for concerts, they were not specifically designed as concert rooms and the rooms, long and narrow to accommodate long sets of dancers, and high-ceilinged, were far from ideal; the accommodation for the musicians was merely a gallery set at one end of the room, often raised above floor level. (The original design of the York Assembly Rooms may not have made any provision for musicians at all; a minute of July 1732 records an order 'that a Gallery be built for the Music betwixt ye Middle Column in ye Great Room next ye Recess, And that the Same be borne up by Iron Cramps'.)[45] The dancing assembly band itself was small – the accounts for the New Assembly Rooms in Newcastle show that four musicians only were employed for the usual winter subscription nights with eight on special occasions.[46] This band may have been identical to a band that advertised in the *Newcastle Courant* in 1801 calling itself the Country Dance Band; this latter body, of which William Wright was a member, played at the theatre, at the balls that often followed concerts in Newcastle and at private functions. The advertisement, the only known reference to the band, states:

> The Musicians composing the Country Dance Band of Newcastle return their sincere thanks for the Many Favours conferred on them in that Part of their Profession; and as the Ladies and Gentlemen have frequently been disappointed, particularly on a Play Night, they take this Opportunity to inform their Friends, that they are now disengaged from Mr. Kemble, and are at Liberty any Night in the Week to serve any Party of Ladies and Gentlemen, who may please to Employ them, by applying at Mr. Wright's Music-Shop, High-Bridge, or to any other of the Band.[47]

In York, a larger band was customary for dancing assemblies, probably around ten musicians, and the waits in York were often augmented for large-scale events such as Race Week by waits brought in from other areas: from Skeldergate, Ripon, Leeds and Wakefield.[48]

For those who did not know how to dance or who wished to improve their skills, dancing masters were available; the activities of these men can be deduced from their frequent advertisements. At the beginning of the century they were peripatetic, covering large areas of country in the course of their teaching activities; Hugh Demsey, who taught dancing and fencing using Durham as a base from at least 1723, advertised in the *Newcastle Courant* in June 1727 that: 'Being desir'd by his friends, he will attend at the City of Durham 6 Months in the Year ensuing, and will teach at Lancaster and Preston the other 6 Months'.[49] Many of the dancing masters have names that suggest a French origin – in 1731 a Monsieur la Motte advertised his services, claiming that he taught in several places, such as Carlisle, Lancaster and Kendal; a Mr La Glace advertised in the *Cumberland Pacquet* in the 1790s.[50] It was a frequent selling point for these men that they could teach the latest and most fashionable dances; Demsey's travels included frequent visits to London, and an occasional trip to Paris, to learn the latest steps. But this peripatetic lifestyle lent itself particularly to rumours, often maliciously inspired; Demsey was repeatedly forced to rebut claims that he was not returning to the area – for these rumours he usually blamed a Newcastle dancing master, a Mr Lax. Lax was presumably trying to poach Demsey's pupils.

The usual practice was for the dancing-master to open a school in town, teach for two or three months, then hold a ball at which the pupils would perform their steps for their admiring parents, and at which the dancing master himself would give demonstration dances as advertisements for his services. The organizational ability demonstrated at these balls was occasionally transferred to concerts; a Signor Campioni, competing with Edward Avison's events in Race Week 1771, offered the novelty of a breakfast concert at which he 'will do himself the honour of exhibiting in such dances as the Ladies and Gentlemen shall require'.[51] Two years later, a Mr Hogg – a dancing master probably working from North Shields – also put on a Race week concert in Newcastle but did not repeat the effort, suggesting it had not been particularly successful.[52] Towards the end of the century, most of these dancing masters became more settled, giving up their extended circuits for residence in one particular town, from which they travelled several days each week to nearby towns or villages. Although, as Thomas Bewick's *Memoir* makes clear, these men frequently employed fiddlers to play at their lessons, many were good instrumentalists in their own right; at least one dancing master played in Avison's concert orchestra of 1736 as a violinist, and in 1790s Newcastle Alexander Munro Kinloch (son of another Scots dancing-master, Adam, who came to the town from London in 1780), acted as principal cellist in local concerts and as Master of Ceremonies in the winter subscription series.

The tunes these men played for their lessons tended to be traditional but some dancing masters clearly composed their own tunes, and with the increase in domestic music-making at the end of the century, saw – like Peacock – an opportunity to increase their income by publishing books of the tunes they used, exploiting their pupils as a ready-made and willing market. The most blatant attempt to cash in on this partisan audience was made by Abraham Mackintosh, a Scots dancing master who came to the town around 1798; just after the turn of the century, he produced a book – entitled *A Collection of Strathspeys, Reels, Jigs, &c.* which included some pieces diplomatically named after pupils – 'Miss Rickaby's Reel', for instance. (The book also included one or two tunes of local interest, including 'The New Tyne Bridge' by T. W., probably Thomas Wright.) Mackintosh was not however the only dancing master to try to take advantage of the burgeoning domestic market: Alexander Munro Kinloch and Ivie Gregg (a dancing master who had worked in Newcastle for many years) both produced books of tunes around the turn of the century, published locally by William Wright. The Scottish ancestry of these men may have been an additional selling point, guaranteeing the authenticity of the country dances they taught, although the many Scots in Newcastle were not on the whole regarded favourably. It is impossible to know how many copies of these books were sold, but the fact that they continued to be produced suggests that they were profitable. Thus, many of the traditional tunes that had started life with the despised pipers and fiddlers at outdoor fairs and weddings for the poorer people came into middle-class homes, eagerly accepted and adapted for people of the 'genteeler' classes.

Notes

[1] *NJ* 4–11 November 1768.
[2] Wilkinson, *Wandering Patentee*, 220.
[3] The Smith family seem to have been resident within St Oswald's parish from the early 1750s and in the parish of St Mary the Less in the 1770s.
[4] *NA* 10 September 1796.
[5] *NC* 7 February 1767.
[6] EP/Du.SO/112/2/47.
[7] *NA* 3 March 1792.
[8] *NCh* 6 October 1770.
[9] *The History of James Allan, the celebrated Northumberland Piper* (Newcastle: John Ross, c1850). Many editions, mostly almost identical, exist of this pamphlet.
[10] Chapter Archives of Durham Cathedral, Church Commissions, Bishopric Estates, Receiver General's Accounts, 1684-1802, Box 133: will made 23 September 1761, proved 19 December 1761.
[11] Registers of Hexham Parish Church, passim.
[12] YHB 4 December 1769.
[13] *NC* 25 January 1755.
[14] *Memorials of St Giles, Durham*, Surtees Dociety, vol. 95 (Durham/London: Andrews/Quaritch, 1895), Grassmen's Accounts, 1727, passim.
[15] DCAB 20 November 1733; DCTA 1733–4.
[16] Mayor of Durham's accounts, passim.
[17] CCN 8 October 1705.
[18] Ibid., 15 September 1702, 25 June 1746, 26 September 1763.
[19] Registers of St. Nicholas, Newcastle, 9 October 1759. Charles Avison was a witness to this wedding.
[20] CCN 8 October 1705.
[21] Ibid., 17 April 1711.
[22] Burial registers of St Nicholas, Newcastle, 24 April 1737.
[23] YHB 23 October, 6 November 1693.
[24] CAY vol. 35, 18 October 1736 *et al.*
[25] ARA 27 July 1732.
[26] ARM 2 February 1764.
[27] Idem.
[28] YHB 4 December 1769.
[29] Brown, *Dissertation*, 158–9.
[30] Joseph Ritson, *The Bishoprick Garland, being a Choice Collection of Excellent Songs, relating to the above country, full of agreeable Variety and pleasant Mirth, A New Edition, corrected* (Newcastle: Hall and Elliot, 1792); *The Northumberland Garland; or, Newcastle Nightingale, A Matchless Collection of Famous Songs* (Newcastle: Hall and Elliot, 1793).
[31] Bewick, *Memoir*, 46; accounts of Thomas Bewick, 15 June 1798. Bewick paid Peacock one guinea for teaching his son.
[32] Accounts of Thomas Bewick, 3 June, 2 November 1798.

[33] Brian Crosby, 'Private Concerts on Land and Water: The Musical Activities of the Sharp Family, c1750–1790', RMA Research Chronicle, 34 (2001), 67.
[34] *NJ* 28 March 1741; *NC* 10–17 October 1741.
[35] *NCh* 11 October 1777, 20 June 1778.
[36] Ibid., 9 April 1774. A similar type of concert had been presented only a month earlier by Miss Marshall, a 14-year-old who had 'had the honour to perform before the Nobility and Gentry at Bath, London, Cambridge, &c. with great applause'. Miss Marshall combined 'Lovely Nancy' and 'Maggie Lawder' (performed with variations on piano and five stringed cello) with more conventional concert pieces by composers such as Bach, Piccini, Handel and Just [NC 12 March 1774].
[37] *NC* 27 September 1760.
[38] Ibid., 6 April 1771, 16 February, 20 July 1782.
[39] Playbills, 11 December, 21 December 1795; Brown, *Dissertation*, 75.
[40] *NC* 4 August 1787, 19 December 1795; *NA* 3 November 1798, 5 March 1791.
[41] *NA* 7 October 1797.
[42] *NJ* 8 September 1750.
[43] *NC* 2 June 1770.
[44] *YC* 17 January 1749.
[45] NARA 28 July 1732.
[46] Ibid., passim.
[47] *NC* 21 November 1801.
[48] ARA 23 August 1733.
[49] *NC* 3 June 1727.
[50] *CP* 30 April 1793.
[51] *NC* 15 June 1771.
[52] Ibid., 5 June 1773.

PART TWO

MUSIC AS ART AND SCIENCE

Chapter 4

Gentlemen and Amateurs

Private activities never received the same kind of publicity as public entertainments; when attendance was by invitation only, there was no need for the general populace to be told how their betters were enjoying themselves although occasionally local newspapers hinted admiringly at the entertainments of the wealthy. 'On Wednesday evening at the Concert and Ball given at the Assembly Rooms, York, by the lady of Walter Fawkes, Esq.; there was a numerous and brilliant assemblage of ladies and gentlemen: More of beauty, more of elegance, than were displayed on this occasion, will seldom be seen.' The concert, for which between two and three hundred invitations had been sent out, 'was in the first stile of musical excellence, and did the greatest credit to the abilities of Mrs. Hudson, Mr. Meredith, Mr. Wilton, &c.' and the refreshments 'consisted of every thing that could please the eye, and gratify the taste'.[1] Mrs Fawkes, as wife of York's mayor, had a reason for publicizing her musical entertainments but many a private ball and concert must have been noted only in the day-to-day diaries of the wealthy, or in the occasional letter between friends.

As a result, the identities of the wealthy amateur music-lovers and the nature of their activities can be difficult to establish, and must be gleaned from a number of fragmentary sources – dedications of music, subscribers' lists, references in private papers and correspondence. But it is hard to imagine that many, if any, of the richer families of the region did not indulge in some sort of musical activity. Few went as far as Lord Delaval of Seaton Delaval Hall who built a theatre at his house and held theatrical evenings there *à la Mansfield Park*, performing plays and comic operas with members of his family and guests filling leading roles,[2] or George Bowes, local MP and landowner, who in 1750 invited Maurice Greene to his house at Gibside to perform his opera *Florimel*, but many took up musical instruments and played to a higher or lower standard.[3] Earl Cowper, brother of the Dean of Durham Cathedral, was an excellent violinist who took the Cathedral band in hand on his visits north; the Reverend Mr Nesfield, vicar of Chester-le-Street, was a notable performer on the flute.[4] In 1792, the *Newcastle Courant* detailed a number of such gentlemen who played at the Durham Musical Festival, naming, in addition to Mr Nesfield, two other vicars and five members of local gentry families – the Metholds, Jacksons, Bainbridges, Viners and Forsters.[5] Avison's pupils included Lady Milbanke, wife of a local baronet and an excellent harpsichordist (Avison talked of her 'graceful performance')[6] and Ann Ord, whose husband had been High Sheriff of Northumberland and who herself had been a member of the Blue Stocking Club in London, attending meetings of 'both sexes eminent for learning, science, general literature, and the fine arts'.[7] (According to Avison, Mrs Ord's playing was 'elegant'.)[8] John Garth was patronized by fourteen gentlemen of County Durham including Lord Barnard (later the Earl of Darlington), whose children he taught at Raby Castle near Staindrop; he dined with the Milbankes and Noels, gentry families of County Durham. William Herschel was whisked south by the Milbankes to entertain the Duke of York at their estates at Halnaby in Yorkshire.[9] The Blackett and Ridley families of Northumberland record the purchase of oratorio tickets late in the century; of the 210 subscribers to Thomas Wright's *Six Songs* of c1788, seven were titled (chiefly members of Lord Delaval's family), 11 were of local gentry families and 15 were professional men (chiefly attorneys and surgeons).[10] The subscription lists of Garth and Avison are full of titled gentlemen and ladies – Sir Walter Blackett, the Duke of Cleveland, the Countess of Carlisle, Sir Thomas Clavering, the Countess of Scarborough and Sir Henry Mainwaring – and gentlemen of gentry families – James Garland Esq., Ralph Jenison, John Milbanke, Nicholas Lambton – in addition to a considerable number of clergymen.[11] Avison was friendly with the prominent Ellison family of Newcastle – clergymen, merchants and landowners; one of the maiden ladies of the family, Jane Ellison, who lived on family estates near Bishop Auckland, was the godmother of Avison's only surviving daughter.[12] Even allowing for a certain proportion merely wishing to be seen to be fashionable, or charitable, or merely performing what they saw to be a social obligation, many of these gentlemen and ladies exhibited a real interest in music.

The prebendaries at Durham Cathedral formed a small and extremely active clique of gentlemen with substantial interests in music. They were all pluralists and spent only a small proportion of the year in Durham, dividing the rest of their time between their southern benefices and the capital; in his letters, Spencer Cowper, Dean of the Cathedral and brother of Earl Cowper, recounts his visits to concerts in Hertfordshire, London and Bath and details his admiration for, amongst others, the castrato Senesino.[13] The Sharp family, who provided several Archdeacons of Northumberland, are perhaps best known from the painting by Zoffany, which depicts them with a variety of musical instruments. Their interests were eclectic, encompassing traditional music and the oratorios of Handel, and they enjoyed waterborne concerts, for which they bought and outfitted a barge.[14] On their visits north, they were fond of the extravagant, dramatic gesture; freed from the necessity to consider commercial success, they put on a variety of concerts 'for their own amusement': an outdoor concert in the gardens at Old Durham, a large house just outside the city (1754); a mini-festival of concerts – two concerts on the River Wear and its banks, and two more in the Cathedral (1756).[15] Between them, Dr Sharp's sons played the double-bass, bassoon, oboe and kettle-drums in these concerts but an inventory of the family's possessions taken in 1759, and the Zoffany painting, make it clear that they were much more versatile; the 1759 inventory included kettle drums, fifes, flutes, Northumbrian pipes, the Welsh harp, cello, violins, viola da gamba, serpent and even a boatman's whistle. Like almost all the prebendaries, they were devotees of Handel's music and patronized the Handel Commemorations in London in the late 1780s and early 1790s. Another prebendary, Dr Knatchbull, enjoyed a quieter type of musical evening – dinner, followed perhaps by a little music from some of his guests:

Avison, Garth and Hesletine.[16] Probably all the prebendaries attended the private concerts in the Deanery and in the Archdeacon's house in the College behind the Cathedral, where mid-century concerts included works by Corelli and Geminiani – now becoming a trifle old fashioned – and apparently complete performances of oratorios such as *Messiah* in which the singing men took principal vocal and instrumental roles.[17] Some prebendaries even 'borrowed' the organist and a singing man or two from the choir and bore them south to provide private entertainment at their homes; in March 1748, James Hesletine was given leave of absence, while repair work was being carried out on the organ, to accompany one of the prebendaries to his home in the south – a week later the Dean and Chapter of the Cathedral granted permission for Hesletine to take one singing man and three choristers with him.[18] Hesletine seems to have been absent until the beginning of September.[19]

As the activities of the Sharps show, the prebendaries were prepared to make political statements by their musical activities. The Dolben family of Finedon in Northamptonshire (Sir John Dolben was a prebendary of Durham Cathedral in the first half of the century) was active in the movement to revive the so-called 'ancient' music as undertaken by the Academy of Ancient Music in London from the 1720s; Dolben owned copies of motets by Palestrina, Byrd and others.[20] Later in the century, the ideals of the Concert of Ancient Music were close to the prebendaries' hearts, particularly in its adulation of Handel, whose music had never gone out of fashion in Durham. The fact that many prebendaries were the sons of noble or gentry families made them particularly receptive to the implicit messages of the 1784 Handel Commemoration – that the aristocracy were the arbiters of good taste and that revolutionary ideals such as those rife in America and France were anathema.

Musical societies

In some cases, the kind of musical get-together favoured by Dr Knatchbull in Durham developed into a more formalized and regular arrangement. Eneas Mackenzie, in his history of the area published in 1827, mentions a regular music-meeting that he claims was held in the vicarage in Newcastle in the early 1760s. Mackenzie paid the penalty for writing so long after the event and the deaths of the people involved – some of his facts are demonstrably incorrect – but he may well be correct in his general points. The people he names as taking part in these friendly meetings were certainly active in music-making at this period: John Brown; Avison; James Hesletine (perhaps unlikely as Hesletine and Avison were on bad terms at this period); the Beilbys (engravers and later employers of the better-known Thomas Bewick); Lady Milbanke; and Mrs Ord.[21] This group may have been identical with the Newcastle Musical Society. Musical societies had originated in Oxford during the Commonwealth when prohibitions on public music-making had encouraged a group of gentlemen to meet privately, paying a small subscription towards the cost of accommodation, refreshments and the occasional visit of professional musicians from London.[22] The idea spread quickly; a recent study lists no fewer than 377 18th century societies in England, Scotland, Wales and Ireland, including formally-named musical societies, societies of singers, choirs, Sunday school choirs and glee clubs. In the north-east, the study lists musical societies in Newcastle, Durham, Sunderland and Darlington; further west, Carlisle and Whitehaven also possessed societies with another in Douglas, on the Isle of Man. In Yorkshire, several societies flourished in York (including a Glee Club at the George Inn), and others in at least ten other centres, ranging from substantial towns and cities, such as Ripon, Hull and Rotherham, to smaller places, such as Rastrick, Sowerby and Wadworth.[23]

The north-eastern societies remain shadowy entities, known only from scattered references in subscription lists and tradesmen's accounts. The Newcastle Society had been in existence and buying music from at least the 1740s – if Mackenzie's recorded meetings in the vicarage are accurately reported, they were only the latest manifestations of a well-established group. The society was still in existence in the late 1790s and may have survived into the 19th century and a second society met at the Sun Inn in the town in the early 1760s.[24] In Durham, the musical society is known only from a single purchase of music in 1766, and the Darlington Musical Society is known only from its purchase of Avison's Opus 9 in 1766.[25] Perhaps significantly, the Darlington Musical Society seems to have been active at the time of the only known subscription series in the town; the series may have been organized by the gentlemen of the Musical Society or have been a separate manifestation of a relatively brief surge of interest in music. The Sunderland Musical Society was active from the late 1770s until around the end of the century, buying music from Thomas Ebdon amongst others and purchasing from Thomas Bewick a medal for unknown purposes at a cost of 15 shillings.[26] The society's purchases were made by a man called John Thompson; this may have been the breeches shop owner who later moved to Newcastle, or a member of his family. Thompson's purchase of tickets for the society from Bewick suggests that this society occasionally held public concerts.[27]

The societies met in private, to allow the gentlemen members to escape the cares of business and the home, and to enjoy the twin pleasures of company and music. Taverns were popular venues, although John Marsh of Salisbury, visiting York in 1796, attended a meeting of the York Society in a dancing school, reporting that Haydn's symphonies were followed by a convivial dinner.[28] Although membership was closely controlled – members generally had to be elected – and confined to the wealthier portions of local society, professional musicians were often hired to give direction and strength to the playing. Many societies employed a professional violinist to direct the ensemble and, occasionally a cellist too; the Newcastle society in the 1790s employed Thomas Wright as leader, and hired a cellist from the local theatre. The theatre also provided the Sunderland Society with its leader at the same period in Mr Brown, the London-born musician who led the band of the North Shields Theatre Company and directed the gentlemen in their exploration of sacred music at the Freemasons' Hall on Sunday evenings.[29] (The Society had bought Thomas Ebdon's *Sacred Music* on its publication in 1790.)[30] A musician who handled his employers well could reap the reward not only of a regular salary but also of an annual benefit concert, on one of the rare occasions that the gentlemen, as a society, appeared publicly. Thomas Wright received several such benefits from the Newcastle Musical Society.[31]

Elsewhere, professional musicians could be a more integral part of the society, members rather than employees; this system operated in the York Musical Society, the only Northern society for which detailed records survive.[32] These records – chiefly attendance lists – cover the period from 1767 until almost the end of the century and indicate that the Society, which met weekly throughout the year (except in December), included both performing and non-performing members, regulating strictly the numbers in each category – in 1769, a proposed new member was refused admission because there were no vacancies for non-performing members. Performing members were greatly in the majority; in 1776, a proposal put forward to increase the number of non-performing members suggested an increase to 12 at a time when the usual attendance seems to have been between 28 and 30. Non-attendance and the frequent presence of casual visitors on a guest basis makes a calculation of the number of members difficult, but membership clearly grew steadily, from around 25 in 1767 to around 57 in 1796, and members included almost all the principal professional musicians in the city (including some singing men from the Minster), outnumbered roughly two to one by gentlemen amateurs – a rash of clergymen, several doctors, shop-owners and merchants and a dancing master. These gentlemen invited such notables as Felice Giardini to attend while he was in the area and acquired his concertos to play, to add to Carl Abel's symphonies and Geminiani's versions of Corelli's concertos and music they had bought earlier in the century: concertos by Festing, Avison, Jomelli and John Hebden, who had once run the public concerts in York.

Although these musical societies rarely gave public concerts, with the exception of benefits for their professional musicians and charitable concerts for indigent musicians, the gentlemen who were their members frequently appeared on the concert-stage, augmenting the relatively small numbers of professional musicians in bands such as Avison's Newcastle orchestra and Garth's Durham band of the 1750s. Bands for special occasions could be enlarged by calling upon amateurs from neighbouring towns and their help was always carefully acknowledged; for a concert in Sunderland in 1792, Thomas Wright advertised that the band would be larger than normal 'as the Gentlemen Performers, not only of Sunderland, but of Newcastle also, have kindly promised Mr. Wright their assistance on the night'.[33] The previous year, the *Newcastle Courant* had commented that for Wright's benefit in Newcastle, 'the kind assistance given by Gentlemen performers is deservedly the subject of much praise'.[34] The amateur status of these gentlemen was jealously guarded, with their names withheld from publication on almost every occasion; the leader of the band at the Darlington Subscription concert in 1765 was referred to merely as 'a private gentleman'. This attitude was more prevalent at the beginning of the century, however, and may have been changing towards the end of the century when local newspapers named a number of gentlemen amateurs at the Durham Musical Festival of 1792.[35] The tendency for the gentlemen to appear in the subordinate roles of rank-and-file members of the orchestra, rather than to act as soloists, may have been owing to a like reticence; in addition, a general feeling that it was beneath a gentleman's dignity to excel in playing an instrument – suggesting as it did that he had indulged in the sort of hard work more commonly associated with the lower classes – may have meant that there were relatively few gentlemen of a requisite standard to play solos.

The motives of these gentlemen for financing concerts and subscription series remain, in the absence of direct evidence, uncertain, although an element of philanthropy certainly existed in the gentlemen's willingness to promote benefits or series for favoured musicians or for those in need. In York, the subscription series grew out of a meeting of gentlemen but their reasons for making a public entertainment out of a private pleasure are unknown. In Newcastle, the gentlemen who organized the first subscription series of 1735 intended it for the 'entertainment of the town' but that would not preclude a desire to improve the facilities of the town and its appearance in the eyes of visitors (one of the justifications Avison brought forward for public music-making), or a desire to educate. The organizers of the Newcastle subscription series in the late 1790s kept firm control of the repertoire performed, as if to imply that their judgement was better than that of their musicians or their audience. But these gentlemen *were* the audience and were still running the subscription series for their own private pleasure; the small number of the subscribers in the 1790s may have itself been seen as a guarantee of exclusivity, ensuring that everyone knew everyone else and could be assured of their gentility. Unlike concert series earlier in the century, advertisements for these series rarely appeared and then only at the very beginning of the season, thus ensuring the likelihood that 'strangers' who bought tickets for the concerts on the night would be few, and most likely to be friends or guests of those already subscribers and therefore socially acceptable.

Studies and writings

In 1808, the *Gentleman's Magazine* published an obituary for Ann Ord that makes clear that, for her, music had not been merely a pleasant pastime or a practical accomplishment but also a subject for serious study.[36] Gentlemen, and Lady, Amateurs had money and leisure enough to read widely and to indulge themselves in a serious study of any subject that engaged their interest, and many seized the opportunity; in William Hayes's view, only such an impartial and disinterested amateur could be a 'learned and judicious Friend to Music'. The upper-class education that gave gentlemen in particular a command of several languages, ancient and modern, and encouraged them to be familiar with a range of authors, gave them the tools with which such serious study could be undertaken. Clergymen were especially voracious readers and debaters. In York, William Mason, one of the Vicars Choral, wrote about cathedral music and produced his own works, *Caractacus* and *Elfrida*, based on classical models of the Greek drama; *Caractacus* was performed at Covent Garden in 1776 and 1778 and in York in 1777 – the music was 'partly selected from the most celebrated *Composers*'.[37] John Jortin, the London clergyman who wrote to Charles Avison about the music of the ancient world (published in the 2nd edition of the *Essay* under the title of 'A

LETTER to the AUTHOR, concerning the music of the ANCIENTS') quoted or referred to a whole host of ancient authors including Horace, Pliny, Seneca and Ptolemy, as well as more modern writers such as Milton and Pope. John Brown quotes in his writings a similar list of authorities, with the addition of such luminaries as Voltaire.

The desire to study the theoretical aspects of music was not confined to the gentlemen but extended to at least some of the region's musicians. Charles Avison was not merely a practical musician; his writings indicate that he was widely-read and well-educated, although whether this was as a result of schooling or a self-imposed course of study cannot be decided on surviving evidence. He too had studied classical authors such as Polybius and Horace, quoting them in the original language and in translation, and had also read contemporary or near-contemporary writers, citing French writers such as Montesquieu, the Abbé du Bois, English commentators such as Shaftesbury and Milton, and such oddities as Tosi, the Italian castrato who had settled in England. Although Tosi's book had been translated into English and published as *Observations on the Florid Song* in 1742 and Avison also helpfully pointed out that Rameau's book on composition had recently been published in English translation, some of the works Avison quotes in his writings were not available in English translations and he may well have read the works in their original languages; a quotation from the poetry of Salvatore Rosa, in its original language, is placed on the title page of the first edition of his *Essay on Musical Expression* and it is plausible to speculate that Avison might have learnt the rudiments of that language from his teacher, Geminiani.[38] He was not the only musician whose erudition was commented on locally; at Thomas Wright's death in 1819, the *Newcastle Courant* commented that he was widely known as a man well-read in both classical and modern literature.[39]

In the early 1750s, Avison conceived the idea of putting his views on the theoretical and aesthetic aspects of music into print. The idea seems to have originated around 1751 when he was writing an extended preface for his Opus 3, *Six Concertos in 7 Parts* (which he dedicated to Ann Ord); the task, once started, began to attract more of Avison's attention than he had anticipated. 'I found my first Design, of writing Directions to Performers only, grew so much upon my Hands, that I could not resist the Temptation, however unequal to the task, of extending them also to the Practice of Composition.'[40] It was, therefore, with the purely practical aim of giving advice to performers and composers that Avison's most extended writing – the *Essay on Musical Expression* – began, although Avison widened its scope somewhat to draw an extended analogy with another art, painting, and to include an assessment of the value (or lack of it) of works by other composers.[41] By discussing considerations pertinent to composers, Avison was led into a discussion of aesthetic matters in which he put forward his belief that the purpose of music was to convey the 'passions' or emotions, and that this was not merely a musical consideration but a means of rational and social benefit. 'It is music's peculiar and essential Property, to divert the Soul of every unquiet Passion, to pour in upon the Mind, a silent and serene Joy, beyond the Power of Words to express, and to fix the Heart in a rational, benevolent and happy Tranquillity'.

Moreover, although music's powers might be misused, the emotions it aroused were nevertheless of the 'benevolent and social kind' – since music encouraged the benevolent feelings, it must inevitably deter the malevolent emotions. 'I would appeal to any man,' he wrote, 'whether ever he found himself urged to Acts of Selfishness, Cruelty, Treachery, Revenge or Malevolence by the power of musical Sounds.'[42] And the benefits, to individuals and to society as a whole, which followed from the pleasurable aspects of music, were always at the forefront of Avison's mind. He spent the first few pages of the *Essay* explaining how music could rouse the beneficial emotions and soothe those that were anti-social, and in 1758 wrote a letter to the *Newcastle Journal* in which he explained that one of the chief benefits of public music-making was the way in which it could encourage the friendly social intercourse of friends and neighbours.[43] In short, it was – at its best – a civilizing influence.

The first edition of the *Essay*, which appeared in 1752, prompted an acid reply in the form of a pamphlet – *Remarks on Mr. Avison's Essay on Musical Expression* – published anonymously, although its author was widely known to be William Hayes of Oxford.[44] Hayes's grounds for attacking the *Essay* were many, including the assertion that it should not have been written by a professional – and therefore biased – musician, but by a disinterested gentleman amateur. Hayes also doubted whether Avison had written the *Essay* without assistance, calling him the 'nominal' author and demonstrating a considerable snobbishness towards someone he plainly regarded as a provincial nonentity who could not even write harmony correctly. Avison added an addendum to the second edition of the *Essay* published in 1753, in the form of a reply to Hayes's pamphlet, disarming Hayes's criticisms by admitting the help he had had in forming the book. 'Having … attempted a Province of Writing which was new to me,' he commented, 'I thought I could not engage in it with too much Caution; and therefore, had recourse to my learned Friends,' adding that he was 'proud to embrace the generous Countenance which those Gentlemen of Integrity and Genius showed it'.[45] In short, he had consulted some of those 'learned and judicious' gentlemen amateurs of whom Hayes so much approved, and it is reasonable to suppose that he was expressing in writing views that had been formed in discussions with patrons and friends over a period of years; the *Essay* may be regarded therefore as broadly representative of the beliefs and opinions of many informed gentlemen amateurs in the north-east at that period.

A decade later, John Brown, vicar of Newcastle, also produced a book on music. Brown had come to Newcastle in 1761, too late to take part in the discussions that had given rise to the *Essay*, although he may have been, like Jortin, one of Avison's correspondents. The two men clearly shared many views, most notably on church music, and Brown cites Avison in his own book. But Brown's intentions could not have been more different from Avison's. Avison aimed to produce a practical guide for composer, performer and music-lover, concerning himself with matters of good taste and good music, and the qualities necessary to produce both; his subject was music with a sideways glance at the social benefits it might promote. Brown aimed to produce a didactic tool that would help to correct what he saw as the evils of his society; his subject was morality, with an examination of the way in which music and poetry might help promote that virtue in a decadent age. He viewed his own era with profound pessimism (he committed suicide in 1766), and looked back to a golden age when music and poetry were inextricably bound together and used as a means of inculcating the highest moral precepts – concerns that found their expression in the prolix title of his book: *A Dissertation on the Rise, Union, and Power, the Progressions, Separations and Corruptions of Poetry and Music, as they are found to exist in their several Kinds and Gradations among Mankind; thence to consider the Course which have produced that Separation under which they now lie, and have often lain, amongst the more polished Nations; and, in conclusion, to point out the Circumstances in which, and the Means by which, they may possibly be again united.*

The music of the Ancients, which had been a passing concert for Avison (he included only brief comments on the subject in the first edition of the *Essay*, and expanded this in the second edition, not by any writings of his own, but by including a rambling and amiable letter from John Jortin), was for Brown an ideal from which present-day society had fallen. Music and poetry, he claimed, had developed when man was in his most natural state (*unnatural* was one of his preferred adjectives for music he did not like). Man had developed from 'uncouth inarticulateness' to 'Action, Voice and articulate Sound' represented by dance, music and poetry respectively – these were the instruments by means of which laws had been promulgated and taught, and by which tales of heroes had been kept alive as a moral example to succeeding generations.[46] This original, and best, function of the arts had reached its apotheosis in ancient Greece; Brown wrote of Pindar that 'we find, in his sublime Songs, the fullest and most perfect Vision of salutary Principles, thrown out in Maxims, religious, political and Moral'. Euripedes 'carried the legislative Power of Song to its best Perfection'.[47] Moral purpose was to Brown the *raison d'être* of music; to Jortin's innocent question (posed in his letter to Avison) 'Why should not a man amuse himself sometimes?' Brown would have answered acerbically.[48] *Amusement* was music's worst enemy, though an inevitable result of the decline in modern morals and manners. 'In a great and powerful Kingdom, where additional Degrees of Wealth should flow in with every Tide, these, especially in a Time of Peace, must inevitably be followed by new Degrees of Inventive Luxury and an unwearied Passion for Dissipation, and Amusement.'[49] Opera pandered to this craving for amusement; likewise, a love of amusement prompted extravagances in composition and performance, encouraging ridiculous conventions such as the inappropriate repetitions of *da capo* arias, and virtuoso displays that were 'gaudy, flaunting, and unnatural'.[50] Music was not only capable of being a civilizing influence; it had no other purpose.

Surface agreements in the writings of Brown and Avison hid fundamental differences of opinion. Their agreement on the state of church music led them both to condemn what they considered to be old-fashioned practices of strict counterpoint and plead for a simple music that would allow worshippers to hear and understand the texts clearly. But, at a deeper level, they disagreed on the precise relationship between words and music. Brown believed that all evils stemmed from the separation of music and poetry and the oversetting of a natural order in which music must be subordinated to the text; moreover, the poet must always take precedence over the composer, for the words carried the moral message which the music must serve. Harmony, in Brown's opinion, was the devil's invention – too elaborate a setting must inevitably obscure the text, and lead the composer and listener into a contemplation of the music rather than the message. The absence of words altogether was unacceptable; Brown quoted, with approval, Plato's definition of instrumental music as 'an unmeaning thing, and an Abuse of Melody'.[51]

Avison's views on the subject, as a composer principally of instrumental music, were inevitably different, although cautiously expressed. He too spoke of the Greek period as a time when the art of song – music and poetry in partnership – had reached its high point, but he was not prepared to insist that this was the only form music might acceptably take. Music might be considered as a subject in its own right, rather than a mere adjunct to another art such as poetry, and harmony was 'the Perfection of Music as a single Science', although he admitted that it might detract from a listener's understanding of a text if used badly.[52] Moreover, he was more cautious than Brown about the possibility, or desirability, of restoring the simple perfections of Greek music. 'In our Days, the Ear being accustomed to the harmonic Institution of many Parts, the Attempt to approach too nearly to that most happy and simple Melody of the Ancients, might prove no less difficult than dangerous.'[53] Modern audiences, he feared, would find the plain unadorned simplicity of Greek melodies too strange to be comfortable. Harmony, used well, could enhance the pleasure to be gained from music: 'Let us not … suppose, that the modern music does not give us great Pleasure by its Harmony, for surely, if harsh and discordant Sounds strike the Air with a jarring Shrillness and wound the Ear, those which are smooth and concordant, must fill it with Pleasure.'[54] For Avison, the pleasure of music, and therefore its civilizing influence (in that it roused the 'benevolent Affections') was in its careful balance of harmony, melody and 'musical expression'. All three elements must be present for music to have its greatest effect. Too great an emphasis on melody produced vapid and extravagant tunes designed only to show off the performer's dexterity; too great a dependence on harmony was dull and lifeless. 'Musical Expression' was a nebulous quality, which he nowhere precisely defines; he wrote merely that it was 'such a Concurrance of Air and Harmony, as affects us more strongly with the passions or Affections which the Poet intends to raise'.[55] It was something that could better be felt than expressed. 'After all that has been, or can be, said, the Energy and Grace of *Musical Expression* is of too delicate a Nature to be fixed by Words; It is a Matter of Taste rather than of Reasoning and is, therefore, much better understood by example than by Precept.'[56] Taste could therefore best be cultivated by intelligent listening and studying the works of the best composers.

Nevertheless, in his writings on vocal and instrumental music, Avison might at first consideration seem to be supporting Brown's claims that music was merely the servant of the text. In his preface to the edition of the psalms of Benedetto Marcello, brought out by his friend John Garth, Avison endorsed many of Brown's views on the need for simplicity in vocal music; he stressed that in setting the psalms, the intention had been at all times to enable the words to be clearly understood and that, to this end, the number of parts had been kept to a minimum. His comments in the *Essay* that 'the finest Instrumental music may be considered an imitation of Vocal' and that the violin family was perhaps superior to other instruments in that 'with their expressive Tone and the minutest Changes they are capable of in the Progression of Melody, show their nearest Approaches to the Perfection of the human Voice' seem to echo Brown's belief in the supremacy of vocal music over instrumental.[57] Yet his own compositions were primarily instrumental in nature and he wrote in his *Reply* to William Hayes's pamphlet that 'I have always thought, that the Passions might be very powerfully expressed, as well by instrumental music, as by vocal'.[58] Tacitly, rather than evangelically, he was contributing towards a change in attitudes that was to accelerate towards the end of the 18th century and in the beginning of the 19th century, by which vocal music lost its supremacy, and instrumental music, by severing its connections with the text, became autonomous.

Audiences in the north-east would have sympathized with Brown on this issue, rather than Avison. Although instrumental music formed the greater part of all local concerts and was plainly much enjoyed, a popular prejudice in favour of vocal music was nevertheless still evident. In the rare reviews of concerts that appear in local newspapers, vocal soloists were often commented upon at great length while instrumental performers received little or no attention. Following the Newcastle Musical Festival in 1791, the *Newcastle Chronicle* dissected the performance of each of the principal singers in turn (coming to complimentary conclusions each time) but of the instrumental players, the writer could only remark, somewhat condescendingly: 'As we profess not a very refined knowledge of instrumental music we can only say, that the band was sufficiently full, and the execution of some pieces in a very superior stile, and as far as we could judge, might be said to approach the summit of excellence'.[59] The famous names that meant most to audiences and which brought them flocking to concert-rooms were those of singers: Madame Gertrude Mara, Signora Cremonini, Michael Kelly, Charles Incledon. Only a few instrumental players had the same drawing power when their names appeared in advertisements: Johann Peter Salomon, Felice Giardini and one or two local favourites such as Thomas Wright. But even Wright turned to singing a glee or two in concerts, and Madame Louisa Gautherot, the famous violinist, thought it best to include a song or two in her concerts in York in 1792, although this may also have had much to do with popular expectations of appropriate behaviour for female performers.[60]

Despite their differences in matters of theory, Avison and Brown found common ground when it came to practical considerations of contemporary performance – they were united in condemning the worst excesses of virtuosity displayed by singers and instrumentalists alike. Brown saw this as a distraction from the meaning of the text; Avison perceived it as a hindrance to the true expression of the passion or emotion the music should be conveying. Both believed it to be an exhibition of vanity and believed that it showed a lack of dedication to the spirit of the music. Large parts of Avison's *Essay* dealt with virtuosity of one kind or another, criticizing composers and performers (professional and amateur) alike, suggesting that in composition virtuosity was often a means of disguising lack of ability, and, in performance, of disguising a vulgar lack of taste. He referred to it as 'that Deluge of unbounded *Extravaganzi*, which the unskilful call Invention, and which are merely calculated to show an Execution without Propriety or Grace'.[61]

Brown blamed the public taste for virtuosity on the desire for amusement, on an 'unwearying Passion for Dissipation';[62] Avison identified a number of other factors. He believed that some performers had too much power – 'at once the Misfortune and Disgrace of Music'.[63] These performers pressed composers to produce works that showed off their talents to best advantage, which led in turn to those composers who complied being valued more than others of better quality who did not. 'Through the inordinate Vanity of a few leading Performers,' he wrote, 'a disproportionate Fame has been the lot of some very indifferent Composers, while others, with real Merit, have been almost totally unknown.'[64] Secondly, audiences did not, on the whole, have much taste or musical knowledge and were too inclined to be impressed by mere show. Avison's thinking in this regard may have been influenced by the reaction of Newcastle audiences to the Swiss violinist with whom he had clashed at the time of the first subscription series in 1736; one of Avison's anonymous supporters at the time described the violinist as 'a certain nimble-finger'd Swiss' who 'upon his receiving every Night an extravagant Demand for his Dexterity that Way, imagined himself a Person of so much Consequence'.[65] Avison's criticism of another group of musicians who sometimes indulged in misplaced virtuosity – church organists – might also have been directed at an acquaintance, Solomon Strolger of All Saints' Church, Newcastle, whose playing was some years later described by a parishioner as extravagant.[66] Strolger's continuance in post for 53 years, however, suggests that his playing satisfied at least the churchwardens of the church who had the power to hire and fire him. This lack of taste exhibited by audiences also, in Avison's view, encouraged composers to indulge in tasteless compositions, in the name of making a living; one of Avison's criticisms of Handel was that he composed too much and pandered 'to the vitiated Taste of the Age'.[67] In summary, he quoted his old teacher Geminiani, who had stated that, during the 34 years he had lived in London, 'the Hand was more considered than the Head, the Performances than the Composition; and hence it followed that instead of labouring to cultivate a Taste which seemed to be all that was wanting, the Public was content to nourish Insipidity'.[68]

It is a curious dichotomy that Avison seems to have been writing, in his theoretical works, with his mind turned towards new ideas, but acting, in his professional life, with his feet planted firmly in the past. His advocacy of the autonomy of music, divorced from words and from judgements based on its effectiveness in imitating non-musical phenomena, looks forward to the ideals of the Romantic era and the 19th century, as does his stress on balance and on music as an art rather than as a science. Yet he admired the music of Rameau, that firm believer in music as a science based solidly on the rules of harmony, describing his music as 'graceful and spirited' and full of musical expression.[69] 'His *Chorusses*, *Airs*, and *Duetts*,' he wrote, 'are finely adapted to the various Subjects they are intended to express. In the first, he is noble and striking: In the latter, chearful, easy and flowing; and when he would sooth, most expressively tender.'[70] He quoted Rameau's views on imitation with approval. Moreover, his own compositions looked back to the Baroque practices of his teacher, Geminiani, and Geminiani's teacher, Corelli, in both style and form; he was still composing *concerti grossi* – the so-called concertos for violins – at a period when his friend John Garth of Durham (20 years his junior) was producing cello concertos of a more modern style. In this, he was almost certainly influenced by the necessity to write for a concert band that was largely composed of amateurs;[71] practical considerations must also have led him to copy works by Hasse into his commonplace books, despite castigating him in the *Essay* as one of a number of composers, who indulged in 'an endless repetition of their *Subject,* by wearing it to Rags, and tiring the Hearer's Patience'.[72] Nevertheless, the band for which Avison composed also played in Durham concerts during the 1750s at which Garth's cello concertos were played and must therefore have been capable of tackling such music. Avison's adherence to the old forms, while influenced by practical considerations, was certainly also a matter of personal taste.

Apart from brief prefaces to psalters, dealing principally with the practicalities of singing in church, no further writings on music were published in the north-east until 1801, when Thomas Thompson, organist of St Nicholas's Church in Newcastle, published a dictionary of musical terms.[73] Thompson had been a child prodigy who had performed in public since his early teens and who had later studied with Clementi in London. On his return to Newcastle in the early 1790s, he established a teaching practice despite his youth – he was only 15 years old when he became organist of All Saints in 1793 and 17 when he moved to St Nicholas in 1795.[74] His book was clearly intended as a practical guide for his pupils; most of the entries are short and factual – an explanation of Italian terms such as *accelerando* and *lento*. But in a few entries, he discussed issues of more general and theoretical interest. Under the entry for 'cadence', for instance, he condemned the tendency of some performers to go to extremes, criticizing virtuosity in terms of which both Avison and Brown would have approved. 'Art, in this particular,' he wrote, 'is apt to prevail too much over nature, in consequence of a miserable ambition in performers to excel their rivals, in such rapid transitions and movements, as can have no better pretension to merit than the difficulty of execution.'[75] Thompson's need to condemn this practice showed, however, how prevalent this tendency continued to be.

Thompson also included a short entry on harmony, tracing its practice back to the ancient Greeks, and talking of its representation in ancient treatises in a manner that suggests that he had either personally studied them or read critiques of them. He quoted Quintilian in defining music as 'the Art of the Beautiful' but went on to say that 'this Art becomes a science, and even very profound, when we attempt to find the principals [sic] of the combinations [of sounds] and the causes of the pleasures which they inspire us with'.[76] In this respect, Thompson appears to be voicing sentiments of which Hayes and Rameau would have approved; under the heading of 'Taste', however, his views were more inclined towards Avison's and towards the modern view that music was an art which only good taste and judgement could define. Like Avison, he found taste impossible to define: it was 'that which is most felt and least explained'.[77] He pointed out that some conflicting opinions concerning the value of individual pieces of music were merely owing to personal preference: 'Each man has his peculiar taste, by the which he gives to things, which he calls beautiful and excellent, an order which belongs to himself alone'.[78] Differences in opinion in this respect could be attributed to an individual's character or disposition, age or sex. 'But there is also a general taste,' he wrote, 'on which all organized persons agree, and it is this only to which we can absolutely give the name of taste. Let a concert be heard by ear sufficiently exercised, and men sufficiently instructed, [a greatest number] will generally agree on the judgement of the pieces, and on the order of preference convenient to them.'[79] Part at least of this 'order of preference' could be assessed by pre-agreed rules – such things as whether a piece of music adhered to the rules of harmony – but much depended on an instinct that some men possessed and some did not. Thompson saw the development of this sense of 'taste' as a necessary balance to the musician's art. 'Genius creates, but taste makes the choice, and a too abundant genius is often in want of a severe censer [sic], to prevent it from abusing its valuable riches'; in this, Thompson may have been echoing Avison's reservations concerning Handel.[80] He concludes: 'We can do great things without taste, but it is that alone which renders them interesting. It is taste which makes the composer catch the ideas of the poet; it is taste which makes the executant catch the ideas of the composer' – again Avison had written something very similar in the second edition of the *Essay*, commenting that 'playing in good Taste does not consist of frequent Passages, but in expressing, with strength and Delicacy, the Intention of the Composer'.[81] It is likely that both Avison and Thompson would have regarded such good taste as limited only to a small number of people of the 'genteeler Sort'; Avison would no doubt have criticized the large and uncritical audiences who frequented the populist benefit concerts of Thompson's time, where exciting, showy military music and loyal, nationalistic sentiments were the chief attraction, and approved the much smaller number of subscribers to the turn-of-the-century subscription concerts, who admired the symphonies of Haydn and Pleyel, the songs of Mozart and, occasionally, Avison's own works.

Notes

[1] *LI* 6 March 1787.
[2] *NCh* 31 December 1790: 'On Thursday evening, Lord Delaval's elegant theatre at Seaton Delaval was opened for the admission of a certain Number of Ladies and Gentlemen to whom tickets had been sent, and the tragedy of *The Fair Penitent* performed in a stile that would have done credit to a regular theatre: The afterpiece called "*You may like it or let it alone*" was written for the occasion and consisted of a number of songs, selected from other pieces and introduced in an original plot … In the after-piece, Lord Tyrconnel [heir of Lord Delaval] gave the audience a proof

of his comic powers; he was throughout a fund of rich humour, and his songs were sung with considerable power and infinite Taste. The songs by the Miss Daniels were also highly deserving of praise'.

[3] Burrows and Dunhill, *Harris*, 272: I am grateful to Matthew Gardner for drawing my attention to this information.

[4] Burrows and Dunhill, *Harris*, 251–3, diary of George Harris, 21–5 October, 28 October, 19 November 1748; *NC* 20 October 1792.

[5] *NC* 20 October 1792.

[6] Charles Avison, *8 concertos in 7 parts ... dedicated to Lady Milbanke*, Op. 4 (London: John Johnson, 1754).

[7] *The Gentleman's Magazine*, July 1808, 581–3.

[8] Charles Avison, *Six Concertos in 7 parts... dedicated to Mrs Ord*, Op. 3 (London: John Johnson, 1751).

[9] Lubbock, Constance A., *The Herschel Chronicle: The Life-story of William Herschel and his sister Caroline Herschel* (Cambridge: Cambridge University Press, 1933), 22.

[10] Thomas Wright, *Six Songs with a Thorough Bass for the Harpsichord, humbly dedicated to Miss Carr of Dunston-hill*, Opus 1 (n. p., c1788).

[11] Avison, Opus 4.

[12] DRO D/Br/D 939: will of Jane Ellison of Durham City, 9 April 1757.

[13] Cowper, *Letters*, passim.

[14] For details of the Sharps' activities, see Crosby, 'Private Concerts'.

[15] These were the only concerts known to have been held in the Cathedral itself during the 18th century.

[16] Burrows and Dunhill, *Harris*, 279, diary of George Harris, 1–31 October 1751.

[17] Ibid., 252, 278, diary of George Harris, 19 November 1748, 25–8 September 1751.

[18] DCAB 26 March, 2 April 1748.

[19] Ibid., 20 July 1748.

[20] Burrows, D, 'Sir John Dolben, Musical Patron', *MT*, cxx (1979), January, 65–7; 'Sir John Dolben's Music Collection', *MT*, cxx (1979), February, 149–51.

[21] Mackenzie, *A Descriptive and Historical Account*, 590.

[22] Burchell, J., *Polite or Commercial Concerts? Concert Management and Orchestral Repertoire in Edinburgh, Bath, Oxford, Manchester, and Newcastle, 1730–1799* (New York/London: Garland, 1996), 171–4.

[23] Burchell, 'Musical Societies', passim.

[24] Ibid., 29.

[25] Ibid., 13.

[26] Ibid., 38; accounts of Thomas Bewick, 18 September 1777.

[27] Accounts of Thomas Bewick, 4 October 1779.

[28] *The John Marsh Journals: The Life and Times of a Gentleman Composer (1752–1828)* ed. Brian Robins (Styvesant, New York: Pendragon Press, 1998), 625.

[29] *NC* 19 March 1791.

[30] Burchell, 'Musical Societies', 38.

[31] *NC* 7 January 1797; *NA* 21 April 1798.

[32] YMS, 14 September 1767–27 December 1792. All the information about the York Musical Society in the following paragraphs is taken from this document.
[33] *NC* 26 May 1792.
[34] Ibid., 26 March 1791. It was an invariable practice for dancing masters and, rather less so, for musicians to insert a paragraph of thanks in local newspapers the week following a ball or concert, to thank their patrons for their attendance. Wright and the Volunteer Band did so after almost every concert in the 1790s.
[35] *NC* 20 October 1792.
[36] *The Gentleman's Magazine*, July 1808, 581–3.
[37] *YCh* 4 April 1777.
[38] Pier Francesco Tosi (transl. J.E. Galliard), *Observations on the Florid Song; or, Sentiments on the Ancient and Modern Singers* (London: 1742).
[39] *NC* 9 January 1819.
[40] 'Mr Avison's Reply to the Author of Remarks on his Essay on Musical Expression &c.', in Avison, *Essay*, 2nd edition, 3.
[41] The Preface to Opus 3, slightly expanded, formed the last section of the *Essay*.
[42] Avison, *Essay*, 1st edition, 3, 5.
[43] *NJ* 4-11 November 1758.
[44] Printed in full by P. Dubois, together with both editions of the *Essay*, Avison's Prefaces to his musical works, Garth's Marcello's Psalms, and a detailed examination of Avison's philosophical and aesthetic views: Dubois, P., *Charles Avison's Essay on Musical Expression, with Related Writings by William Hayes and Charles Avison* (London: Ashgate, 2004).
[45] Avison, 'Reply', 3–4.
[46] Brown, *Dissertation*, 27.
[47] Ibid. 82.
[48] John Jortin, 'A Letter to the Author, concerning the Music of the Ancients', in Avison, *Essay*, 2nd edition, 25.
[49] Brown, *Dissertation*, 241.
[50] Ibid., 205.
[51] Ibid., 47.
[52] Ibid., 65.
[53] Garth, *Psalms*, Preface.
[54] Idem.
[55] Avison, *Essay*, 61.
[56] Ibid., 70.
[57] Ibid., 101.
[58] Avison, 'Reply', 33.
[59] *NCh* 3 September 1791.
[60] *YCh* 23 August 1792.
[61] Avison, *Essay*, 1st edition, 35.
[62] Brown, *Dissertation*, 43.
[63] Avison, *Essay*, 37.
[64] Ibid., 38.
[65] *NC* 10 April 1736.

[66] Ibid., 13 January 1780.
[67] Avison, 2nd edition, 50.
[68] Avison, 'Reply', 45–6.
[69] Avison, 1st edition, 52.
[70] Ibid., 52–3, fn.
[71] Burchell points out that, in the second half of the century, some members of the Edinburgh Musical Society continued to prefer the older repertoire to the modern as it was considered to be more suitable for players of lesser ability. *Polite or Commercial*, 63.
[72] Ibid., 43.
[73] Thomas Thompson, *A Dictionary of Music, Containing an explanation of the French, Italian, and other Words, &c. Made Use of in that Science* (Newcastle: William Wright, 1801).
[74] It was not uncommon for organists to be appointed at a relatively young age; other local organists such as Thomas Hawdon and George Barron also obtained posts in their teenage years although most organists were older, generally in their mid-twenties or early thirties. Matthias Hawdon was probably in his late forties when he became organist of St Nicholas in 1776. Thompson was slightly unusual, however, in being appointed to such a prestigious post at that at St Nicholas – previous occupants of the post had tended to be older, more experienced musicians.
[75] Ibid., 1–2.
[76] Ibid., 13.
[77] Ibid., 19.
[78] Ibid., 20.
[79] Ibid., 20–21.
[80] Ibid., 21.
[81] Idem; Avison, *Essay*, 2nd edition, 140fn.

PART THREE

MUSIC AS AN AID TO PIETY

Chapter 5

Music in the Cathedral

Musical personnel

Music in English Cathedrals was, John Brown believed, 'not of the first Rank in the great Quality of Expression; nor yet so improper or absurd, as to deserve a general Reprobation'.[1] Brown's experience of such music was probably extensive – he had been a clergyman in London for some years before travelling north – but had clearly not been entirely happy; he wrote: 'We have no grand established Choirs of Priests, as in FRANCE; whose Dignity of Character might in a proper Degree maintain that of the divine Service. This Duty is chiefly left to a Band of *Lay-Singers*, whose Rank and Education are not of weight to preserve their Profession from Contempt'.[2]

The only cathedral in the north-east was at Durham; it was a cathedral of the new foundation, dating from the Reformation and, as such, it did not build its musical life around Vicars Choral, as did old foundation cathedrals such as York Minster, but around the triarchy of minor canons, lay clerks and choristers. The minor canons, 12 in number, were clerics, usually holding benefices in or near the city, the ten lay clerks were professional singers, and the choristers, also ten in number, were local boys. In addition, a number of deputies and supernumeraries and probationary singing men probably swelled the numbers or stood in for those singing men too aged or infirm to sing – the job was for life unless some misdemeanour resulted in dismissal, which it sometimes did. When all members of the choir were present, the preponderance of adult singers must have produced a bottom-heavy sound, although some of the male voices would have sung alto.[3]

Minor canons were required to sing in the choir by an order of 1690; the Dean and Chapter ordered that 'the Minor Canons be admonished to learn to sing and as soon as they are qualified for singing in the Quire that they doe sing as often as Occasion offers'.[4] This requirement may not have been strictly enforced; a century later, the Bishop of the time wrote to the Dean and Chapter reminding them that when they came to choose minor canons, they should consider not only their moral character but also their abilities as singers. He was a tactful man and stressed that 'his request might be understood not to convey any Reflection on the present very respectable Body of Minor Canons' but was to be regarded as an expression of concern to ensure 'the better and more solemn Performance of divine Service'.[5] The two most musically competent minor canons in mid-century were the brothers Abraham and Edward Gregory; Abraham was precentor of the Cathedral and Edward, a fine bass, was considered excellent as a soloist in anthems and oratorios.

The ten choristers, all local boys and often members of a limited number of families whose children followed each other into the choir over a number of years, were educated at the Song School, under a Master of the Choristers who was often (though not invariably) the organist; if more than usually intelligent, they could graduate to the Grammar School as a King's Scholar. For their singing, they were paid £3 6s. 8d. each per annum and were granted 40 shillings as a contribution towards the cost of finding an apprenticeship.

Some choristers returned in later years as adult singing men. In the first half of the 18th century, such local men made up the majority of the ten lay clerks, or singing men, and a substantial proportion of the singing men remained local in origin throughout the century, but the Dean and Chapter also pursued an active policy of recruiting professional singers from outside the area. In 1704, a Mr Budney of Cambridge was paid 'for his Care in supplying the Quire with good voyces'; Budney evidently trawled southern cathedrals for suitable singers – amongst those he may have recommended were a Mr Gryffin from Lincoln (who came to Durham in 1694) and Thomas Laye (1710), and John Ash (1722) whose origins are unclear.[6] These imported singers were paid considerably higher wages than the local men, their yearly salary averaging £30 rather than the £20 of locally-born singers. The Dean and Chapter were also prepared to allow exceptional singers to name their own terms; in 1693, the Dean was authorized to write to 'Mr. Blundeville the Singing Man at York to know upon what terms he will come to serve this church'. John Blundeville, however, took ten years to make up his mind to move and by the time he reached Durham in 1703, he may have been past his best – his terms were remarkably reasonable at £25 per annum.[7]

Wages rose as the century wore on. James Houseman, who was probably a countertenor, was sworn in as a singing man in 1732 at a salary of £40 on account of 'his extraordinary Voice'.[8] The first singer offered £50 a year was Thomas Mountier, previously popular in London concerts and briefly to become Charles Avison's vocal soloist in Newcastle concerts; Mountier was sworn in at the Cathedral in 1735. In mid-century, the Chapter also paid £50 per annum for Jasper Clark, from Winchester, described by the Dean, Spencer Cowper, as one of the best singers he had ever heard.[9] In the last quarter of the century, such high wages became commonplace; in 1782, no singer was paid less than £40 a year and four received £50. This increase in wages no doubt reflected inflationary pressures but was also an acknowledgement of the improved quality of the singing men themselves. William Evance (from Oxford) and Edward Meredith (from London) were the best-known of these late-century singing men, much admired and in considerable demand for singing at events both sacred and secular, outside the Cathedral.

But for these high salaries, the Dean and Chapter did not always receive good value. Complaints about non-attendance were frequent, particularly in the first three decades of the century. Some or all of the singing men were fined for non-attendance on no less than ten occasions between 1696 and 1796; in the latter year, the Dean and Chapter seem to have decided that if the stick of fines did not work, they would try the carrot of rewards; they offered every singing man who attended both services daily an extra shilling on each occasion.[10] Some individuals were persistently troublesome; Mountier apparently had domestic problems, including the illness of his wife, and was eventually threatened with dismissal for non-attendance – he was not paid after late 1741. Houseman, despite his 'extraordinary' voice, was accused of being 'Useless to the Quire' and 'very Negligent' and his abilities did not save him from being threatened with dismissal for drunkenness.[11] More than one singing man was expelled for adultery (which included sexual relations even where both parties were unmarried) and drink was a common failing: 'Laye, now appearing [before the Chapter] often before being Admonishd fror Drunkenesse and Disorderly Living aswel as negligent attend^{g} his Duty in the Quire and not reforming was Expell'd'.[12] Samuel Marlor in the 1790s committed the most spectacular offences; in April 1795, he was suspended from his duties 'in consequence of gross and disorderly behaviour at Church in a state of great intoxication by loud Talking and the most shocking imprecations by which the Reader was Prevented for a considerable time from proceeding in the Service'.[13]

Non-attendance may have been owing in part – particularly where weekday services were concerned – to the fact that singing men, despite their high salaries, were only part-time musicians. Throughout the century, they were expected to supplement their income from the Cathedral by taking on outside jobs. Jasper Clark was a barber who shaved his fellow singing men; John Marshall, a local man who died in 1782, was a watchmaker.[14] The Chapter did not apparently object to any of these activities, presumably judging that they did not interfere with the performance of the men's duties, but they took care to regulate apprenticeships for the choristers, insisting, in 1704, that they would not accept any boy as a chorister unless the child's parents first agreed that they would not enter into any apprenticeship agreement for him without the consent of the Dean and Chapter, clearly to ensure that the employer would guarantee the child's attendance at service.[15]

Towards the end of the century, the outside employment undertaken by the singing men more frequently took the form of other musical activities. William Evance composed and published music, and performed at various concerts around the area, both as a singer and as a harpsichordist; he travelled as far as Aberdeen for concerts and also undertook some teaching of the Durham choristers.[16] Edward Meredith's activities took him to Newcastle, Tynemouth, Sunderland, Morpeth, Leeds and Wakefield for winter subscription series, and Edinburgh, Manchester and Liverpool for individual concerts and musical festivals. These men and others frequently asked for leaves of absence to cover these activities; on no occasion was this refused although the absence of such key singers must inevitably have affected the quality of the choir. In addition, Meredith was parish clerk at the church of St. Nicholas in the Market Place; this too must have reduced his appearances in the Cathedral.[17]

Further problems may have been caused towards the end of the century by the general ageing of the choir. Meredith moved on in 1788; Evance and several others reliable stalwarts of the choir were perhaps past their best. Meredith's replacement also did not stay long, and other men imported into the choir from southern Cathedrals proved problematic: Marlor was always drunk, Radcliffe and

Stanley permanently on the verge of bankruptcy. In August 1796, Jonathan Grey of York heard a service in the Cathedral and noted in horror that 'it was slovenly chaunted & wretchedly hurried more than in any Place I ever was at'.[18] It is only fair to add, however, that only a month after Grey's visit, John Marsh of Salisbury heard the choir singing at the local Festival of the Sons of the Clergy and judged their three anthems very well sung.[19]

The outward-looking attitudes of the Dean and Chapter that had led them to search southern Cathedrals for acceptable singers also found expression in their willingness to allow leaves of absence for training, allowing singing men of local origin to travel to London for 'improvement'; this was especially significant early in the century, when the proportion of imported and ready-trained singers in the choir was smaller. A typical case was that of Robert Softly who in 1701 was given 'leave to go to London for a Yeare to improve his Skill in Singing and his Handwriting and Art in Pricking Songbooks' (that is, in music copying).[20] For some singing men, this leave could extend over a period of several years. William Smith, admitted a singing man in 1722 on the lowest possible annual salary (£6 13s. 4d.) was given leave eight months later to go to London for an indefinite period; two years later, he was given another 12 months' leave – it is not clear whether this was a continuation of the former leave or whether he had returned to the Cathedral in the meantime.[21] He had certainly returned before October 1727, as in that month he was allowed to go to Newcastle for a month to learn to play on the organ.[22] His salary had risen by this time to £20 per annum and he remained a singing man until his death in 1734.

The Dean and Chapter's willingness to countenance these absences was all the more remarkable in view of their experiences with one singing man, Richard Elford. Elford, a countertenor, was sworn in as a probationary singing man in 1695 and as full singing man three years later; his origins are not known but he was probably a local man. Given leave of absence to go to London, he spent most of his time in the capital trying his luck as an actor in the theatres; the Dean and Chapter dismissed him from the Choir in February 1698/9 'for neglecting ye Quire, and Singing in ye Playhouse and … for his Manyfest Contumacy'.[23] Elford pleaded the penitent and was reinstated but the uneasy truce did not last long – the lure of London was too great and although Elford forsook the theatres, he became a singing man at St Paul's and at Westminster Abbey.[24] Most singing men, however, behaved more conscientiously during their time in London and returned to Durham as better singers and copyists. This policy of sending singing men to London for training, the hiring of experienced and excellent singers from southern Cathedrals and the nature of the prebendal body itself – all of whom also held benefices in the south and who generally chose to spend most of their time there – ensured that the choir was not an isolated, inwardly-turned body, but had wide and frequent links with other ecclesiastical musical establishments, and with the latest musical developments in the capital.

The outward-looking policy was maintained in the early part of the century when the Dean and Chapter came to search for an organist. As had been the case in many cathedrals, the organ had been vandalized during the Commonwealth and a temporary organ, put up after the Restoration by George Dallam, had been replaced in 1685 by a larger instrument built by Renatus Smith. Two local organists, probably recruited from the ranks of the singing men, were succeeded in 1682 by the first organist appointed from outside the area since the late 16th century. William Greggs had been a singing man and master of the choristers at York Minster, but may not have been entirely satisfactory as he was on at least one occasion reprimanded for his teaching of the choristers and advised to be 'more careful hereafter'.[25] His conduct was not sufficiently heinous to put the Dean and Chapter off imported musicians, however; on Gregg's death in 1711, they appointed another outsider, the Londoner James Hesletine. Hesletine, who was around 19 years old at the time of his appointment, had been a chorister in the Chapel Royal under the tutelage of John Blow and throughout his time at Durham, also held the appointment to the post of organist at St Katherine by the Tower in London to which he had been appointed in 1709. His youth was by no means unusual – many organists were appointed at a surprisingly early age – but his elevation to such a prominent post was an indication of the respect with which his abilities were held. Hesletine was a man of difficult temperament, exacerbated perhaps by the early death of his wife (he never remarried); in 1727 he came close to dismissal for 'notoriously abuseing' one of the prebendaries and was only persuaded to apologize after nearly a month of arguments, during which period he was suspended.[26] Near the end of his life, he is said to have destroyed many of the manuscripts of his compositions as an obscure act of revenge after another argument. Despite these difficulties, he remained in post for 52 years, until his death in 1763.

His successor was the subject of considerable controversy. The Dean of the time, Spencer Cowper, wanted to promote one of the singing men, local man Thomas Ebdon, but the Chapter objected, not, it appears, from any doubts as to Ebdon's abilities, but at the Dean's high-handedness in taking the decision without reference to them. They refused to confirm the appointment. beginning a dispute that lasted a year, during which Ebdon carried out the organist's duties but was regarded by the Chapter as merely a temporary expedient while the Dean, determined to carry his point, paid Ebdon's salary as organist out of his own purse.[27] The resolution of the argument, a year after Hesletine's death, left Ebdon in post and he continued as organist, amply fulfilling the Dean's estimation of his abilities, until his own death in 1810. Hesletine and Ebdon between them served the cathedral as organists for 99 years; both also acted as the master of the choristers, although some of the training of the boys seems to have been undertaken by various singing men, particularly from the 1790s onwards.

Duties of the choir

The Dean and Chapter's Act Books for the 18th century make only rare references to the exact duties of the choir but a service sheet of 1680 shows that, at that period, morning and evening prayers were sung daily by the choir and that anthems were performed on each day except Wednesdays and Fridays.[28] A note dated 20 November 1711 in the Act Books indicates that prayers were held at '6 a clock' (presumably in the evening) and that the singing men were each expected to attend in turn to chant the psalms; the neglect of this duty was one of the most frequent causes of dispute between prebendaries and singing men. Additional particularly elaborate services were held on the great festivals of the Christian year – Christmas, Easter Day and Whitsunday – as well as on special occasions – the arrival of a new bishop in the city, the funerals of prebendaries. The singing men were expected to be in their stalls before the beginning of the service (the fact that the Chapter felt obliged to mention this in the Act Books suggests that the requirement was generally honoured in the breach), and were required to chant the psalms and responses, and to sing anthems. The service was most frequently the so-called short service, with the second, or communion, service reserved for the first Sunday of every month and for festivals.

In addition to these duties within the Cathedral, the choir made a regular appearance at the annual festival of the local branch of the Sons of the Clergy, a charitable organization originally set up in London in the late 17th century. The organization is known to have been active in the north-east from at least 1711, holding an annual service late in the year at which the choir from Durham sang the *Te Deum, Jubilate* and two or three anthems.[29] In the first half of the century, this service was always held at St Nicholas's church in Newcastle but in the second half of the century alternated between St Nicholas and the Cathedral in Durham; the service took place in the morning or early afternoon, allowing the choir on one occasion to combine the trip to Newcastle with the money-making venture of a concert in the evening.[30] The Dean and Chapter seem to have regarded the Sons of the Clergy service as a legitimate use of the choir, and those clerics who were in residence at the time also attended, but there is some evidence that the visit did not always go smoothly – in 1791, the Act Books record that the Chapter agreed that the expenses of the choir for the trip should be strictly limited, suggesting that some earlier bills had been unacceptably high and that the choir had been perhaps overindulgent.[31]

From time to time, particularly in the second half of the century, the choir was called upon to help inaugurate organs at local parish churches. In 1759, singers from Durham were present at the dedication of a new organ in Stockton Parish Church and in 1794 almost all the choir, adults and boys, travelled to Tynemouth, under the direction of the Cathedral organist, Thomas Ebdon, to celebrate the new organ there.[32] The celebration was a concert rather than a service; a selection of sacred music sung by the choir was accompanied by a band (described by one advertisement as the band of the West York Regiment of Militia but which certainly also included other performers), led by Thomas Wright of Newcastle. The vicar, the Reverend Mr Charlton, seized the opportunity to deliver a sermon in praise of the use of instrumental music in church, tracing its use since the earliest days of the Jewish religion and pointing out (in terms that suggest he may have been familiar with Avison's *Essay on Musical Expression*) its ability to 'stifle the malignant, and excite the best emotions, in the human mind'. The *Newcastle Courant* considered he had 'considerable strength of argument'.[33] The choir visited Sunderland on a similar errand in 1769, when they were called upon to assist at the opening of St John's Chapel in the town but this was not a concert – they performed 'Cathedral Service and proper Anthems'.[34] This visit had an unexpected consequence. The response from the congregation seems to have convinced Thomas Ebdon that there was an appreciative audience for music in the town; the following year, he and the choir put on a performance of Boyce's oratorio, *Solomon*, in Sunderland and a subscription series followed quickly.[35]

Individual singing men were also in demand to sing anthems at charity services; throughout the 1780s, William Evance and Edward Meredith regularly sang at sermons for a variety of charities in Newcastle and Sunderland. The sermon held in 1794 at All Saints, Newcastle, was typical – 'A sermon will be preached at All Saints' Church tomorrow forenoon, by the Rev. Mr. Lindow, of South Shields,' commented the *Newcastle Chronicle* in its local news column, 'for the benefit of the charity for relief of poor married lying-in women at their own houses in this town.'[36] Singing men customarily performed free of charge on such occasions and their motives may have been genuinely philanthropic but there was no doubt that such occasions could be a useful personal advertisement. Meredith also sang frequently at Freemasons' events, both formal and informal, singing anthems at anniversary feast and glees at convivial dinners; as he and many other musicians in the area were freemasons, these appearances may also have been unpaid.[37] His performance, with William Evance, at a charity sermon in York in March 1785, when the two men sang an anthem at a charity sermon for the Lunatic Asylum at St Michael le Belfrey, was also gratis, but the visit was paid for by their performances in two successive nights of oratorios to celebrate the opening of the organ in the church.[38] The singing men were also occasionally 'loaned' to other Cathedrals where resources were limited; two sang at the burial of the Bishop of Carlisle in 1787 when, as the *Newcastle Courant* reported: 'Dr. Nares's anthem, *The Souls of the Righteous*, &c. was performed to a very numerous Congregation, by Messrs Friend and Banks, from Durham, accompanied on the organ by Mr. Hill. The performance was solemn and affecting, and particularly the solo by Mr. Friend, which was executed with great taste and judgement'.[39]

Repertoire

If John Brown was disapproving of the employment of lay singers in Cathedral choirs in England, he was equally condemnatory of the music performed in the services. He was wholeheartedly in favour of the customary use of texts from Scripture which allowed congregations to hear the 'sacred writings', and approved the use of the vernacular, believing that the English language was 'generally round and sonorous, clearly accented, and capable of being adapted to a Variety of musical Expression'.[40] But the music to which these excellent words were set was a very different matter; his belief in the primacy of the words and his advocacy of the virtues of simplicity led him to remark that 'too studious a Regard to *Fugues*, and an artificial *Counterpoint* appears in the *old* [music], and too *airy* and *light* a Turn, to the neglect of a grand Simplicity in the *New*'.[41] He spoke well of some passages in Purcell's anthems, however, and of Handel's 'greatness and Sublimity of Style'.[42] Avison was equally critical, particularly of what seemed to be a rigid adherence to 'a dry rule of Counterpoint'; 'many an elaborate Piece, by this Means, instead of being solemn, become formal; and while our Thoughts, by a *natural* and pleasing Melody, should be elevated to the proper Objects of our Devotion, we are only struck with an Idea of some artificial Contrivances in the Harmony'.[43] He did, however, feel that many excellent compositions for the church had recently appeared 'which might be easily procured and adapted to the Purposes here mentioned'.[44] Both men wanted a general reform in church music; Avison felt that a lead for this reform must come from the organists of Cathedrals who, he wrote, 'are, or ought to be, our Maestri di Capella, and by whom, under the Influence and Protection of their Deans, much might be done to the Advancement of their Choirs'.[45] He cited, as an example of a reformer, Dr. Henry Aldrich, Dean of Christ Church, Oxford, who had introduced works by Palestrina and Carissimi into church services (albeit in arrangements by Aldrich himself).

The music performed at Durham Cathedral was firmly rooted in the past. The late 17th-century bishop, Dr John Cosin, had been a prebendary of the cathedral in the 1630s and much preferred the music of that period; his desire to return to what he regarded as an ideal music led to almost a century of musical stagnation fuelled by the conservative tastes of the prebendaries and by the general inclination against the new exhibited by the Church of England as a body. The service sheet of the 1680s indicates that the services and anthems performed at that time were principally of 16th- rather than 17th-century origin. G. W. Harris, in his diary during the 1740s and 1750s, records his visits to Durham Cathedral for services, citing performances of music by Henry and Daniel Purcell, Blow, Croft and Handel (particularly music from *Messiah*). The most up-to-date composer he cites is Robert Creighton who died in 1734.[46] A book published seventy years after the service sheet – *A Collection of Anthems As the same are now Perform'd in the Cathedral Church of Durham* – shows that the Cathedral repertoire was still firmly backwards-looking.[47] The book published the texts of the verse and full anthems sung in the Cathedral, together with the names and dates of their composers; although it does not indicate the frequency with which the individual anthems were performed, it does give an indication of the range of material used. 107 full anthems are listed and 120 verse anthems. Although at first sight there are a large number of anthems by 18th-century composers (51% of the whole), three composers – Aldrich, Croft and Greene – account for almost all of these works; Croft's anthems alone account for 22% of the anthems in the book. The appearances of Hesletine and John Garth are explained by the local connection and Handel's occasional anthems were also in evidence – *Zadok the Priest*, other Coronation anthems and the funeral music for Queen Caroline. The remaining 49% of the anthems are pre-18th century, with 19% of the whole dedicated to pre-Restoration works. Twelve anthems by Byrd, four by Tallis and three by Orlando Gibbons are included, as well as a number by lesser-known Gentlemen of the Chapel Royal. In the second half of the century, this trend appears to have continued; as late as 1788, Thomas Ebdon was publishing a communion services – 'Composed for the Use of the CHOIR of Durham' – very similar to those composed and published in the heyday of High Churchism in the reign of Queen Anne.[48]

Notes

[1] Brown, *Dissertation*, 213.
[2] Ibid., 214.
[3] Details of the Durham Cathedral Choir are taken from the Act Books of the Dean and Chapter (for appointments and details of salaries) and from the Treasurer's account books (for details of payments), unless otherwise stated.
[4] DCAB 20 November 1690.
[5] Ibid., 20 September 1794.
[6] Ibid., 20 July 1704.
[7] Ibid., 15 May 1693, 6 January 1702/3.
[8] Ibid., 14 October.
[9] Cowper, *Letters*, 169, 23 October 1753.
[10] DCAB 20 November 1796.
[11] Ibid., 30 November 1745.
[12] Ibid., 13 June 1717.
[13] Ibid., 11 April 1795.
[14] Details of Clarke's activities are in the Treasurer's Account Books; *NC* 6 July 1782.
[15] DCAB 20 July 1704.
[16] Farmer, H. G. *Music Making in the Olden Days: the story of the Aberdeen Concerts 1748–1801* (London: Hinrichsen, *c*1930), 71.
[17] Churchwardens' account books, St Nicholas, Durham, passim.
[18] Diary of Jonathan Grey, 11 August 1796.
[19] Robins, *Marsh Journals*, 624.
[20] DCAB 24 September 1711.
[21] Ibid., 24 September 1722, 10 July 1723.
[22] Ibid., 14 October 1727. Smith probably studied with Thomas Powell, organist of St Nicholas, Newcastle.
[23] Ibid., 18 February 1698/9.
[24] Charles Burney, *A General History of Music* (London, 1776) ed. Frank Mercer (New York: Dover, 1957), vol. 2, 481, 482n, 488.
[25] DAB 20 November 1704.
[26] DAB 19 August, 2 September 1727.
[27] Details of this dispute can be found both in the Dean and Chapter's Act Books and in the Dean's own papers, in the Chapter Archives: DCAB 1 October 1763, 17 November 1764; DRA/17, Deanery Accounts, 1763–4 passim. An account is also given in the diaries of G. W. Harris, 12 January 1764 [Burrows and Dunhill, *Harris*, 413–14].
[28] Brian Crosby, 'A Service Sheet from June 1680', *MT*, 121 (1980), 399–401.

[29] These services were reported annually from 1711 in local newspapers for most of the century. A book by John Smith (a prebendary of Durham Cathedral) entitled *A Sermon preach'd to the Sons of the Clergy at their First Solemn Meeting at St. Nicholas's Church, Newcastle, September 10, 1711* was published by J. White of Newcastle, late in that year. [Richard Welford, 'Early Newcastle Typography, 1639-1800', *Archaeologia Aeliana*, Series 3, 1907, vol. 3, 59].
[30] *NC* 3 September 1763; *NJ* 27 August–3 September 1763.
[31] DCAB 20 November 1791.
[32] *NG* 26 April 1794.
[33] *NC* 19 April, 26 April 1794.
[34] *NCh* 1 April 1769.
[35] *NC* 9 June 1770.
[36] *NCh* 26 April 1794.
[37] *NC* 12 June 1784.
[38] *LI* 29 March 1785.
[39] *NC* 25 August 1789.
[40] Brown, *Dissertation*, 213.
[41] Ibid., 213–14.
[42] Ibid., 214.
[43] Avison, *Essay*, 1st edition, 47.
[44] Ibid., 82.
[45] Ibid., 81.
[46] Harris's visits to the Cathedral were at random – merely the days he happened to be in Durham – and it may be presumed that he heard a representative selection of music. Burrows and Dunhill, *Harris*, 215, 262, 278, 279, 284, 285, 293, 326, *et al.*
[47] *A Collection of Anthems As the same are now Perform'd in the Cathedral Church of Durham* (Durham: Isaac Lane, 1749).
[48] *NCh* 12 April 1788. For a discussion of the significance of Ebdon's music, see Fellowes, E. H., *English Cathedral Music*, revised J. A. Westrup (London: Methuen, 1969), 29–30.

Chapter 6

Organs and Psalms

The provision of organs in north-eastern churches at the beginning of the 18th century was erratic – rare outside the large towns and not omnipresent within them. Outside the cathedral, Durham's six parishes had no organs until 1792 when an organ was built in St Mary le Bow, the small church in the lee of the cathedral;[1] St. Nicholas in the Market Place had had an organ before the Commonwealth but it had been torn down at that time. The small town of Sedgefield to the south of the city, had an organ built in 1708, of moderate size but no great quality; John Garth of Durham was organist there for some time in the 1740s and 1750s, and possibly longer; Garth also played the much older private organ, dating from 1688, in the Bishop of Durham's residence in Bishop Auckland.[2] Two of Newcastle's four parishes – St Nicholas and All Saints on the Quayside – had had organs since the 17th century; of the others, St John's acquired an instrument in 1735, but St Andrew's did not possess one until 1783. Gateshead Church also had an organ from the late 17th century and Newcastle's Roman Catholic Chapel had one from the late 18th century. Outside Newcastle and Durham, the existence of organs was even more patchy. Stockton on Tees had an organ – built by Thomas Griffin of London – from 1759, when John Garth and the Durham choir helped the parishioners to inaugurate it.[3] Sunderland, North and South Shields and Tynemouth do not appear to have obtained instruments until well into the last quarter of the century. Country parishes were even less well served unless a wealthy benefactor offered the necessary finance as in 1787 when the Earl of Darlington financed an organ for Staindrop, the village at the back door of his home at Raby Castle.[4] In 1795, two local notables combined to provide an organ at Earlsdon, north of Newcastle; Ralph Grey provided the money for the organ and Thomas Fenwick paid for the gallery upon which it was mounted.[5] Elsewhere, particularly in the larger towns, parishioners took the initiative in providing instruments. The Stockton organ was financed partly by the sale of pews in the newly erected organ gallery and partly by subscription. Around 80 subscribers (including Lord Darlington) subscribed £250 12s.; Griffin was paid £200 for building the organ and the rest of the money went towards boatage and porterage, painting and gilding, and the cost of hiring Garth and the Durham singers to perform at the dedication.[6] At St John's in Newcastle, the parishioners, having made a collection, asked the Corporation to contribute towards the cost of the organ and to pay the salary of the organist once appointed; the Corporation agreed to pay 20 guineas. A year later, the parishioners contacted the Corporation again to say that they had themselves managed to raise all the necessary funds but wished to hold the Corporation to its promise to pay the salary of the organist, as the

Corporation had 'upon all former Occasions of the like nature in the other churches of this town not only encouraged but provided for the continuance of the use thereof'.[7] The Corporation appointed the newly returned Charles Avison. Avison moved on within six months to a more lucrative appointment at St. Nicholas but 13 years later was in a sufficiently stable financial situation to return the favour to the parishioners. By this time, some years after the death of Avison's replacement, the organ was 'long useless' and needed repairs at an estimated cost of £160; Avison offered to contribute £100 of this if the parishioners raised the rest. In return, Avison required – and got – the post of organist for a second time although, as he remained organist of St Nicholas, he must have put in a deputy.[8] (In later years, his sons acted as his deputies: his elder son, Edward at St Nicholas and his younger son, Charles, at St John's.) Almost 30 years later, the parishioners of Newcastle's fourth Anglican parish, St Andrew's, set up a similar scheme for voluntary contributions to buy an organ; as with St John's, the Corporation agreed to pay the organist's salary. However, economic pressures in the 1790s led the Corporation to rethink their expenditure and insist that the parishes pay the organists' salaries themselves.[9] Only the salary of organist of St Nicholas's Church remained in Corporation hands.[10]

The builders of these organs were a mixture of local and national men. Dallam and Smith built successive instruments at Durham Cathedral and one of the Smiths was called in on three occasions between 1707 and 1711 to carry out repairs to St Nicholas's organ in Newcastle; when Avison recommended in 1749 that a swell be added to the St Nicholas organ, Richard Bridge of London carried out the work.[11] But the area had its own organ-builders, many of whom carried out repair work on church organs, but seem to have worked principally on the production of chamber organs. In 1734, William Prior – active in Newcastle during the first three decades of the century, making and repairing instruments of all sorts (as well as false teeth) – advertised a chamber organ (although it was not specifically stated to have been of his own building): 'a NEW ORGAN, Consort Pitch, fit for Church, Chapel, or Chamber, with two Sets of Keys, long Eights, and eight Stops, viz. *Open Diapason, Stop Diapason, Principal Flute, Fifteenth, Cornet, Sesquialter,* and *Trumpet*; so contrived that four of the said Stops with proper Handles are play'd in the lower Set of Keys; and for greater Variety, several of the Stops drawn in Halves'.[12] A John Oliver offered another chamber organ in 1740, described as having six stops and 335 pipes; nothing is otherwise known of Oliver – he may have been related to Thomas Oliver of York, a dancing-master who also sold musical instruments.[13] The chamber organs that these men produced were chiefly designed for use in the home, although the possession of one of these instruments by the curate of St Andrew's Church, long before the church itself had an organ installed, raises the possibility that the chamber organ may have been used in the church.[14] The usual practice was to raffle these instruments; the organ was displayed in a public hall for viewing or for playing, after which would-be purchasers bought a ticket – once the desired number of tickets had been sold, the winning ticket was drawn. William Bristowe (who was active in the region in the 1720s and 1730s, carrying out work on the 'little organ' in the Song School at Durham Cathedral and elsewhere) advertised in 1730 such a viewing for one of his chamber organs ('containing several Stops, with some uncommon Varieties') displaying it in the Cordwainer's Hall in Newcastle and inviting all music-lovers to try it out, excepting only the organist of All Saint's Church, with whom he had quarrelled 'for particular reasons'.[15] Bristowe did not advertise the cost of his organ; Prior raffled his organ in 1734 with 100 tickets at one guinea each and Oliver's went for considerably less: 50 lots at 10s. 6d. each.

These men seem to have worked over a smaller area of country than did Thomas Haxby of York who from mid-century began to travel over a wide area of Yorkshire and the Midlands repairing and building organs; not until the 1780s did the north-east region boast an organ builder of similar standing to Haxby. John Donaldson – almost certainly of North-eastern origins, possibly from Newcastle or North Shields – had followed the usual practice for a man with ambition and travelled to London for training, initially as as a clock and watch maker, spending 'some years with Mr. Dale of Coldbath Fields, principal Finisher to the celebrated Messrs. Mudge and Dutton, Watchmakers in Fleet-street'. On his return to Newcastle, he set up two shops, one a watch-making business, in the Bigg Market, and the second an organ manufactory, not far away in Northumberland Street. Donaldson advertised that he made and repaired 'all Sorts of Church, Chamber and Barrel Organs, to play Psalms, Concertos, Minuets, &c. in the neatest Manner, and on the most reasonable Terms'.[16] The reference to barrel organs was no doubt aimed particularly at country parishes, where such easy-to-play instruments, provided with all the most popular psalm tunes, could take the place of a more expensive and challenging church organ.

Donaldson probably gave up the watch-making business at an early date but the organ manufactory thrived. Throughout the next decade, he and his assistant, Robert Boston, worked on organs throughout the north-east, carrying out work on all four of Newcastle's organs – repairing All Saints' in 1781, building the first organ at St Andrew's in 1782-3, working on St John's in 1785, and carrying out extensive repairs at St Nicholas in 1786-7 during a complete renovation of the church; in addition, they carried out repairs on Stockton Parish Church after the theft of some pipes (1784), supplied a new organ for the rebuilt Freemasons' Hall in Sunderland (1785) and built a new organ for St Hild's Church in South Shields (1786). Work further afield included organs in Whitehaven, Aberdeen and Bradford. Some of this work may have been obtained through personal contacts; the organist of Whitehaven was probably related to a Newcastle family of waits, and the organist at Aberdeen was a former apprentice of the organist of St Nicholas, Newcastle.[17] In 1790, for reasons that are not clear, Donaldson moved his centre of operations from Newcastle to York, even though this brought him into direct competition with Thomas Haxby whose business was still thriving there. His best known organ was built just at this point of transition – an organ for the Earl of Belvedere's house in Dublin, which was later transferred to the Holywell Music Room in Oxford, where it still remains.[18] Donaldson opened a shop outside Micklegate Bar in York, later moving into the city to Petergate, selling instruments of all kinds, and travelling round the region making and mending organs; he returned to the north-east on at least one occasion, in 1792, to carry out repairs to the organ in Durham Cathedral.[19] He prospered, was admitted a freeman of York in 1797 and by 1800 was sufficiently prominent to be elected a common councilman of the city.[20]

The instruments constructed by these men are only infrequently described in local sources, owing in part to lack of technical knowledge but principally to a concern only with the general effect the organ made on the congregation in worship.[21] It is clear, however, that the three manual organ, without pedals, was the model for many organs in the region, certainly in the larger towns. Specifications for the St Nicholas organ in Newcastle indicate nine stops on the great, six on the choir and five on the swell organ; St John's was rather smaller with nine stops on the great, three on the choir and two on the swell. Both organs had a range of mixture stops, and trumpet and cornet stops on the great; St Nicholas's also had cornet, trumpet and hautboy stops on the swell. But few of the local papers were interested in such details. Of Donaldson's new organ at St Andrew's in Newcastle, the *Newcastle Courant* could only comment that 'the elegant construction and powerful effect of the new organ … does great credit to Mr Donaldson … and will be the means of recommending him to other parishes for that business, which has been hitherto, executed in the country by artists brought from London'.[22] The *Courant*'s only reference to the organ installed in St Mary le Bow, Durham, in 1792, was that 'by the by, it was too small'.[23] The *Cumberland Pacquet*'s writer was rather more interested in technical matters, and better informed concerning Donaldson's Whitehaven organ built after the old instrument (built by Snetzler) had been vandalized: 'The organ,' he wrote, 'will be taken down, thoroughly cleaned and tuned, rebuilt and augmented with three new stops, viz. a Thorough Trumpet in the full-organ, and a Principal and Stop'd Diapason in the Swell.'[24] The following year, on the organ's inauguration, he added that: 'The Swell may indeed be said to be almost new being enriched by two new stops, a cornet, and principal and the Great Organ has received the addition of an excellent trumpet'. The latter, however, was not used, to the great regret of the writer; 'we suppose, through an apprehension of its being too powerful for the voices'.[25]

Despite a general lack of knowledge concerning the technical workings of organs, it was a matter of civic pride to keep these instruments in good condition and to keep up-to-date with the latest developments. Avison's reason for adding the swell to the organ in St Nicholas's Church in Newcastle in 1749 was that 'a swell stop is now universally esteemed and made use of in most capital towns and that an addition of it to the organ of Saint Nicholas would make it one of the finest instruments in England'; even if Avison had other, more practical or personal, musical reasons for wanting a swell, he correctly judged that an appeal to civic pride would be the argument most likely to carry weight with the Corporation.[26]

Organists

The men, and one or two women, who took up these organists' posts were almost all professional musicians; the only known amateur player in Newcastle during the 18th century was Charles Avison's replacement at St John's, James Clark, a saddler, although it is likely that many country churches such as Earlesdon and

Staindrop employed amateur organists.[27] The post was frequently held by successive members of the same family: the Wright family, Thomas, his son Robert and grandson Thomas, were organists of Stockton parish church from 1759 until the second Thomas argued with the churchwardens in 1818 and resigned;[28] the Avison family, Charles, and his two sons Edward and Charles, were organists of St Nicholas, Newcastle from 1736 until 1795 with a 12 year break (from 1777 until 1789) when the post was filled by one of Charles Avison senior's pupils.[29] The Avisons were also connected with St John's in the same town from 1735 until 1776. Elsewhere, particularly later in the century, some churches experienced a very high turnover of organists, for a variety of reasons – untimely deaths, arguments between organists and vestrymen, and musicians moving on in search of better-paid or more prestigious posts. St Andrew's in Newcastle had five organists in the 13 years following the installation of its organ in 1783; the first, Thomas Hawdon, moved on to a better post after only six months, the second, George Barron, died within four years of appointment, the third, George Carr, after only three. The fourth, Thomas Wright, then held the post for six years before an argument arose, principally over his frequent use of deputies. Henry Monro then held the post until well into the 19th century.[30]

Some organists were surprisingly young on their first appointment; of the St Andrew's organists, Thomas Hawdon was 18 years old when appointed, George Barron only 15 (and 19 when he died in-post). Thomas Thompson, son of a local wait, was appointed in 1795 to the post of organist at All Saints at the age of 15 and to the post of organist at St Nicholas two years later; he remained at the latter church until his death in 1830.[31] Extensive travelling in search of the elusive perfect post was commonplace; Avison's friend John Garth might have found organists' posts not too far from home at Sedgefield and Bishop Auckland, but Avison's pupil, Matthias Hawdon (father of Thomas) travelled to Hull, then moved onto Beverley Minster before returning home to St. Nicholas.[32] Thomas Hawdon started at St Andrew's Church, Newcastle, moved to Dundee, took up his father's old post at Holy Trinity, Hull, then returned to All Saints in Newcastle, before dying, in 1793, at the age of only 28.[33] Edward Edmund Ayrton, organist of Gateshead Parish Church between 1790 and 1793, was the nephew of the organist of Ripon Cathedral and came to the north probably from Cambridge, after some obscure misdemeanours (probably involving a clandestine marriage) which caused his family to search for some remote place to find him gainful employment. After three years at Gateshead, he moved on to Swansea and, eventually, to Little Bolton in Lancashire, where he arrived, ill and dying, in 1811, able to play only once before his death. His illness was probably exacerbated by heavy drinking.[34]

Two women are also known, or thought, to have been organists. The first, Ann Avison, mother of Charles, is alleged to have been organist at Gateshead Church, almost certainly looking for a source of income after the death of her husband in 1721. The second, Ann Howgill, is a unique example in the north-east of a woman instrumentalist who was apparently a career musician. She was the daughter of the organist of Whitehaven, William Howgill, and the only girl in a family of six; her eldest brother took over from his father on the latter's death in 1790. Ann was appointed organist of Staindrop in County Durham in 1793 at the age of 18 and moved on to Penrith Church in 1797. Her later career is not at present known.[35] Neither of these appointments was thought odd enough to be commented upon by local newspapers suggesting that, unlike public performance elsewhere, playing the organ in church was not considered 'unfeminine'; women organists were possibly more frequent than is immediately apparent from surviving evidence.

By far the most surprising appointment was that made to All Saints' Church in Newcastle in 1714. In January of that year, the Corporation minutes recorded the new organist as 'Mr. Francis de Prendecourt'.[36] 'Captain' Francois Prendcourt had been one of the Catholic musicians at the court of James II in London; after James was deposed in 1688, Prendcourt appears not to have followed the former king to France but to have remained in England. He seems to have worked his way north, reaching Derby in 1705 and possibly briefly holding the post of organist in Kendal Parish Church before coming to Newcastle. His employment in the Anglican church he did not profess was certainly out of poverty and need; he is reputed to have said in more affluent times that he could never bring himself to play in, or compose for, the Anglican church.[37] He held the post at All Saints, however, until 1725 and seems to have been constantly in debt – Corporation Minutes record a number of charitable payments to him.[38]

The salaries paid to these men and women – on average £20 or £25 per annum in most churches – were small and generally formed only a part of an organist's income; economic uncertainties could also mean the possibility of a reduction in wages, as Charles Avison junior found to his cost in the early 1790s. Even Charles senior found his £40 per annum as organist of St Nicholas was not sufficient to support a growing family; in the early years of his marriage, his wife advertised her services as a teacher of needlework to bring in extra income.[39] For all these organists, a variety of other income-generating activities was essential: as wait, music teacher, performer or concert-promoter. The association between the organist of St Nicholas's Church in Newcastle and the role of concert promoter in the town was probably an accidental result of Charles Avison's pre-eminence, but the post of organist was very generally associated with that of concert promoter throughout the region; in Sunderland, Tynemouth, North and South Shields, Durham, Newcastle and Stockton all regular concerts were organized by the local organist. In many cases, this was almost inevitable given the fact that in many smaller towns the local organist was probably the only resident professional musician but even in larger towns, boasting a number of musicians, the association of principal organist in the town with concert-giving was taken for granted. In 1751, during the election for the post of organist at Holy Trinity, Hull – an election eventually won by Matthias Hawdon – the two short-listed candidates were required, not only to play the organ but also to give a concert; Hawdon won by demonstrating his ability to play concertos on harpsichord, violin and cello.[40] In Newcastle, the role of concert promoter was so bound up with the position of organist that Thomas Wright, well-known as an orchestral leader and soloist, promoted benefit concerts for himself in towns such as Sunderland and Morpeth, where he could be considered as a visiting musician, but did not feel able to do so in Newcastle, where he lived, until after he had taken up the post of organist at St Andrew's Church in 1790. Even then, he did not attempt to revive the flagging subscription series in 1794 until he had both been solicited to do so and had been assured that the present organist of St. Nicholas was not intending to do so himself.

One of the consequences of the situation in which an organist's post represented only one of a number of income sources for a professional musician was an occasional neglect of the organist's duties. There is no reason to suspect that most organists were not devout and sincere in their own beliefs – Avison's comments in his *Essay* certainly suggest that he was – but for many financial considerations may have been paramount. Prendcourt, as has already been shown, was sufficiently pragmatic to accept a job in a church contrary to his own belief; at much the same time, Samuel Nicholls at St Nicholas may have been implicated in the illicit sale of pews in the organ loft. Later in the century, both Thomas Wright and Alexander Munro Kinloch, a dancing master, accepted organists' posts at time of financial stringency; Wright was attempting to build up his career at the time, while Kinloch was acting as his father's assistant and may not have been financially secure. By 1798, Kinloch's position had greatly improved with the establishment of several new bands of which he was a member, and he gave up the post, inheriting his father's practice the following year after the latter's death in an accident.[41] Wright's departure from his post at St Andrew's was more acrimonious; he resigned his position in October 1796 after an apparently spectacular argument with the churchwardens one Sunday evening. One of the chief complaints against him was that, in Wright's words, he had 'two or three Sunday afternoons employed a young Man to do the Duty for me'. Complaints about the quality of the young man were probably spurious as he had also acted, without objections, as deputy at St Nicholas; the churchwardens' real concern may have been a more general feeling that Wright was neglecting his duties.[42] Wright had the previous year taken on the leadership and organization of two new bands, for which he was also composing a very large amount of music; these new activities, together with an increase in the amount of performance that he undertook and his teaching activities, may have left him with little time for his duties at St Andrew's.

Performance practice

The role of the organist in church music was twofold: to provide voluntaries and to accompany psalm-singing. Two voluntaries were usual within each service; the first, after the psalms, often employed solo stops and showed off the full range of the instrument, and the second, a more solemn affair towards the end of the service, was usually a fugue. Two-movement works were common and voluntaries might last around ten minutes. They were almost always improvised, and published collections of voluntaries such as those of John Garth (*Six Voluntaries*, Opus 3, published 1771) and Matthias Hawdon (*Six Sonatas Spirituale or Voluntaries*, Opus 4, published 1784) were probably not intended for the church organist (except beginners who wanted models to follow) but for the domestic market, as the wording in Hawdon's advertisement makes clear; he intended the

Voluntaries for 'the Harpsichord, Organ, or Piano Forte', that is, for playing at home, perhaps on one of the chamber organs made by local builders.[43]

The second role of the organ in church was to accompany the congregational singing of psalms. Charles Avison wrote that the organist should discharge this duty conscientiously in order to 'relieve, with religious Chearfulness, the calm and well-disposed Heart'.[44] Brown argued that, played well, the use of the organ could only enhance the atmosphere of a service: 'In great Towns, where a good Organ is skilfully and devoutly employed by a sensible Organist, the Union of this Instrument with the Voices of a well-instructed Congregation, forms one of the grandest scenes of unaffected Piety that human Nature can afford'.[45] However, all too often – if contemporary complaints can be trusted – this ideal union of thoughtful and restrained organist and well-instructed congregation, this 'calm' and decorous display of music, was far from reality. A writer to the *Gentlemen's Magazine* in February 1731 accused organists of a number of abuses in terms that, if exaggerated, were often echoed elsewhere. 'For half an hour together, they divert their auditors by scouring up and down the whole compass of the organ, and skipping from one subject to another, till they have given us a different air in every key of the Gamut … By this means, the pretty Gentlemen and fine Ladies below, are reliev'd from the danger they were in of growing hideously dull, and an opportunity given them of displaying their fine taste and rings.' Organists were alleged to indulge in a number of practices which encouraged entirely the wrong emotions in their congregations: they introduced popular airs such as *Lilliburlero* into the accompaniments of the psalms 'to the confusion of the audience'; they displayed a gaiety which 'dissipated that drowsy disposition which good christians are apt to sink into on such occasions'; they displayed – particularly in the case of the second voluntary which came directly after the sermon – a liveliness whereby the Congregation was 'soon eas'd of any irksome impressions receiv'd from the pulpit'.[46]

That this was not merely the jaundiced view of a few straight-laced clerics but was also the concern of practising musicians is attested by Avison's comments in his *Essay*. He warned that the conscientious organist should 'be extremely cautious of imitating common Songs or Airs in the Subjects of this … Kind of performance; otherwise he will but too much expose Religion to Contempt and Ridicule'; and condemned the organist who eschews the proper 'Sublimity of Style' in favour of 'absurd Graces and tedious and ill-connected Interludes' by which he 'misleads or confounds his Congregation'.[47] The only other organist in Newcastle at this time, Solomon Strolger, organist of All Saints Church, appears to have indulged in precisely this type of performance. Strolger, a Londoner who had probably come to Newcastle in his late teens or early twenties, had obtained the post of organist at All Saints in 1725 on Prendcourt's death, and held it for 53 years until his own death in 1779; in a letter to the *Newcastle Courant* the year after Strolger's death, an anonymous writer referred to his playing as 'those unmeaning rants from the Organ-loft' – precisely the kind of playing Avison condemned in his *Essay*.[48] Strolger's successor was Avison's younger son, Charles, whose performance was directly contrasted with Strolger's by the anonymous letter-writer; Charles junior was credited with introducing 'divine harmony' and was highly recommended to the parishioners even though the writer thought that they might find his playing 'a little singular' after their previous experiences.[49] It seems probable that the son practised his father's maxims.

The constant complaints against such extravagant and extrovert playing, however, suggest not only that it was commonplace but also that it was widely appreciated by congregations. Precisely the kind of voluntary deprecated by the writer to the *Gentleman's Magazine* was played by Avison's pupil, Matthias Hawdon, in January 1783 on the organ of St Andrew's Church, Newcastle. 'The Voluntary composed and performed by Mr. Hawdon,' commented the *Newcastle Courant*, 'was much applauded being calculated to display the various powers of every different key in the instrument, so as to give a full scope of criticism to the nicest ear.' Hawdon might be forgiven this extravagance as he was inaugurating a new instrument and might be expected to show off its capabilities as comprehensively as possible; nevertheless it is clear that the result was greatly appreciated by his audience. Not only was it 'much applauded' but the *Courant* remarked that it 'conveyed, we are happy to say, the fullest conviction of the Artist's judgement in his Profession'.[50]

In Whitehaven two years earlier, the *Cumberland Pacquet* had commented equally favourably on the performance of the son of the organist who, aged 11, 'performed the Whole service on the organ both parts of the day, which consisted of six psalm-tunes and four voluntaries'. The complex and showy voluntary performed in the middle of the evening service, consisting of four movements 'with frequent and easy transitions, from the chair organ, to the swell, and the full organ' both 'afforded great pleasure to those who are alive to the divine impressions of music' and 'excited real amazement in those who are acquainted with the construction of that instrument'.[51] Young William Howgill was following the example of his father who, in his psalm-playing, displayed on the organ, 'such a sweetness and sprightliness of tone … as to give a spirit to that part of the Service, not known before in this place'.[52] This was very much approved of both by the *Pacquet* and by the congregation; the *Pacquet*'s only regret was that Howgill senior had not gone far enough – 'we hear it is the wish of many, that he would fill up the chorus in that grandest part of the Christian Worship, by taking up the trumpet too'.[53] In 1784, Howgill and his son played a double voluntary composed by the latter; this consisted of two movements (*andante* and *allegro*) and was described by the *Pacquet* in terms more appropriate to the concert room than to the church: 'whether it is thought more pleasing in its effect or ingenious in its construction, it is entitled to an uncommon share of notice, both from its being the further prosecution of a subject, which has as yet been very slightly investigated by the greatest masters, and from the age of the composer, which is only fifteen years. – We shall have credit with the learned in this science, when we assert that the piece … is perfectly correct to the rules of composition'.[54] A second double voluntary performed by the Howgills the following year was found to contain 'a great variety' and 'uncommon beauty'; its effect was 'solemnly grand and pleasing'.[55] Despite the reservations expressed in certain quarters, large numbers of worshippers clearly felt that such elaborate and entertaining compositions were perfectly acceptable in divine service.

Psalm-singing

The singing of metrical psalms – with or without the accompaniment of the organ – dated from the Reformation, and the passing centuries had seen the establishment of a number of practices that were seen in many quarters as undesirable, raising strong feelings in clerics, musicians and congregations alike. Brown's opinions were strongly expressed in his *Dissertation*; he condemned the psalter still commonly in use in many parish churches – the 16th-century Sternhold and Hopkins version – as one that 'hath quenched all the poetic Fire and devout Majesty of the royal Psalmist' (that is, the original Psalms of David in the King James version of the Bible). 'There are few Stanzas,' he wrote, 'which do not present Expressions, to excite the Ridicule of some part of every Congregation.'[56] He preferred the Tate version of the early 18th century 'which though not excellent, is however not intolerable'.[57] He also criticized the tunes to which the psalms were sung, calling them 'as mean and meagre as the Words that are sung'.[58] However, despite these strictures, he felt that the music of the parish church needed no reform: 'Its Simplicity and Solemnity suit well its general Destination; and it is of Power, when properly performed, to excite Affections of the noblest nature'.[59] Avison was less sanguine; he expressed considerable reservations about the performance of the psalms, in particular with reference to the organ accompaniments, the speed of singing, the use of too many parts, and the over-ornamentation of the tunes. All these were detrimental, Avison believed, to what he and Brown considered the essential constituent of psalm-singing – an understanding of the words.

Their objections were to what has become known as the 'old' way of singing; this included a number of practices which had been taken to ridiculous lengths and which now brought ridicule on metrical psalm-singing. The practice of lining-out, by which the parish clerk sang or spoke the lines of the psalm before they were repeated by the congregation, was dying out by mid-century but still lingered in some country parishes and even attracted occasional support. A correspondent to the *Gentlemen's Magazine* in February 1741 regretted its loss, even though he had heard it condemned as 'indecent and uncouth'; he advocated its use as an aid to understanding, pointing out its assistance to those members of the congregation who could not read or did not possess books.[60] A more common criticism, however, was that it destroyed the sense of the words by pausing at the end of lines regardless of whether the sense continued. The magazine's correspondent was more concerned with another practice commonly found in many churches, of drawing out the individual notes of psalm tunes to enormous length – often of several seconds each – thus eliminating the forward momentum of the tune and obscuring the sense of the poetry, a practice that Avison also disapproved of, condemning the 'present Method of Singing the Common Psalm-Tunes … which are everywhere sung without the least Regard to *Time* or *Measure*, by drawing out every Note to an unlimited Length', and commenting that 'it is evident, that both the *Common* and *proper Tunes* were originally intended to be sung in the *Alla-Breve* Time, or the regular pointing of two, three or four *Minims* to a *Bar*'.[61] In this he was probably at fault, as references in Elizabethan times to psalms as

'Geneva jigs' hardly suggests the sedate pace even Avison's emendations recommend. He offered as a good example, worthy of copying, the style of psalm-singing in Protestant congregations in continental Europe, whose excellence he attributed to 'the exact *Measure*, in which those Tunes were sung'. He was also adverse to the ornamentation that was an inevitable consequence of such long-drawn out performances of psalm-tunes, as a result of uncertainty amongst individual singers as to when to change note; he spoke in favour of 'Plain and unadorned harmony'.[62]

Avison put his ideas into practice in a collection of psalm-tunes which appeared as a supplement to an edition of Isaac Watts' Psalms published by the Newcastle bookseller, William Charnley. Avison's tunes accompanied the 18th edition of the book, which is undated; several advertisements for the tunes however appear in local newspapers in 1757 and succeeding years.[63] The preface to the book – called an 'advertisement' – is unattributed but its comments on psalm-singing almost certainly reflected Avison's views on the matter. The book, the preface said, was intended for use both in church and in the home, for the saying or singing of psalms both in public and in private. In public performance, the author condemned the practice of lining-out but suggested that, if it could not be avoided, the worshipper should follow the words in the psalm book while they were being spoken in order to 'make the sense compleat'; the parish-clerk should be encouraged to read out the psalm in its entirety before going back to line out, thus mitigating the problem of interrupting the sense of the words. The practice of lingering on every note 'to such a tiresome extent' not only 'disgraces the Musick' but also, on a practical level, 'puts the Congregation quite out of Breath in singing five or six Stanza's'. If a faster speed was observed, the author commented, 'we might often enjoy the Pleasure of a longer Psalm with less Expense of Time and Breath'.[64] Avison's tunes accompanying the psalter were all arranged so they could be sung to both the old – Sternhold – version of the psalms and the newer early 18th-century version of Nahum Tate. Thirty-eight tunes were included in the supplement, in a variety of metres; treble and bass lines are given for all, with occasional figures to assist the organist or other accompanist to fill in the harmony. Ornaments are conspicuous by their absence, with the exception of one or two inserted passing notes clearly intended to make the tunes easier to sing. True to his maxim in the *Essay*, Avison wrote mainly in minims, although some tunes have crotchets and were obviously intended to be sung at a faster pace.

The columns of Newcastle's papers were full of advertisements for such psalters, for church or private use. Many advertisements were for works published in London; the 19th edition of Playford's Psalms, for instance, was advertised in the *Newcastle Courant* in 1738 with the advice that it included 'A New INTRODUCTION TO PSALMODY, *in a clear and easy Method for the Use of young Beginners*'.[65] This was intended for use with the old version of the Psalms but was offered with a supplement for use with the new version. Both versions could be bought bound together with the Book of Common Prayer. In the same edition of the *Courant* was offered the fourth edition of 'A compleat MELODY; or, the HARMONY of SION', edited by William Tansur. This comprised three volumes. The first volume was 'a new and compleat Introduction to the Grounds of MUSICK, Theoretical and Practical, Vocal and Instrumental, teaching all its Rudiments, and Composition in all its Branches'; volumes two and three concentrated on sacred music – volume two was an edition of the Psalms and volume three presented a number of new hymns and anthems in two, three and four parts. Less familiar editions of the psalms were also advertised, such as 'Divine Recreations, a collection of psalms, hymns and canons in two, three and four parts' which was printed in London and issued in four parts between Christmas 1736 and November 1737.[66]

But the book in which Avison's psalm-tunes were included is evidence that many similar books were published in the provinces, not only including psalm-collections but also hymns and anthems for public and private use. One of the earliest 18th-century publications of this type in the north-east was that of Benjamin Bennett, minister of the Hanover Square Unitarians, who in 1722 published *Occasional Hymns, Chiefly for the Lord's Day and Lord's Table being a Collection from Others, with an Addition of New Hymns.* Bennett's book, like most of these publications, included a preface commenting on issues raised by music in worship – Bennett clearly doubted whether music had any value at all; his definition of a hymn was poetic not musical. He commented: 'The Fathers [of the church] sometimes complain of a fondness in People for Tunes, Measures, and Rules of Art and a vain Curiosity, as they call'd it, in Singing, which they thought resembled the Theatre, and savour'd of the Corruption and Effeminacy of secular Musick, tending to please the Ear, without raising the Affections' [that is, the Emotions].[67] Bennett stressed that he himself did not go quite so far as this but nevertheless he was inclined against the use of music. 'No question to some, the Niceties of Poetry of Tune, &c. may be helpful; but to most, I'm afraid, they are rather a snare: Too much attention [is] apt to detain the mind from that which is its chief business – that is, devotion'.[68]

In the first half of the century, Bennett's views seem to have been extensively held by north-eastern publishers; the many psalters that appeared in the area were published without tunes, clearly intended to be read, either silently or aloud, rather than sung. Publishers may also have considered publication of music an unnecessary extra expense in view of the fact that a very limited number of tunes were in constant use and would all be familiar to regular church-goers. But in the second half of the century, a number of psalters were published locally with tunes. Avison's edition of 1757 was followed in 1763 by a psalter published in Hexham: *Several Select Portions of the Psalms, from Tate and Brady's Version, Collected for the Use of Churches, By a Clergyman.* The clergyman who compiled the volume was almost certainly William Totten, Vicar of Hexham, and he enlisted a local music teacher, William Thompson, to revise and correct the psalm tunes; Thompson also provided a new tune of his own called, appropriately, *Hexham.* The psalter was unusual in that the tunes, engraved by Joseph Barber of Newcastle, were not provided in a supplement at the end of the book, but were on alternate pages with the text, so that words and tunes could be seen at the same time, although this meant that a number of tunes appeared three or four times in the psalter. All the tunes are presented in two parts, in Avison's preferred minims, and are enlivened by occasional passing notes; no figures for the bass are given and no ornamentation provided.

In 1778, an itinerant psalm-teacher working in the north-east, Matthew Proctor, published an advertisement for another psalm book with music. This ambitious project was to consist of three volumes with an astonishing amount of music. The first volume, which included the subscribers' list, was intended as an introduction to church music and was to include no less than 74 psalm tunes mostly in four parts, 'as Fuges, Rounds, and Solos, &c. &c.'. (Many of these tunes would clearly not have passed Avison and Brown's requirement that the intelligibility of the words was paramount.) Volume two was to include the most commonly sung canticles (such as *Jubilate* and *Nunc Dimittis*) and 12 anthems by Michael Wise, organist at Salisbury in the late 17th century. Volume three offered 'upward of 56 of the most celebrated old Tunes, in two parts, for the use of congregations who do not chuse to sing the new music as they will suit either old or new version', plus 30 hymns, three Christmas carols and a paraphrase of the Lord's Prayer. Eight of the hymns would be adapted to the violin or German flute 'with a thorough bass for the Harpsichord and Organ, &c.' and the volume would also include a number of blank sheets of manuscript paper for practical use by the purchaser. It is not clear whether this work was ever published.[69]

A further book of psalms with tunes appeared seven years later, printed in Berwick. This was edited by a William Armstrong and was entitled *Psalms and Hymns with their proper tunes in the Tenor Part, Collected from various Authors*. In the preface, Armstrong commented: 'Singing, as it is conducted in many Churches, tends rather to create disgust, than to help devotion'; he therefore presented a number of psalms and hymns that had brought himself 'pleasure and edification' in the hope that they might help others.[70] The 40 tunes for these psalms were placed in a supplement at the back of the book in the melody line only, and they are notable for the inclusion of a relatively small number of ornaments, generally in the form of passing notes, anticipations and trills on the penultimate note. Those tunes in common time were almost invariably marked with pauses on the last notes of the first and third phrases, suggesting a slow and stately manner of delivery with some mannerisms of the delivery typical of the old practice of lining out.

Choirs and teachers

Despite all these publications, it is difficult to establish the exact practices of north-eastern churches, and the performance of psalms was no doubt very different in country churches such as Staindrop and Earlsdon, and in town and city churches in Newcastle, Durham and Sunderland. Brown's views and Avison's may certainly be taken to suggest the practice at St Nicholas's Church in Newcastle, where they both guided the service in the early 1760s; a plain, unornamented and relatively brisk delivery of the psalms with a simple and temperate organ accompaniment was probably the norm there. In addition, Avison may have introduced the use of rather more elaborate canticles than was generally the practice; a manuscript volume of his adaptations of *Twelve Canticles taken from the Compositions of Carlo Clari and adapted to English Words Selected from the Psalms* is dated the year before Avison's death (1769) and is labelled *Collection the Second.* The Canticles in normal use in the church – the *Jubilate*, *Magnificat*, *Nunc Dimittis*, etc. – are not represented here and Avison may have arranged Clari's works for use as anthems. In accordance with Avison's expressed views, the canticles never feature more than three parts (with added bass); ten of the 12 are for two parts (plus bass). Of these, four are for two sopranos, four for soprano and bass, and one each for soprano and alto, and soprano and tenor. Each of the canticles, which vary considerably in length, has a number of sections, often in contrasting tempi and keys although the modulation is rarely surprising – Avison was content to move from tonic to dominant or relative minor, and back again. The canticles have been used in performance at some period as an anonymous hand has marked in pencil extra repetitions of some sections and omissions of others; this is clearly not Avison's doing, however, as the writer has also marked various sections, rather condescendingly, as 'very good'. If they were indeed performed at St Nicholas, Avison must have had access to two or three very good solo singers (including perhaps Ann Ord).

He certainly did not, however, have access to a choir, at least during Brown's tenure as vicar; the singing of psalms was very definitely in Brown's view, a matter for the entire congregation. He spoke contemptuously of the situation where 'a Company of illiterate People form themselves into a *Choir* distinct from the Congregation. Here,' he said 'Devotion is lost, between the impotent *Vanity* of those who *sing,* and the ignorant *Wonder* of those who *listen*'.[71] (Avison's views, in light of the composition of the Canticles, may not have been so extreme; it is perhaps significant that the volume of the Canticles is dated three years after Brown's death.) One kind of choir was nevertheless known in Newcastle – and other towns in the north-east – from the beginning of the century; choirs of children from the local charity schools (and later in the century, from Sunday schools) were regularly taught to sing psalms and anthems, and at least once a year performed what they had been taught at special charity sermons; collections from these services were then dedicated to the running of the schools. Local newspapers regularly reported on these sermons, although, perhaps significantly, none were reported as taking place at St Nicholas, but rather in St John and All Saints, Newcastle, and at Sunderland. The earliest known service dates from 1725 but the publication of a book two years earlier by a local man, Prideaux Errington – *Copies in Verse, for the Use of Writing SCHOOLS, and HYMNS for Charity Schools* – suggests that the practice was significantly older. The book gives a flavour of the sentiments which the charity children were required to entertain. After a fulsome preface dedicated to the Mayor, Sheriff and Aldermen of the town, and to the Vicar and other trustees of the Newcastle charity schools, Errington printed pious verses for dictation to the children as writing exercises and a number of hymns of conventional devotion:

O God of all our Joy,
Our Bliss and Happiness,

Our Lips we will Employ
Thy Goodness to express.
Hallelujah.

One hymn specifically referred to the charity and the philanthropists who kept the children alive:

How glorious is that Charity
That you, our Friends, express;
Preventing future Misery,
And present Woes redress!

The children were expected to be properly grateful and to allow their benefactors to be comfortably self-congratulatory – newspaper reports frequently comment on the pleasure such performances must inevitably afford the ladies and gentlemen who contributed to the charity.

At least in Newcastle, the charity children were initially trained to sing with the intention of interspersing them with the adult members of the congregation, to lead the singing of those around 'so that the whole Congregation may join in one intire Harmony'.[72] This practice might have answered some of Brown's objections to the use of choirs, but the idea seems to have disappeared early on, and the charity children were formed into a small independent choir that sang on its own on special occasions once or twice a year. But by the 1730s, local newspaper reports suggest that the charity children – if they continued to be taught to sing – were no longer encouraged to sing in services, even for their own benefit; by 1736, when Avison was in the last months of his first tenure as organist of St John's, the annual sermon for the charity schools had become one for the general benefit of the poor of the parish, and the anthem was sung by the Durham singing man, Thomas Mountier, a friend of Avison's and vocal soloist at the subscription concerts.[73] In mid-century, the charity sermons, if they continued, were rarely reported in local newspapers; not until the year after Avison's death (1771) is any such sermon reported at St Nicholas; in that year, the mid-year sermon for the charity children was graced by a hymn sung by the choir of Durham Cathedral. The practice of using the Durham choir, or individual members of it, on such occasions continued until the end of the century; they were particularly popular at a sermon held annually at All Saints in October or November to raise money for pregnant poor women giving birth at home, and also appeared at charity sermons in Sunderland. The idea of using charity children in charity services, and at other times, only became common again towards the end of the century when Avison's younger son, Charles, became organist of All Saints in 1780; in November of that year, at the annual charity sermon, Charles junior directed an anthem that was sung by six of the charity boys and four of the charity girls. This practice continued until the end of the decade and was extended to other occasions; in January 1784 and 1785, the children sang anthems in church and a collection was taken for Avison (who was perpetually in financial difficulties) 'in consideration of his Teaching them'.[74] By 1787, the children were referred to solely as 'boys' and were also singing at a benefit for the Sunday Schools at St John's, suggesting that the standard of singing was sufficiently high to be welcome elsewhere; the children were also lent to St Ann's Chapel, Newcastle, on Easter Sunday 1788, by which time they had been joined by Sunday School scholars, a practice also followed at St John's Church.[75]

Avison moved from All Saints to St Nicholas in 1788 but in his six years as organist there before his death in 1795, no record survives of charity or Sunday school children singing at any services; after Avison's death in 1795, a number of charity sermons were reported at St Nicholas but on each occasion the choir from Durham sang anthems. The practice of using charity children continued at St John and at All Saints, in the latter place under the direction of Avison's friend, Thomas Hawdon, son of Matthias; in 1791, the *Newcastle Courant* reported that 'a new Anthem, composed for the occasion, will be sung by a part of the boys and girls, accompanied by Mr Hawdon, on the organ'.[76]

Other churches in the region also used charity or Sunday school children in charity and other services: Sunderland, Staindrop, Houghton-le-Spring, Tynemouth, North Shields, Bedlington and Stockton. In some of these churches, the local organist was responsible for teaching the children; at Stockton in October 1795, for instance, the children sang 'God Save the King' in church under the guidance of the organist.[77] But most of the children, particularly in country areas, were taught their psalms and anthems by peripatetic psalm teachers. The earliest known of these was Thomas Guilding who taught the charity children of All Saints and St John, Newcastle, and of Sunderland; Guilding's 1726 advertisement in the *Courant* described him as a 'Musick-Master who hath taught Vocal and Instrumental as well as Church Musick, in many of the Chief Cities, Counties, Market, and other great Towns; but last at Whickham and its neighbouring Villages'.[78] He was unusual, however, in not regarding himself solely as a teacher of psalms, also offering tuition in vocal and instrumental music, cantatas, operas and songs, and in ornamentation, and in 1727, he accepted a post as singing man at Durham Cathedral. Four years later, he moved on to Lincoln Cathedral.

More typical of most psalm teachers was Matthew Proctor who in 1778 advertised his 'thirty years constant experience, as a teacher of psalmody, throughout the northern counties of England'.[79] Such men could, like dancing masters, travel substantial distances; William Askew, whose death in Bootle at the age of 40 was reported in the *Newcastle Courant* in 1778, had 'taught psalmody in the counties of Cumberland, Westmorland, and Lancashire, near 20 years'.[80] The psalm teacher usually remained in a town or village for two or three months teaching local children, then put on one or more performances for the benefit of local notables; Proctor taught in the 1770s at Staindrop and then at Houghton-le-Spring where he enrolled 45 pupils in his school.[81] Proctor's 200 pupils in Staindrop sang in church before Lord and Lady Darlington, whose benevolence probably provided Proctor's wages. 'What pleasure must every thinking man feel,' said the *Newcastle Courant*, 'to see so many poor children reap the benefit of his Lordship's benevolence.'[82]

Elsewhere, the parish clerk may have continued to exercise a great deal of influence over church psalm-singing. Some were prominent, well-respected musicians, particularly in the larger towns. St Nicholas's Church in Durham, which had lost its organ during the Commonwealth, appointed as parish clerk in the 1780s the popular singing man, Edward Meredith. (Meredith's duties included reading out the parish poor rate from the porch twice a year, for which he received one shilling one each occasion in addition to his yearly salary of 30 shillings.)[83] John Thompson, the Newcastle breeches maker and music teacher, who had been a chorister at Durham Cathedral under James Hesletine, was parish clerk at St Nicholas in Newcastle from the early 1790s; arguments between parish clerk and organist over psalm-singing at this period are unlikely – Thompson's teenage son, Thomas, took over the position of organist at St Nicholas in 1795.[84] Particularly in country parishes, however, the quality of clerks was probably significantly lower.

Generally, very little evidence survives on the performance of these men but the eager interest of the *Cumberland Pacquet* in events at the Old Church in Whitehaven (where John Donaldson's organ was installed) preserves an unusually clear picture of the activities of a parish clerk and his relationship to the organist in his church, which may be typical of the situation in other town churches in the region. The Whitehaven organist in the later 1770s and 1780s was William Howgill who was probably related to the Newcastle family of waits of the same name; William died in 1790 and his son, also William, took over his position. The *Pacquet*, founded in 1773, began to take an interest in the singing at the church in 1785 on the death, at the age of 73, of the incumbent parish clerk, Joseph Wilde, who had held the post for over 30 years. After an encomium on his private virtues, the *Pacquet* commented on his demeanour in church: 'there was a becoming decency and unaffected reverence in his manner, and a sweet solemnity in his voice, which, while they engaged his constant auditors, never failed of attracting the notice of strangers'.[85] His successor was Isaac Wilkinson, who seems immediately to have attempted to take the singing in church in hand, suggesting that, despite the *Pacquet*'s comments, it had been sedate and not of a particularly high quality.[86] Two months after his appointment, Wilkinson directed a performance of a 'Choral Hymn' with words taken from the 96th Psalm, and music by William Jackson of Exeter. Wilkinson clearly intended his choir to stand apart from the congregation rather than to lead them in a manner of which John Brown might have approved; the *Pacquet* commented: 'The attempt to distinguish particular times [i.e. Easter] by such performers, is certainly very laudable, and ought to be encouraged; – it is therefore to be wished that some place could be appropriated for his singers, who, we understand, were on this occasion, greatly incommoded by the intrusion and rude behaviour of some people who separated them; by which the fine effect of the chorus was hurt in some parts'.[87] Apart from expressing a wish that the choir had been a little larger, the *Pacquet* was well-pleased both with the singing and with the accompaniment on the organ.

The success of this event encouraged Wilkinson and his scholars to sing another anthem on Christmas Day of the same year and to perform again at Easter the following year. On this last occasion, Wilkinson augmented the children's voices with bass and tenor adult voices, again using an organ accompaniment. The *Pacquet* remarked that the event would 'no doubt, from the applause it has received, operate as a powerful incentive to practise other pieces of this sort'.[88] Wilkinson was spurred on to over more ambitious efforts and at Christmas 1786 directed 46 men and boys in singing an anthem, chorus, and the Hallelujah Chorus.[89] From August 1786, Wilkinson also directed a choral version of some psalms every second Sunday; 160 Sunday school children performed these immediately after the evening services, 'ranged in the middle aile'. The *Cumberland Pacquet* remarked that they, and the accompanying organ, kept very good time.[90] The singing had been introduced to the children, the *Pacquet* claimed, as 'a kind of relaxation' and 'the solemnity was much heightened from the reflection that the tongues employed in that exercise might, and, probably would have been engaged … in exercises very different from the present, and disgraceful to a christian country'.[91] Sunday schools and psalm-singing were thus a means of combating social evils; Wilkinson's activities occupied idle minds and hands that might otherwise have been about the devil's business.

Throughout the 1780s, Wilkinson directed his scholars in psalms and anthems at Christmas and Easter and on special occasions such as the Day of Thanksgiving for George III's return to health in 1789.[92] In addition, he continued to perform his everyday duties; an anonymous writer to the *Pacquet* in December 1786 praised his industry if not his voice: 'We have a *musical professor* in our parish; indeed he is none other than the parish clerk; – and he sings tolerably well through his nose … I have calculated that, in the line of his duty … for the godly solace, comfort and edification of his auditors, he has sung *three thousand, two hundred and forty psalms*'.[93] By 1791, however, the situation had changed; the elder William Howgill had been replaced by his son, evidently a much more energetic man. William junior took over the instruction of the scholars, suggesting that Wilkinson's prominence in this had been at least partly the result of the indolence or incapacity of the elder William.[94] In February 1791, the *Pacquet* had noted with approval the publication of a psalm book by Edward Miller, organist of Doncaster, quoting the preface at length; Howgill was quick to see the virtues of the book and within two months was using it to instruct the children, choosing 'a certain number of the best voices from the Sunday Scholars, who are to be instructed in singing the correct and fine melodies in Miller's Psalms, according to the plan laid down in the preface to that excellent work'.[95] In July, the principles of Miller's Book were introduced into the church service. The *Pacquet*'s comments on this occasion suggest that, even under Wilkinson's energetic and ambitious direction, the psalms had been performed at the very slow tempi condemned by Brown and Avison. 'The effect of the performance showed,' wrote the paper's correspondent, 'that whatever constitutes the essence of music (air, measure and expression) is to be found in the plain and simple melodies of the church, when rescued from the odious absurdities of giving the same unmeaning length of sound to every syllable.'[96]

Notes

[1] *NA* 22 September 1792.
[2] Geoffrey Brown, 'John Garth, the *Galant* Organ Voluntary, and the Organs at Sedgefield and Auckland Castle in County Durham', *Journal of the British Institute of Organ Studies*, 26, 2002, 138–9.
[3] Vestry Book, Stockton Parish Church, 1762–1926, December 1759 [note in back of book].
[4] *NJ* 8 September 1787.
[5] *NCh* 25 February 1795.
[6] Vestry book, Stockton Parish Church, December 1759.
[7] CCN 7 October 1734, 13 October 1735.
[8] Ibid., 10 October 1748.
[9] Ibid., 15 April 1776.
[10] CAN, passim.
[11] CCN 26 June 1749.
[12] *NC* 1 February 1724, 5 October 1734.
[13] Ibid., 23 February 1740; *YC* 21–8 August 1739.
[14] *NG* 15 June 1765.
[15] *NC* 1 February 1724.
[16] Ibid., 12 August 1780.
[17] For details of Donaldson's career, see R. Southey, *Commercial Music-making in 18th century north-eastern England: a pale reflection of London?* PhD Dissertation, University of Newcastle upon Tyne, 2001, 194–7.
[18] Stephen Bicknell, 'The Donaldson Organ in the Holywell Music Room, Oxford', BIOS, *Journal*, 11 (1987), 32–49.
[19] CCN 16 June 1792; *YCh* 21 May 1795; *YC* 10 April 1797.
[20] *NCh* 1 March 1800.
[21] The specifications for the organs of St Nicholas and St John, Newcastle can be found in Dubois, *Charles Avison's Essay*, 203.
[22] *NCh* 18 January 1783.
[23] *NC* 20 October 1792.
[24] *CP* 20 August 1782.
[25] Ibid., 24 July 1781, 1 April 1783.
[26] CCN 26 June 1749.
[27] Ibid., 20 October 1736; *NC* 9–16 April 1743.
[28] Stockton Vestry Book, December 1759. The younger Thomas Wright of Stockton was an entirely different person to Thomas Wright of Newcastle, who led many bands in the region in the 1780s and 1790s. Their dates of birth and death are almost identical, however; both were violinists and composers, and were confused even in their lifetimes and shortly afterwards, much to the annoyance of Thomas Wright of Stockton's widow, Elizabeth. Wherever the name Thomas Wright is used without attribution it refers to Thomas Wright of Newcastle.
[29] Details of appointments of organists in Newcastle are all taken from the Chamberlain's Accounts of Newcastle Corporation [CAN]. The Corporation

employed all organists in the town until the early 1790s when financial constraints led them to offload their responsibilities onto the church vestries. After 1794, they were responsible only for payment of the salary to the organist of St Nicholas.

[30] Vestry Minute Book, St Andrew, Newcastle, passim.

[31] CAN, passim.

[32] *NJ* 15–22 June 1751; *NC* 21 December 1766.

[33] *NC* 12 June 1783, 29 November 1788; G. H. Smith, *Hull Organs and Organists* (London/Hull: A. Brown and Sons, 1910), 14–15; *NJ* 22 December 1787; *NA* 30 November 1793.

[34] John Hugh Thomas, 'Edward Edmund Ayrton. The Swansea Ayrton', *Morgannwg, The Journal of Glamorgan History*, xxxix, 30–49.

[35] *NA* 3 June 1797.

[36] CCN 17 January 1714.

[37] Wilson, *Roger North*, 53.

[38] CCN 19 December 1716, 18 December 1717, 25 July 1720, 2 October 1721, 17 December 1722, 30 September 1725.

[39] *NC* 21 January 1738.

[40] *NJ* 15–22 June 1751.

[41] *NC* 4 July 1795. Kinloch was appointed organist of All Saints, Newcastle, after Thomas Thompson moved on to St Nicholas in 1795.

[42] Vestry minute book of St Andrew, Newcastle, 10 October 1796.

[43] *NC* 29 May 1784.

[44] Avison, *Essay*, 1st edition, 75.

[45] Brown, *Dissertation,* 214.

[46] *The Gentleman's Magazine*, February 1731, 51.

[47] Avison, *Essay*, 1st edition, 75, 77–8.

[48] CCN 30 September 1725, 21 December 1779; *NC* 13 January 1780.

[49] *NC* 13 January 1780.

[50] Ibid., 25 January 1783.

[51] *CP* 24 July 1781.

[52] Ibid., 1 April 1783.

[53] Idem.

[54] *CP* 28 September 1784.

[55] Ibid., 10 May 1785.

[56] Brown, *Dissertation,* 130.

[57] Ibid., 131.

[58] Ibid., 214.

[59] Ibid., 131.

[60] *The Gentleman's Magazine*, February 1741, 82–3.

[61] Avison, *Essay*, 1st edition, 76.

[62] Idem.

[63] *NJ* 9–15 July 1757.

[64] I. Watts, *The Psalms of David, Imitated in the Language of the New Testament, And applied to the Christian State and Worship* (18th edition) (Newcastle: William Charnley, c1757).

[65] *NC* 4 November 1738.
[66] For a detailed discussion of various editions of the psalms and their purchasers, see Ian Green, *Print and Protestantism in Early Modern England* (Oxford: Oxford University Press, 2000), 503–52.
[67] Benjamin Bennett, *Occasional Hymns, Chiefly for the Lord's Day and Lord's Table, being a Collection from Others, with an Addition of New Hymns* (Newcastle: J. Button, R. Akinhead, M. Brison, 1722), xiii.
[68] Ibid., xiii–xiv.
[69] *NC* 27 June 1778.
[70] William Armstrong, *Psalms and Hymns and their proper Tunes in the Tenor Part, Collected from various Authors* (Berwick: for the author, 1784), 2.
[71] Brown, *Dissertation*, 214–15.
[72] *NC* 28 May 1726.
[73] Ibid., 25 December 1736.
[74] Ibid., 31 January 1784, 16 April 1785.
[75] Ibid., 29 March 1788.
[76] Ibid., 19 November 1791.
[77] Ibid., 7 November 1795.
[78] Ibid., 28 May 1726.
[79] Ibid., 27 June 1778.
[80] Ibid., 25 April 1778.
[81] Ibid., 25 April 1772.
[82] Ibid.,10 August 1771.
[83] Churchwardens' accounts of St Nicholas, Durham, passim.
[84] *NC* 20 June 1795; CCN 18 June 1795.
[85] *CP* 11 January 1785.
[86] Ibid., 25 January 1785.
[87] Ibid., 22, 29 March 1785.
[88] Ibid., 19 April 1786.
[89] Ibid., 27 December 1786.
[90] Ibid., 9 August 1786.
[91] Idem.
[92] *CP* 29 April 1789.
[93] Ibid., 13 December 1786.
[94] It is probable however that William junior had been acting as organist in his father's place for some years.
[95] *CP* 15 February, 26 April 1791.
[96] Ibid., 5 July 1791.

Chapter 7

Oratorio Performance

John Brown devoted seven pages of his *Dissertation* to the genre of oratorio. He shared the Bishop of London's view that sacred subjects ought not to be treated in such a theatrical manner and his disapproval led him to assign the genre a pagan origin, tracing it back to ancient celebrations at the tombs of departed warriors, a practice St Augustine had condemned – from such disgraceful roots in Greece and Asia, Brown supposed it had found its way back to Europe by means of returning crusaders. But he also, correctly, attributed the modern origins of the genre to dramatic representations in Italy and ascribed its musical form to the influence of the Italian opera. In this latter fact lay its worst defects, in Brown's opinion. He expressed a very English dislike of sung dialogue – 'a circumstance so repugnant to modern Manners and therefore so far out of Nature, that no Audience can be much affected by the Representation, or take part in an Action so improbably feigned'.[1] Moreover, this 'glaring Improbability' led the listener to concentrate on the music rather than on the words and the subject matter – and it was Brown's first article of faith that in music the text must always take precedence over the tune. Some of the material used as librettos for oratorios – the poems of Metastasio, for instance – were admirable, he said, but the 'Simplicity, Majesty and devout Expression' of the poetry was 'sacrificed to the Composer's Vanity or ill-directed Art'.[2] Worse, the circumstances of performance, in the theatre, tended to lead to oratorio, like opera, being regarded merely as an amusement – Brown's worst insult.

In his discussion of the oratorio in England, Brown found himself in a dilemma, faced with the necessity of condemning the genre without being unduly critical of its chief practitioner for whom he clearly had a great admiration. Handel possessed 'exalted Genius', he wrote with enthusiasm; 'no Man ever possessed greater Powers of musical Expression'.[3] How then could Brown explain his involvement in a genre so unacceptable? Brown managed to imply that the real fault lay in the poor quality of the librettos which forced Handel to undesirable musical tricks to hide their deficiencies – had they been of a better quality, he could have allowed his natural abilities full expression. Brown suggested the existence of a vicious circle: because texts were so bad, oratorio had acquired such a low reputation that writers of quality refused to become involved, which in turn led to the involvement of hacks, a further worsening of texts and a 'degradation' of the genre. Handel, Brown said, had been forced to employ '*Versifiers* instead of *Poets*' for his librettos. 'Most of the Poems he composed to, are such as would have sunk and disgraced other Music than his own … He was in the Situation of a great Painter, who should be destined to give Life by Colours, to a dead and unmeaning

Design.'[4] Even where the poet was of indisputable excellence, as in the case of Milton, problems beyond Handel's solving had arisen. The libretto for *Samson* had been 'so much changed in the Attempt toward accommodating it to Music' that it could hardly be said to be the poet's work. Poems like *L'Allegro* and *Il Penseroso* were elegant but 'merely descriptive' and therefore incapable of arousing the affections as the best poetry, and music, should.[5] Only *Messiah* gained Brown's wholehearted approval but the texts for that work were taken from the only truly acceptable source – Scripture. This, Brown said, meant that *Messiah* should not be classified as an oratorio at all but as a collection of hymns and anthems.[6] To demonstrate his views as clearly as possible, Brown wrote his own text for an oratorio; *The Cure of Saul* was doubly appropriate in being taken from Scripture and in dealing with a musical topic – David's use of music to soothe the maddened King Saul.[7]

Charles Avison had nothing to say on the genre of oratorio but his comments on Handel, as has already been noted, caused much controversy. In the first edition of *An Essay on Musical Expression*, he had remarked that the composer, although capable of the 'noblest Harmonies', had, in his opinion, produced too much material because of commercial pressures, and that therefore there was much dross amongst the gold. Indeed, Avison said, he was astonished that Handel had produced so much excellent material 'as could hardly have been expected from one who hath supplyed the Town with musical Entertainments of every Kind, for thirty Years together'.[8] These relatively temperate comments roused such protest – including the pamphlet by William Hayes of Oxford – that Avison amplified his comments in the second edition of the *Essay*, published a year after the first. He compared Handel to the poet Dryden. 'Their Abilities equal to every Thing; their Execution frequently inferior. Born with Genius capable of *soaring the boldest Flights*; they have sometimes, to suit the vitiated Taste of the Age they lived in, *descended to the lowest*.'[9] Even this was too much for some of Handel's uncritical supporters. But Brown, despite professing unreserved support for Handel's 'exalted Genius', went much further in his criticisms, devoting a page to a discussion of six faults in Handel's oratorio writing. Brown disliked 'too much musical Division upon single Syllables' which in his opinion obscured the meaning of the words; he condemned a too literal imitation that concentrated on depicting individual words rather than permitting 'a proper Expression of the ruling Sentiment'. Some solos were too long, and he considered the *da capo* form, with its obligatory repetitions, ridiculous. Choruses (called 'choirs' by Brown) were often too long and much too forceful – he described himself as 'apt to be fatigued and disgusted by such a long-continued and forcible Impression'. However, the use of instrumental introductions to such choruses was to be condemned for an exactly contrary reason; where a change of mood took place, they took away the element of surprise which the choir's sudden entrance, unprepared, could provide – this in turn destroyed the '*Impression* and *Effect*'. (Brown's dislike of instrumental music may have prejudiced him further in this regard.) Finally, he deplored the use of fugues and canons which he considered were used merely to show off the composer's abilities rather than to express the words.[10] Brown hastened to excuse himself for this detailed criticism of Handel's work by using Avison's reasoning –

that the fault lay not in the composer but in the tastes of the age in which he lived. Then, having been brutally explicit in his criticisms, he remarked that he chose 'to cast them into Shades, referring them to the Observation and Regard of musical Professors, rather than to fix a Mark of Disrespect on any particular Composition of a Man whose exalted Genius he reveres'.[11]

The reservations of Avison and the disapproval of Brown may have had its effect on the performance of Handel's works in Newcastle. Avison was clearly not adverse to Handel's music *per se*; he performed songs by Handel in his only known concert in London in 1734, and extracts from the oratorios were included in concerts in Newcastle, particularly in situations where the music's patriotic elements were appropriate (in the concert to mark the outbreak of the War of Jenkins' Ear in 1739, for instance). No record survives, however, of a complete oratorio performance in Newcastle under Avison's direction.

In Durham the situation was very different. Here, the combination of a resource of excellent singers, and the conservative tastes of the clerics and the prebendal body they made up, led to Durham's musical life being dominated by Handel's music. The earliest reference to repertoire in Durham concerts, in 1749, records a performance of Handel's *Alexander's Feast* to mark St Cecilia's Day; the Dean of the Cathedral, Spencer Cowper, mentioned the performance in a letter to his brother, commenting with wry amusement on the *Newcastle Courant's* suggestion that the performance was as good, if not better, than anything that could be heard in London.[12] Over the following decade, details of repertoire were published in local papers for 11 concerts, all but one included vocal music by Handel and on several occasions complete performances of oratorios were given – albeit the shorter and more secular works such as *Alexander's Feast*, *Acis and Galatea* and *L'Allegro ed il Penseroso*.[13] Between 1757 and 1768, every winter subscription series in Durham either began or ended (sometimes both) with a concert devoted entirely to an oratorio. As the 1760s wore on, these tended to become more serious in tone, and *Messiah* and *Samson* took the place of the lighter works although the latter continued to be performed in mid-year concerts. The 1763–4 season started with *Samson*, spread over the first three concerts of the series, one act to a concert. But the repertoire remained remarkably limited throughout this period – only six oratorios are known to have been performed. *Acis and Galatea* was by far the most popular and *L'Allegro* (with only one performance) the least; *Alexander's Feast* was performed principally in mid-year concerts and *Messiah* and *Samson* solely in subscription concerts. The only non-Handelian work was Boyce's *Solomon* (equally popular in all types of concerts) – a surprisingly secular and erotic choice for a cathedral choir. The choir was also responsible for the only oratorio known to have been performed in Newcastle before Avison's death in 1770; a performance on 1 September 1763 of *Alexander's Feast*, held on the evening of a visit to the town for the annual festival of the Sons of the Clergy.[14] The fact that this performance was not repeated suggests that it was not particularly popular.

In the late 1760s, the popularity of oratorios in the north was given a boost by a brief and apparently inexplicable upsurge of interest in Yorkshire and Lancashire.

The first sign of this interest surfaced in Wakefield in August 1767 when performances of *Messiah* and *Judas Maccabaeus* were put on to celebrate the dedication of the organ in the parish church; musicians for these oratorios were drawn from a wide area including 'London, Oxford, Cambridge, York, Lincoln, Nottingham, Durham, Liverpool, Manchester, Birmingham and the Parts adjacent'.[15] The popularity of the event must have been considerable and other performances almost immediately followed. Three sets of concerts were advertised in local papers for 1768: in Sheffield in late June/early July; in Halifax in mid-August; and in Doncaster during Race Week in late September.[16] In early 1769, John Camidge, organist of York Minster, held a performance of Boyce's *Solomon* as a benefit in place of his usual vocal and instrumental concert; this may have been designed as a 'taster' for an oratorio festival performed in the city two weeks later during Lent at which two performances of *Messiah* and one of *Judas Maccabaeus* were put on by 'a Band of upwards of 100 Performers' led by distinguished soloists including Tomaso Pinto, 'conductor of the Bands at Vauxhall and Drury-lane', Pinto's wife (the former Charlotte Brent) and Thomas Norris of Oxford.[17] These performances established the pattern for later events in the region: a large number of performers, local instrumentalists, and imported directors and vocal soloists.

The York oratorio performances sparked off a prolonged burst of activity which over the next 12 months saw no less than 11 mini-festivals of oratorios and two individual concerts for a variety of purposes: to celebrate a new organ (Beverley, September 1769); for the benefit of an infirmary (Leeds, October 1769); and for personal benefits (for instance, at Halifax, August 1769).[18] In 1770, the three early-year benefits associated with the subscription series in York took the form of oratorio performances rather than the usual vocal and instrumental concerts, and were followed – as in the previous year – by three oratorios in Lent.[19] In Durham, Thomas Ebdon the organist took up the idea and instituted a new fixture in Durham's musical year, putting on a performance of *Messiah* on Easter Monday to 'a polite and crouded audience'.[20] The passion for oratorios, however, did not reach Newcastle where Avison's death in May 1770 sent musical life on a downward course from which it did not recover for another ten years.

The repertoire at these concerts was overwhelmingly Handelian and, at times, extremely limited; between mid–1767 and mid–1769 only two works – *Messiah* and *Judas Maccabaeus* – were performed with the exception of the performance of Boyce's *Solomon* at Camidge's 1769 benefit in York.[21] Only in mid–1769 did more variety creep into the repertoire. In August, the organist at Halifax put on two concerts; the first was a performance of *Samson* and the second an uneasy compromise between an oratorio performance and a miscellaneous concert – the *Dettingen Te Deum* and *Zadok the Priest* were coupled with extracts from *Judas Maccabaeus* and *Messiah*. (This is probably the earliest example in the area of what later became known as a 'Concert of Sacred Music' or 'A Grand Selection of Sacred Music' – in effect, a concert of Handel's greatest hits.)[22] *Samson*, and the ubiquitous *Messiah* and *Judas Maccabaeus* were put on in Beverley in late 1769, and in September of the same year *Acis and Galatea* was included in a series of concerts in Doncaster.[23] By 1770, *Judas Maccabaeus* had been abandoned and in concerts throughout the area the lighter pieces of the genre were beginning to be favoured: *Acis and Galatea*; *Alexander's Feast*; Boyce's *Solomon*; and James Nares's *The Royal Pastoral*.[24] *Messiah* and *Samson* remained popular, however, and a search for novelty produced performances of pastiches such as *Israel in Babylon* and *Resurrection*.

Some of the performances featured the large bands of singers and instrumentalists that were to become familiar in Victorian productions of Handel. In Doncaster in 1768 the number of performers was estimated at 80; in 1769, the organizers of the Lent oratorios in York and of a series at Tadcaster both anticipated around 100 performers.[25] Lancashire chapel singers were generally used for choruses, except in Durham where the choir of the Cathedral was used. Organizers were willing to pay high sums for well-known vocal soloists – Charlotte Pinto, Frances Hudson of York (who also sang in Arne's oratorio series in London), Thomas Norris and William Matthews of Oxford, Messrs Saville and Warren, singing men from Lichfield Cathedral. The most prominent singer was the castrato Tenducci, hired for the York Lent oratorios in 1770.[26] Money was also spent on eminent instrumentalists such as the Italian violinist, Felice Giardini, who led oratorios in Beverley in 1769.[27]

But the majority of instrumentalists who played in these performances were local men, recruited from a wide area of Lancashire and Yorkshire. The position of leader of the band was most commonly taken by Robert Jobson of Wakefield (later of Leeds), although John Camidge occasionally performed this role; other instrumentalists included Thomas Shaw of York, Stopford the organist of Halifax, Messrs Tinker and Traviss, trumpeters from Manchester, Edward Miller of Doncaster, Haigh, owner of a music shop in Halifax, Thomas Beilby, organist of Scarborough, and Matthias Hawdon, later organist of St Nicholas's Church in Newcastle but at this time organist of Beverley Minster. The performances and the extensive travelling involved created a far-flung network of local musicians across the counties of Yorkshire and Lancashire, which was later to spread into County Durham and Northumberland, and influenced both individual careers and the course of musical life in the north-east.

But after mid-1770, oratorio performance seems to have tailed off. Three concerts put on to celebrate the new organ in St Thomas's Church in Liverpool in July 1770 were the only advertised oratorios in the latter half of that year, and performances in 1771 were limited to a few concerts in York and Durham before March, and three performances in East Retford in August.[28] By 1772, only the Lent performances in Durham remained and by 1773 they had also gone. No clear evidence survives to explain either the rise or the decline of this brief passion for oratorios, but one factor in its demise may well have been the expense of the performances. Even at the height of the fashion, many musicians continued to hold the customary vocal and instrumental miscellaneous concerts as benefits – for them the cost of an oratorio with its expensive soloists and large numbers of performers may have been prohibitive.

In Durham, the genre remained a staple of concerts even after the disappearance of the Lent performances of *Messiah*; the 1778–9 subscription series, for instance, began with *Alexander's Feast* and ended with *Acis and*

Galatea.[29] In addition, Thomas Ebdon began to export the genre to other towns; in June 1770, he put on a performance of Boyce's *Solomon* in Sunderland, a performance whose popularity prompted him to run a subscription series in the town.[30] Oratorio did not establish itself in Newcastle, however, until Edward Avison's death in 1776 brought Matthias Hawdon back from Yorkshire to the town of his birth. Hawdon was clearly out of touch with musicians and musical activity in his home town to the extent that, for his earliest concerts in Newcastle, he imported a vocal soloist – Frances Hudson of York – who had sung for him in Hull and Beverley.[31] But six months after his return, he attended an event which was to lead, indirectly, to the introduction of oratorio in Newcastle; a concert at the Freemasons' new hall in Low Friar Street in October 1777 introduced Hawdon to the virtues of the Durham Cathedral choir who, according to the *Newcastle Courant*, performed 'with great taste and judgement'.[32] With enthusiasm, he incorporated them into his planned winter subscription series (his first in the town), repeating the Freemasons' concert in the first concert, using individual singing men as soloists throughout the series, and inviting the entire choir to the last concert, and to the Race and Assize Week concerts in 1778. With them came the repertoire with which they were most familiar – extracts from Handel and particularly from his oratorios. Hawdon planned several concerts around this material; the sixth subscription concert, for instance, in February 1778, started with the overture to *Messiah*, followed this with an unnamed recitative, song and chorus from the same oratorio, included a song from *Acis and Galatea* in the first half, the overture to *Pharamond* in the second, and ended with a song, chorus, recitative and Hallelujah Chorus from *Messiah*.[33] In the mid-year concerts of the same year, extracts from *Alexander's Feast* and *Judas Maccabaeus* were performed.[34]

The reception given by audiences must have been enthusiastic or at least approving, for in October 1778 Hawdon decided to give Newcastle its first oratorio festival, similar to those in which he had taken part in Lancashire and Yorkshire. Four concerts were planned for the days between Tuesday 6 October and Friday 9 October, alternately performed in the morning and in the evening; a mixture of the serious and the lighter repertoire was included – *Acis and Galatea* and *Alexander's Feast* alternated with *Judas Maccabaeus* and *Messiah*. When it came to hiring soloists, Hawdon thought first of his Yorkshire connections, perhaps wanting performers experienced in this type of festival; he hired Robert Jobson (now organist at Leeds) to lead the band and brought in Lancashire chapel singers to perform the choruses, although he may have used a limited number of these to augment the Durham choir. Frances Hudson of York took one of the female solo parts; the other female singer was Jobson's pupil, Miss Harwood, who was to become very well known as an oratorio singer in the north and in London, singing in the capital with the Concert of Ancient Music. For male singers, Hawdon stayed closer to home, using William Evance and Edward Meredith – technically, the latter was not yet officially a singing man but he may have been singing as a deputy or supernumerary over the winter. Meredith was also experienced in this kind of repertoire, having performed it extensively in London in the earlier part of the decade.

The *Newcastle Journal* was excited at the prospect of the oratorios, unlike the *York Courant* which had not bestirred itself to comment upon or review any of the performances in Yorkshire in the early part of the decade. The *Journal*'s comments on the composer were orthodox and volubly expressed. 'The grand course of oratorios to be performed at the assembly rooms in the first week of October are the noblest pieces ever penned in the musical system, and the works of that immortal genius, Handell. – The affection of Mr. Hawdon, in bringing them forward in a manner to equal the abilities of spirit of their author is evident.'[35] But the *Journal* makes no reference to the religious content of the oratorios or to any perceived political significance, nor did it react to the music on any level other than that of fashion – it hoped that Newcastle could boast entertainment on a par with that available in the capital. 'We flatter ourselves that the public will have the pleasure of hearing them upon an equal footing as when performed at St Paul's Cathedral, London, before the nobility, &c. or at any other Musical meeting in the Kingdom.'[36] Before hearing a single note or word, the *Journal* was prepared to urge that the oratorios should become a septennial event; the paper would have preferred an annual festival but supposed the expense would be too great. After hearing the oratorios, however, the *Journal*, like the York papers, did not print a word of review, enthusiastic or otherwise.

Nevertheless, audiences must have seemed appreciative and their numbers encouraging; three years later, Hawdon decided to hold another series of oratorios. He had in the meantime followed much the same pattern as before with his subscription series, holding a number of relatively small-scale concerts during the winter and three large-scale concerts – the last of the series and the Race and Assize Week concerts – dominated by the Cathedral choir and the music of Handel's oratorios. The increasing popularity of Edward Meredith in the area must also have augured well. In 1781, in the week before Easter, Hawdon offered an oratorio festival very similar to the 1778 event, hiring many of the same performers as before for three evening performances between Tuesday 10 April and Thursday 12 April, with *Messiah* performed twice and *Judas Maccabaeus* once. The success of the previous event and of the subscription series led Hawdon to expect huge audiences and he ordered a total of 950 subscription tickets from the engraver, Thomas Bewick. The *Journal* and other local newspapers were conspicuously silent, however, accepting Hawdon's advertisements but making no editorial comments and printing no reviews.[37] Hawdon's note of thanks after the event, published in the *Newcastle Courant*, offered his gratitude 'for the singular favours he has received on account of his late performances' but concealed the realities of the situation – by July, he was bankrupt.[38] Either audiences had not materialized or, if they had, income was not equal to the expenses.

In Yorkshire and Lancashire, the 1770s and early 1780s saw few oratorio performances. Then the Handel Commemoration in London in mid–1784 – a deliberately patriotic and nationalistic gesture, organized by the members of the Concert of Ancient Music – sparked off a series of imitation concerts and festivals throughout the country. Amongst the first to respond, and to imitate, were the organizers of an oratorio festival in Leeds in November 1784, which offered 'the same Selection of SACRED MUSIC from HANDEL, which was performed in

Westminster Abbey, on the last Day of the Commemoration'.[39] The band was led by the organizer of the oratorios, Robert Jobson, and amongst the soloists was Edward Meredith of Durham Cathedral. This was the first of a very large number of concerts, often in pairs or trios comprising a mini-festival, which were held throughout the north in the last two decades of the century: at Leeds, York, Doncaster, Manchester, Liverpool, Preston, Birmingham, Hull, Sheffield, and dozens of smaller places such as South Shields, Darlington, Knottingly and Malton. This phenomenon was the making of Edward Meredith's career – he was the local singer most frequently in demand – but his move from Durham to Liverpool in 1789 shows clearly that it was still a phenomenon based on Lancashire and Yorkshire, and that Durham was too far north to be convenient as a base from which to travel. Ironically, although several singing men had attended the 1784 London Handel Commemoration, Meredith had not been amongst them.

In the north-east, Durham continued in its accustomed manner, regularly performing oratorios as a part of the subscription series and for mid-year concerts; the repertoire, as before, remained limited: *Alexander's Feast*, *Acis and Galatea*, *Messiah* and *Judas Maccabaeus*, Boyce's *Solomon*. The organist, Thomas Ebdon, took *Messiah* to Sunderland again in 1785 to mark the dedication of the Freemasons' Hall there;[40] a year later, the choir travelled to Darlington to sing the same oratorio, this time under the direction of the organist of Stockton Parish Church.[41] Despite Hawdon's unhappy experiences in 1781, he and Ebdon seemed to remain convinced that there was still an audience for oratorios in Newcastle, and in 1784 the two men collaborated to put on no less than three mini-festival performances of oratorios (two of which took place prior to the London Commemoration in June). The first of these, in February and March, was in effect a truncated winter subscription series of three concerts at fortnightly intervals; *Alexander's Feast* on 10 February was followed by a miscellaneous concert based around excerpts from oratorios and *Zadok the Priest* on 24 February, and by *Acis and Galatea* on 9 March. All the soloists and principal instrumentalists were from Durham Cathedral and the scale of performance was therefore probably quite small.[42] A little later, in the week before Easter, two concerts were held on 6 and 7 April, featuring, appropriately, the more serious works in the genre: *Messiah* and *Judas Maccabaeus*.[43] These concerts were more ambitious than the earlier concerts; Hawdon and Ebdon invited a Lancashire singer, a Miss Wrigley, to sing one of the female vocal parts and William Evance probably sang alto rather than his more usual tenor. Finally, when the Assize Week came round in July, Hawdon's concert featured yet more of Handel's oratorio music – including the Hallelujah Chorus – and finished with *Zadok the Priest*.[44] Hawdon's enthusiasm for oratorio continued unabated; by the autumn of 1784, he was probably too ill to hold a regular subscription series but he advertised a concert on 1 February 1785 – in this, the Durham choir performed *Messiah* at the New Assembly Rooms on Westgate Road on 1 February.[45] The popularity of this feast of oratorio performances – almost the only music to be heard in Newcastle in 1784 and 1785 apart from a few benefits for individuals such as Meredith – is difficult to assess. Local newspapers did not review the performances but it is unlikely that Hawdon and Ebdon should have continued to put on oratorios if support had been slight and income poor. Nevertheless, it is notable that Hawdon's only concert in the latter half of 1785 – an Assize Week concert – was a miscellaneous concert of vocal and instrumental music, and that when Ebdon and Meredith took over control of the Newcastle subscription series in early 1786 (using personnel from Durham Cathedral as singers and instrumentalists), they offered not oratorios but miscellaneous concerts; the brief advertisements for the series make no reference to the music of Handel.[46]

While oratorios continued to be performed on a regular basis in Durham concerts and the multiplicity of oratorio performances in Lancashire and Yorkshire encouraged Edward Meredith to leave his post at Durham Cathedral and move to Liverpool, Newcastle had no further oratorio performances until 1791 when John Ashley's travelling oratorio festival came to the town. Ashley had been assistant conductor in the London Handel Commemoration of 1784 and his company included nationally- and internationally-known singers (Madame Gertrude Mara, Anna Maria Crouch and Michael Kelly) and instrumentalists (the Ashley family, John Mahon, the clarinet player, and Charles Serjeant, the trumpeter). Ashley was aware, however, that he could only benefit from having a local collaborator; in York, less than two weeks previously, he had engaged the son of the Minster organist, Matthew Camidge, as co-director, and in Newcastle he enlisted the help of Edward Meredith (who was also one of the vocal soloists in the company). This ploy was so successful that the first notices of the festival by the *Newcastle Courant* and *Newcastle Chronicle* do not mention Ashley at all but refer to Meredith as the originator of the scheme. 'Mr. Meredith, the worthy Bass singer,' said the *Courant*, 'is determined to entertain us ... There can be no doubt that he will meet with every encouragement, from the Nobility and Gentry, so great an undertaking deserves.'[47]

The festival, spread over six days from Thursday to Tuesday, consisted of a complete performance of *Messiah*, two miscellaneous concerts and two 'Grand Selections of Sacred Music'. The sacred music concerts were extremely long, consisting of three parts of nine or ten items each; almost all of these items were extracts from Handel's oratorios with an occasional overture or concerto to begin individual acts, and works such as *Zadok the Priest* also included. Purists such as John Brown would not have approved of such pick-and-mix tactics, which must destroy the meaning of the words in many cases by taking them out of context, which in any case was clearly made on musical grounds rather than for any reason of devotion, and which in many instances was designed to show off the virtuosity of the singers or to feature the most dramatic and impressive choruses. But this type of presentation meant that audiences heard extracts from oratorios which would never have received an entire performance (*Jephtha*, *Saul*, *Athalia* and *Joshua*), and that extracts from Handel's works could be performed with considerably less expense than a complete performance of an oratorio; by careful choice of items, two vocal soloists could perform an engaging programme at no more expense than the average miscellaneous concert. Thus on 30 March 1790, the Musical Fund in York (the body running the subscription series) presented an extract programme with a limited number of local soloists and chorus singers at considerably less expense and therefore considerably more profit for its own benefit.[48]

The audiences for John Ashley's 1791 Music Festivals in York and Newcastle were excellent. According to the *Newcastle Courant,* a 'numerous and brilliant assemblage of Ladies and Gentlemen [came] from all parts' to attend the York Festival; the *Newcastle Courant* recorded 'an immense concourse of auditors' for the performance of *Messiah* at St Nicholas's church, and the *Newcastle Advertiser* said of one of the miscellaneous concerts that 'the Theatre was more crowded in every part than ever remembered', a sentiment echoed by the *Newcastle Chronicle* which estimated that more than 1000 people had attended *Messiah* (although the second Selection Concert had been less popular).[49] Of the theatre performance, the *Chronicle* said that 'the crowd was so excessive that it was with the utmost difficulty admission could be gained to any part of the house'.[50] But in none of the reports was there any suggestion that the numerous members of the audience were there for reasons of piety; indeed, the *Courant* said explicitly that the Festival 'drew from the neighbouring countries, all those whom taste and fashion could prevail upon'.[51] The principal attraction was not even Handel's music – none of the reviews ever mentioned his name. The attraction was the chance to hear the celebrated soloists, Gertrude Mara above all; as the *York Courant* said: 'All the Musical Amateurs in this County will certainly embrace the only Opportunity of hearing Madame MARA'.[52] The York and Newcastle papers went into raptures over the relative merits of the singers; the *Newcastle Courant*'s correspondent fancied himself a connoisseur, talking of the 'fascinating, simple and elegant notes' of Anna Maria Crouch, 'the all-powerful strains' of Meredith, 'the harmonizined [sic] taste and elegant execution' of Harrison and the 'animated exertions' of Michael Kelly.[53] The *Chronicle* devoted even more column inches to a critique of these soloists, adding praise of the Lancashire chorus singers; when it came to the instrumental performers, however, it could only say that 'the band was sufficiently full, and the execution of some pieces was in a very superior stile'.[54] The message was clear; the fashionable and lauded singers were the real attraction.

In all of this, the choir of Durham Cathedral was notable by its absence, hardly surprising perhaps in view of the fact that the festival had been organized by a London-based musician and had brought its own chorus singers with it. Local instrumentalists, however, almost certainly played as rank-and-file members of the orchestra, and some people were surprised at the choir's absence. A rumour circulated, suggesting that the choir had refused an invitation to participate; the *Courant* hastened to put its readers right – the choir, it said, had never been asked to attend.[55] The Dean and Chapter, and the choir itself, may have felt the insinuation of neglect as unpalatable as the original rumour.

The popularity of the 1791 festival in Newcastle led to an imitation event in Durham the following year. Unlike Ashley's festival, this was a locally organized event, put on – in a manner typical of performances in Lancashire and Yorkshire – to celebrate the dedication of an organ, in St Mary le Bow Church. The profits were to go to charity, for the benefit, principally, of the city's new infirmary. The organizer was the Reverend Edward Parker, rector of St Mary le Bow, and his intention was clearly to try and make the festival the equal of Newcastle's; he could not, however, afford to hire the glittering stars that had appeared in Newcastle and the performances were therefore built around the Durham choir, who were used not only as chorus singers but also as principal instrumentalists. Other local musicians, such as the two Thomas Wrights (of Newcastle and Stockton) and Charles Avison junior, were also invited to play in the band, and, to add a little glamour, nationally-known figures with a local connection were also engaged: Mr Hackwood of the King's Theatre in London, who had led the band in Durham mid-year concerts for some years, was hired as principal viola; locally-born composer William Shield, of the Theatre Royal, Covent Garden, was principal cellist. The contrast between the Newcastle and Durham festivals was most evident in the vocal soloists; Parker relied chiefly on the singing men: William Evance sang alto, John Friend tenor and that old favourite of north-eastern audiences, Edward Meredith, was invited back to the area to sing bass. The only imported soloist was a Miss Worrall from Lancashire. These performers gave three concerts between Wednesday 17 October and Friday 10 October: a selection concert on Wednesday morning, a miscellaneous concert on Thursday evening (including a complete performance of *Acis and Galatea*), and *Messiah* on Friday morning. As these were works in regular performance in Durham, little rehearsal was probably necessary.[56]

The *Newcastle Advertiser* was inclined to treat the festival as a social event. 'It will,' it said, 'be attended by most of the first fashion and consequence in this part of the kingdom' and added that 'it is with pleasure we can announce to the Ladies who intend honouring the Musical Performances at Durham with their presence, that Mr. Parker, with his usual attention, has given directions to have the Chancel and altar fitted up in a very commodious manner for their reception'.[57] The *Courant* agreed, listing the soloists with careful attention. But at least some of its readers regarded the festival as more than a chance to see and be seen; the *Courant* felt it 'ungenerous' not to bring to their attention a letter from one of its correspondents in which the writer spoke of the 'moral' objects of the festival – that is, its charitable purposes – and described the dedication of the organ as 'a very essential ornament and improvement to divine worship. – The congregation of the church of Bow may, now, in thought, ascend to Heaven, with more spiritual animation'. But, although the writer spoke with enthusiasm of the spiritual benefits of music in general, nowhere did he mention the content of the festival or Handel's music.[58] The *Courant*'s reviews were as worldly as its previews, full of praise for individual performers, listing each with care and making some approving comment, if only to say they 'had merit'; an unusual concern to mention by name the gentlemen amateurs who had played may be explained by the familiarity of all of them, as local men, to the *Courant*'s readers. The fact that these men were of the professional classes or of gentry families only added to the impression that the festival was regarded as part of the social calendar.

This emphasis on fashion and on vocal singers, particularly the very well-known performers, was to prove disastrous for Newcastle's next – and last – attempt at a musical festival during the 18th century. In 1796, Edward Meredith collaborated with Thomas Thompson, the young organist of St Nicholas's church, to hold a second festival in the town. This festival was as ambitious in scope as the

1791 festival in presenting six concerts over a four day period: complete performances of *Messiah*, *Judas Maccabaeus* and *Redemption* (a pastiche compiled by Arnold from music sung at the 1784 Handel Commemoration in London), two miscellaneous concerts and one concert of sacred music. But of the glittering array of London stars that had graced the 1791 festival, only three of the lesser lights returned: the violinist Cramer as leader, Samuel Harrison as one of the vocal soloists and Boyce (son of the composer) on double-bass. Meredith himself also sang. But in place of Madame Mara and Anna Maria Crouch were Mrs Shepley from Manchester and Miss Worrall, the young singer hired by the Reverend Mr Parker in Durham – good singers but hardly a substitute for their famous predecessors. Other performers from the Lancashire/Yorkshire oratorio circuit that Meredith knew so well were also engaged – Nicholson the flute player from Liverpool, Hughes the oboist from Manchester. 'The remaining part of the Band,' said the *Courant*, 'will consist of the most approved Performers from Liverpool, Manchester, Durham, Newcastle, and Sunderland, with a complete Set of Chorus Singers, from Lancashire.'[59]

The *Newcastle Courant* was confident that the festival would be a success, believing that 'the performance of oratorios at St. Nicholas Church will, we are persuaded, induce many genteel families residing at a distance to make this town their residence during the week. The Theatre will therefore, we doubt not, next week be crowded with all the people of taste and fashion in this town and of the neighbourhood'.[60] The *Chronicle* was incorrect; the *Courant* later reported that the audiences were 'genteel, but not very numerous'.[61] Income, inevitably, was not equal to expenditure, and Meredith and Thompson lost the considerable sum of nearly £120. It is impossible to come to any other conclusion but that the success of the 1791 festival had been principally owing to the renowned vocal soloists engaged and that, without them, the music and any religious or political message it conveyed was not particularly attractive to Newcastle audiences. Brown's comments – that the circumstances of the performance of oratorio led to it being regarded merely as an amusement – seem to have been only too accurate as far as Newcastle was concerned.

Notes

[1] Brown, *Dissertation*, 216.
[2] Ibid., 217.
[3] Ibid., 218.
[4] Idem.
[5] Idem.
[6] Idem.
[7] The text of *The Cure of Saul* was published as preface to the *Dissertation*. Brown seems originally to have taken music from the works of a number of performers for the work but in the late 1760s it was set to music by Arnold and given five London performances, chiefly at the Haymarket Theatre in early 1768. It was revived in March 1771 but does not appear to have been performed thereafter.

[8] Avison, *Essay*, 1st edition, 53–4.
[9] Ibid., 2nd edition, 50. No-one was apparently anxious to defend another composer, Vivaldi, against considerably more derogatory comments than Avison ever applied to Handel; Avison commented that Vivaldi (together with Alberti and Locatelli) wrote compositions 'equally defective in various Harmony and true Invention'. Vivaldi's works were fit only for children and not even then if you wanted the children to develop good musical taste. Avison, *Essay*, 1st edition, 42.
[10] Brown, *Dissertation*, 219–20.
[11] Ibid., 220.
[12] *NC* 13–25 November 1749; Cowper, *Letters*, 117–18, 7 December 1745.
[13] Although these works are not technically oratorios, they were usually treated as such by north-eastern newspapers (and apparently by concert promoters, too), being listed in advertisements with oratorios such as *Messiah*. Winton Dean, in his discussion of *Acis and Galatea*, lists a number of descriptions of the work taken from 18th-century editions, including 'serenata', 'English Pastoral Opera', and 'masque'. Dean, Winton, *Handel's Dramatic Oratorios and Masques* (London: Oxford University Press, 1959), 183–9.
[14] *NJ* 27 August–3 September 1763.
[15] *YC* 21 July 1767.
[16] Ibid., 14 July, 9 and 16 August, 1768.
[17] Ibid., 31 January 1769.
[18] Ibid., 25 July, 22 August, 19 September 1769.
[19] Ibid., 2, 9 January, 6, 27, February 1769, 9 January, 13 March 1770.
[20] *NC* 7 April 1770. The local newspapers thought it worthwhile to point out that advance sales of tickets for this concert numbered only 45; the rest of the audience paid at the door on the night. Possibly there had been some anxiety over the weather.
[21] *YC* 21 February 1769.
[22] Ibid., 22 August 1769.
[23] Ibid., 29 August, 5 September 1769.
[24] Nares had been organist at York Minster from 1735 until 1756.
[25] *YC* 9 August 1768, 17 January, 13 June 1769.
[26] Ibid., 6, 13 March 1770.
[27] Ibid., 29 August 1769.
[28] Ibid., 31 July 1770, 8, 29 January, 19 February, 23 July 1771.
[29] *NC* 26 September 1778, 6 February 1779.
[30] Ibid., 9 June 1770.
[31] Ibid., 21 June 1771.
[32] Ibid., 18 October 1777.
[33] Ibid., 21 February 1778.
[34] Ibid., 20 June, 8 August 1778.
[35] *NJ* 26 September 1778.
[36] Idem.
[37] *NC* 17 March 1781; accounts of Thomas Bewick, 24, 31 March, 9 April 1781.
[38] Ibid., 14 April 1781.

[39] *YCh* 5 November 1784.
[40] *NC* 5 March 1785.
[41] Ibid., 23 September 1785.
[42] Ibid., 25 January 1784.
[43] Ibid., 3 April 1785.
[44] Ibid., 31 July 1784.
[45] Ibid., 29 January 1785.
[46] Ibid., 19 December 1785.
[47] Ibid., 18 June 1791.
[48] *YC* 30 March 1790.
[49] *NA* 3 September 1791; *NC* 20 August 1791.
[50] *NCh* 3 September 1791.
[51] *NC* 27 August 1791.
[52] *YC* 21 June 1791: According to the *Newcastle Chronicle,* Madame Mara 'positively leaves England on October first' [*NCh* 30 July 1791].
[53] *NC* 27 August 1791.
[54] *NCh* 3 September 1791.
[55] *NC* 27 August 1791.
[56] Ibid., 6, 13 October 1792.
[57] *NA* 6 October 1792.
[58] *NC* 17 October 1792.
[59] Ibid., 25 June 1796.
[60] *NCh* 23 July 1796.
[61] *NC* 6 August 1796.

PART FOUR

MUSIC AS A SPUR TO PATRIOTISM

Chapter 8

In War and Peace

In time of peace

Being non-British was almost always an advantage for musicians in 18th-century Britain – ironically, in view of the often brutally expressed contempt for things foreign. In the early part of the century, the fashion was for all things Italian in music, for Italian opera, Italian singers, Italian violinists. Francesco Geminiani, Avison's teacher, came to England from Naples in 1714, was taken up by leading figures in the social world, and maintained his popularity (although his financial standing was often precarious) until his death in Dublin in 1762. Handel was German but built his reputation on Italian opera; singers such as Cuzzoni, Senesino and Farinelli were idolized by London audiences.

And not in London alone; the fashion spread into the provinces. The works of composers such as Geminiani, and his teacher, Corelli, were always popular, not only for their musical content but also for their relative ease of playing, a serious consideration when orchestras in provincial series included a large number of amateurs of variable ability; in Edinburgh, this consideration kept Corelli and Geminiani popular with certain sections of the Musical Society there until the last quarter of the century.[1] Although the north-east did not boast the resources, or venues, to stage entire Handelian operas, extracts from them were performed in concerts in Newcastle and Sunderland from 1733 and possibly earlier.[2] Individuals traded on the attractions of the fashion. In 1741, a Mr Wright, a violinist visiting Newcastle, thought it worth his while to advertise that he had just returned from a visit to Italy and that he intended to play music by the Italian composer, Tartini; earlier in the same year, the youthful prodigy, Tomaso Pinto, had given a benefit in the town.[3] But by far the most enthusiastic reception for such performers was exhibited in York where, in the late 1730s and early 1740s, the winter subscription series bankrupted itself in its anxiety to follow fashion. No fewer than five Italian performers were hired for the winter series: Signor Cattanei or Cattani (probably Giuseppe Cattaneo, an Italian violinist), Alexander Bitti (composer and instrumentalist), Giovanni Piantanida (a violinist who remained in England for only a short period before settling in Bologna), Piantanida's wife (usually known as la Pasterla but advertised in York as Signora Posterla) and the latter's sister, advertised as Signora Ciara Posterla. Cattaneo and Bitti first came to York in the late 1730s, the others followed later, and their frequent reappearances over a period of five or six years indicates that they were much appreciated by audiences, so much so that local musicians attempted to enjoy some of the same attention; taking all five Italians off to Scarborough for a concert in 1740, John Hebden, musical director of the York series, lightly disguised himself as 'Signor Hebdeni', a ruse which probably deceived no-one.[4] Even after the series collapsed into insolvency and Hebden diplomatically removed himself to London, the new directors looked for Italian soloists, first hiring as leader of the band Antonio Pizzolato (who later suffered the trauma of being robbed by pirates in the Irish Sea), and later, in 1748 and 1749, re-engaging the old favourite Cattaneo.[5] This episode in York marks the high point of Italian popularity in the north but the fashion persisted. Newcastle concert-goers lauded the Passerinis in 1752 and delighted over the singer Signora Cremonini in 1762; the violinist Felice Giardini, a friend of Charles Avison, visited Newcastle, Durham and York year after year to play in summer concerts and recommended his friend, Giovanni Battista Noferi, as replacement when he himself decided to leave England. Nor was Hebden's adoption of an Italian name an isolated instance; the York theatre manager, Tate Wilkinson had started his career in Bath as a singer under the name Tate Wilkinsoni, and as late as 1780, Charles Avison junior appeared in the Newcastle Theatre Royal as Carlos Avisonsini.[6] Admiration was not universal or uncritical however; Spencer Cowper, Dean of Durham Cathedral, was lavish in his praise of the castrato, Senesino, and played Corelli and Geminiani in private concerts in the Deanery but nevertheless condemned modern Italian compositions.[7]

For musicians of other nationalities, the outlook might not be so favourable, though many found it possible to thrive, particularly when, in the latter part of the century, German music came more into fashion: the German violinist, Knerler (briefly the leader of the new York series established after the Italian episode), Madame Lousia Gautherot (one of the few women violinists of the century), Madame Gertrude Mara, the much lauded German singer, and Handel himself. But even Leopold and Wolfgang Mozart found life hard after their initial novelty value had worn off, and for unknowns such as William and Jacob Herschel London could be inhospitable. William Herschel came north in search of employment while his brother returned to Hanover; William's teaching in Sunderland and his performance in Charles Avison's concerts and in the Spring Gardens' concerts earnt him a substantial income, although it is not clear whether this was owing to his nationality and novelty value, or to his natural abilities.[8] For British musicians, the prospect could be bleak in the capital, although some did, like John Hebden, contrive to make a tolerable living; it is interesting to speculate that a realistic assessment of the difficulties faced by British musicians in London may have been one of the factors influencing Charles Avison's return to his native town.

This fashion for all things continental, ironic and unexpected as it was in the light of British xenophobia, extended itself to the repertoire played in concerts, and even to the dances taught to eager assembly-goers – it was always a good drawing point for dancing masters to advertise that they had lately visited Paris to learn the latest steps. In concerts in the north-east from the 1770s onwards (programmes do not survive in large numbers before this date), by far the greater part of the instrumental music played was composed by foreign musicians, from the music of Corelli and Geminiani at the beginning of the century to that of Haydn and Pleyel at the end. Those British composers whose instrumental music was performed were all local men such as Avison and Hawdon, or instrumental players like

Wright and Thompson who followed the usual 18th-century practice of composing their own solos or concertos for performance. Where vocal music was concerned, however, the opposite was true; by far the majority of those songs for which composers were named were written by British composers – particularly such men as Harrington, Cook and Calcott who were best known for their catches and glees. This may have been owing principally to a language problem; songs by non-British composers occasionally appear in translation, and the only Italian songs sung in the original language are associated with the London singers from time to time brought north to lend their glamour to the series.[9]

Against this fashion for foreign music and performers must be set the growing interest in the native music of Britain, represented by folk songs and the inclusion of folk elements in songs and instrumental pieces by composers such as Thomas Wright. It can be argued too that Handel's success, based originally on the attractions of all things foreign, ultimately turned on his ability to make his music more English than many a home-grown product, incorporating elements that were interpreted as nationalistic and patriotic references. His oratorios, despite Brown's dismissal of them as mere fashionable amusement, were nevertheless inextricably linked to political factors, although it is probable that, outside Durham, these factors carried little weight in the north-east. Most concert-goers in the region had apparently no desire to emulate the prebendary, Sir John Dolben, in his involvement with 'ancient music' in London, or to travel to London for the 1784 Handel Commemoration. Such ideas came very late to Newcastle; not until 1798 was a concert of ancient music advertised by Thomas Wright and then he was careful to hedge his bets, offering one act of ancient music and a second of modern favourites, emulating perhaps Rauzzini's concerts in Bath at the beginning of the decade. Wright's definition of 'ancient' music was hardly revolutionary – he offered music by Arne, Avison, Geminiani and Handel – but no national pride or even fashion seems to have brought out audiences for this concert, despite the fact that the country was embroiled in another confrontation with a foreign, revolutionary, enemy.[10] Wright never attempted another concert of this type.

The use of a concert to mark a political event of note was a common practice. The coronation of George II in 1727 occurred before concert life established itself in the north-east (although celebrations in London and Bath were reported in local newspapers), but the celebrations for his grandson, George III, in 1761 – which in Newcastle included the ringing of bells from every steeple capable of it, loyal toasts by town corporations and volleys of celebratory fire from local regiments, fireworks, a fountain running with wine on the Sandhill and entertainments at the Mansion House – culminated in a grand concert for which Avison made an arrangement of one of the psalms of Benedetto Marcello: 'The King shall be joyful in thy strength'.

> Thou, O Lord, shall give him
> Everlasting Felicity:
> Thou shalt make him glad
> With the Joy of thy Countenance …

So will we sing
And praise thy mighty Power,
And glorify thy holy Name for ever.[11]

For several years afterwards, musicians in the town held concerts on the anniversary of the coronation (a practice revived in the 1790s during the French Revolutionary Wars). Elsewhere in the region, similar practices were popular; in York during the 1740s, the winter subscription series was usually timed so that the first concert fell on the anniversary of George II's coronation.[12] Concerts were also held to mark one-off events. In November 1765, Durham Cathedral's choir held a concert in the city in memory of the Duke of Cumberland, performing Handel's anthem for the funeral of Queen Caroline; the concert was crowded according to the *Newcastle Courant* – 'the most brilliant and crowded ever known'.[13] A concert in Sunderland in 1797 commemorated recent naval battles and raised funds for the widows and orphans of seamen killed in them.[14]

Even more common was the practice of holding a concert on the King or Queen's birthday. In the 1750s, Garth's Gentlemen's Subscription Series in Durham regularly held a concert in the third week of November to mark George II's birthday (their opponents in the Cathedral Choir marked St. Cecilia's Day around the same time).[15] In 1760, a concert at Spring Gardens in Newcastle celebrated the birthday of the Prince of Wales barely five months before he succeeded to the throne.[16] This practice could be taken to extremes; a few years later, in 1766, the Darlington subscription series (a summer series) contrived to stretch its season from January (to celebrate the Queen's birthday) to September (the anniversary of the coronation) marking George III's birthday in June in passing.[17] The longest-lasting of these celebrations, however, took place in Sunderland, where in the 1770s Thomas Ebdon of Durham established an annual concert on 4 June (or the weekday closest to that date) to mark George II's birthday, using the proceeds as a personal benefit. When Ebdon withdrew from concert promotion in the early 1790s, the King's birthday concert continued under the direction of Thomas Wright of Newcastle; Wright made these events some of the largest-scale concerts he ever held, enlisting the help of gentlemen amateurs from both Sunderland and Newcastle, using singing men from Durham as vocal soloists, and composing much music for the occasion, including a 'loyal Glee' (the words written by 'a gentleman of Sunderland') and 'An Invocation to the 4th of June', the words and music of which do not survive.[18]

The only surviving programme for a concert of this type is for a concert in Darlington that fell just before the anniversary of the Coronation in 1765. Despite the pretext for the concert, the programme consisted of the usual mixture of songs, concertos and solos, adding only a performance of Handel's 'Grand Coronation Anthem', that is, *Zadok the Priest*.[19] *Zadok* was frequently advertised, even in concerts without notable patriotic overtones; it was even performed in a concert given in Newcastle in 1754 by the Hungarian French-horn player, Charles.[20] Also popular were Purcell's airs 'Britons strike home' and 'To Arms', and Thomas Arne's 'The Soldier Tir'd of War's Alarms', which was frequently performed during the French Revolutionary Wars. 'Rule Britannia', also by Arne, is advertised more rarely, on one occasion forming the subject of the rondo to a piano sonata.[21] Handel's 'See the conquering hero comes' enjoyed a certain popularity after its association with the Duke of Cumberland and the Battle of Culloden but its popularity as an isolated item did not last although *Judas Maccabaeus*, from which it was taken, remained one of the most popular of oratorios.[22] This was one of the works in the repertoire of Durham Cathedral Choir who had a number of 'political' anthems in their repertoire, according to the 1749 collection of anthems.[23] Those by Croft included an anthem composed for the 'Thanksgiving upon the Victory at Audenoard' in 1708, for the 'Suppression of the Jacobite Rebellion' in 1715, for the Peace of Utrecht in 1713 and for the Battle of Blenheim in 1704 as well as coronation anthems for George I. Handel's coronation anthems and his music for the funeral of Queen Caroline were also included in the book.

On many occasions, the only significant addition to the customary repertoire seems to have been a performance of 'God save the King'; a typical example is that of a concert in York in January 1793 to mark the Queen's birthday, which included a rendering of the song, with an extra verse added in honour of the Queen.[24] In time of crisis, the performance of this song became widespread (although the habit of advertisers of referring to the 'Hallelujah Chorus' by the name of 'God save the King' after its middle section, confuses the issue on occasion). The song was rendered in a variety of forms – as the subject for instrumental rondos, as a choral piece and even, on one occasion, as a novelty item when two men from the Theatre Royal in Newcastle played it with variations at a concert in January 1793, 'on one Violin … both bowing and both fingering throughout the whole Piece'.[25] The tune was not just popular in the concert setting but frequently ended theatre performances in the 1790s and was taught to children (particularly those in charity schools), such as those who performed it in the parish church at Stockton on the anniversary of the King's accession on 26 October 1795.[26]

In York, 'God save the King' was frequently played in the late 1780s during the King's illness (referred to by the *York Courant* as 'the melancholy Situation of our beloved Monarch') and again the following year on his recovery.[27] In 1788 and 1789, the King's illness sparked off a number of loyal tributes throughout the north-east. Thomas Ebdon included a special performance of 'God save the King' in a concert in Sunderland in November 1788, which 'was received with a warmth of applause, perfectly consonant to the feelings of a loyal people'.[28] In January 1789, Austin and Whitlock's company in Newcastle 'gratified the audience' by adding to 'God save the King' extra verses 'wrote on the present melancholy occasion'.[29] From January to May, Newcastle newspapers were reporting celebrations throughout the region in thanksgiving at the King's recovery: 'windows and buildings illuminated 'in a manner surprisingly elegant and brilliant' in Framlington; ringing of bells and parades in Middleton in Teesdale; a parade in Warkworth. 'God save the King' was sung on every occasion: in Framlington, a group of singers and instrumentalists and locals paraded through the streets to the tune with 'such cheerful huzzas, that they were heard at several miles distant'; in Morpeth, the Aldermen went to church in procession accompanied by the waits playing 'God save the King'.[30] At Staindrop, the local militia band accompanied the scholars in a parade to church and then to a tea provided by one of the local ladies while the band, bell ringers and adult singers were entertained by Lord Darlington at an inn where 'the song of God save the King was sung in chorus, with the assistance of part of the band, which was repeatedly encored'; a second parade of band and scholars at 2 pm was succeeded in the evening by fireworks and 'music on the green'.[31] Adam Kinloch, a Newcastle dancing master, held a ball which many of his young pupils attended wearing sashes decorated with the words 'God save the King' and 'Long Live the King'; Kinloch opened the ball with 'a Minuet to the Air of God save the King' and ended it with a 'Bath Minuet to the same favourite Air, by a full Band'.[32] In addition, on the Thanksgiving Day itself, a Thursday in April, a service at St Nicholas's church in Newcastle was attended by the Mayor and Magistrates who heard, after the end of the service, a performance of the Coronation Anthem (*Zadok the Priest*) sung by a quartet of male singers – two actors from the theatre, John Thompson, the breeches maker and music teacher, and Thomas Wright – 'accompanied by a full chorus previously instructed for the purpose'.[33]

Towards the end of 1792 and the beginning of 1793, when war with France loomed, local newspapers reported another spate of performances of 'God save the King' in a variety of contexts. Performance in church was again popular: Charles Avison junior played it on the organ after divine service at St Nicholas in December, a performance that met with 'heart-felt satisfaction by the whole congregation';[34] a similar performance was put on 'by the singers of Sunderland church, accompanied by violins, flutes, oboes, and bassoons, and joined by the voices of many of the congregation'. ('The effect,' said the *Newcastle Advertiser*, 'was admirable.')[35] Also in December 1792, a celebration at Alnwick for the birth of an heir to the Duke of Northumberland was marked by a volley fired by the local militia and a performance of 'God save the King' by the militia band; only a few days later, members of the Loyal Society of Chester le Street, accompanied by other local societies, paraded the town's streets to the music of a band playing the tune.[36] Such parades frequently took place at night and culminated in the hanging of an effigy of Thomas Paine, accompanied by a rendering of 'God save the King': at Swalwell at the end of December 1792; in Middleton in Teesdale around New Year 1793.[37] On 14 December 1792, the theatre company in Newcastle added two verses to the words, one of which had been sung at Bristol when 'the Audience applauded eighteen distinct Times, the Ladies joined with their Husbands and Friends, and French Fans fell a Sacrifice to BRITISH LOYALTY'.[38] The second additional verse was specifically designed for a Newcastle audience.

While France her children mourns,
And sorrows o'er their urns,
We happy live.
Hence discord with thy Train,
Thy Ruffian Aims are vain,
For loyal Britons sing
God save the King.

The manly Hearts on Tyne,
O Royal George, are thine,
God save the King.
Northumbria's Sons of old
Were England's Shield we're told
And still are firm and bold,
God save the King.

Local composers wrote a substantial amount of music to celebrate or commemorate specific politically significant occasions. Avison's anthem for the Coronation in 1761 is the only known example of his participation in this genre; a little earlier, James Hesletine of Durham had composed an anthem 'on the taking of Cape Breton' which was performed at the annual meeting of the Sons of the Clergy in Newcastle in September 1758.[39] Hesletine's work has not survived thanks to his insistence on destroying his manuscripts, but the *Newcastle Courant* printed the words of an ode written by Matthias Hawdon to mark the end of the American war in 1783; this ode was sung at a subscription concert in January by Edward Meredith and proved so popular that it was repeated at the following month's concert. The ode was substantial, consisting of a bass recitative and air followed by a second recitative and more verses, and the words, probably written by Hawdon himself, were not much concerned with historical accuracy, as the first recitative demonstrates:

BRITONS! Rejoice! At length, by valour free'd,
Majestic Albion rears her drooping head,
By woe's made greater, see! Sublime she stands,
Snatches fresh laurels from oppressive hands:
Destruction on her helm, in dreadful pride,
See fate and victory attend her side.

In later verses, however, Hawdon probably put his finger accurately on what really concerned his audiences – the problems caused to trade by the war and the opportunities offered by peace. The ode ended:

Thy blessings, peace, again restor'd,
Soon shall our Albion see,
Her ports enrich'd by foreign trade,
Her sons by public virtue made,
Illustrious, great, and free.[40]

Hawdon's own preoccupations may have been elsewhere at a time of great financial difficulties for concert life in Newcastle, for musicians in general and for himself in particular – difficulties which Hawdon later attributed to lack of support for the arts. The words of the second recitative seem to imply that much of the general apathy where amusements were concerned was caused by preoccupation with the war. Hawdon wrote:

> May white-rob'd peace her radiant sceptre wave,
> Rais'd from the ruins of the just and brave.
> The scattered arts shall then not fear decay ...[41]

In time of war

The composition and performance of this type of music enjoyed an upsurge in popularity during the French Revolutionary Wars in the 1790s. At the beginning of the decade, musical life was at a very low ebb in Newcastle with only spasmodic attempts at a circumscribed winter subscription series and a few benefits, such as those given by Thomas Wright. Elsewhere, Thomas Ebdon was pulling out of concert-promotion in Durham and Sunderland. Personal and musical factors (the ageing of the Cathedral choir, for instance) may have had much to do with this, but the political situation – the continuing reoccupation with events such as the King's illness and the worsening relationship with France, as well as the spectre of rising inflation – had their effect too. Little consciousness of this appears in musical programmes or advertisements in the early years of the decade – the programmes for Thomas Wright's 1791 and 1792 benefits, for instance, contain no overtly political items – but from the outbreak of war with France in 1793, the performance of patriotic music, both that composed by local composers and that composed elsewhere, slowly crept into the repertoire, the first sign of a trend that was to blossom spectacularly from 1795 onwards.[42] It was at about this time that the performances of 'God save the King' peak; the concert given by the actors from the Theatre Royal that included their unique version of the national anthem, also ended with *Zadok the Priest*.[43]

In his 1793 benefit, Wright included a popular favourite, *The Battle of Prague*, a piece of imitative music written by the Bohemian composer, František Kocžwara.[44] For this piece, Wright called in the assistance of members of a military band quartered locally, advertising the presence of drums, bugle-horns and trumpets. Military bands had long been popular in the area and newspapers were fond of remarking on their arrival; when Colonel Lambton's Regiment of Foot marched north in 1760, the *Newcastle Courant* commented that 'they have a very fine band of music'.[45] William Herschel came north with just such a band, that of the Earl of Darlington's Militia, quartered in Richmond.[46] Occasionally, these bands gave concerts for their own benefit, as did the Huntingdon Band in March 1780 at the Red Lion in Durham; more frequently they were hired by local concert promoters to augment existing concert bands – brass and woodwind players were few and far between locally.[47] Thus in August 1780, Matthias Hawdon engaged a military band to assist in the Newcastle Assize Concert; the band may have been that belonging to Sir George Saville's Regiment, which certainly played at one of the subscription concerts in October of the same year.[48] Military bands were also popular at Spring Gardens, Newcastle, where their brass and woodwind instruments were better suited to outdoor playing than were stringed instruments, and in the theatre, where military music was popular as interval entertainment, particularly during the 1790s.[49] If the officers of a regiment bespoke a performance at the theatre, the regimental band almost always took part in the performance. They were also occasionally lent to other organizations. In December 1791, when the Freemasons of South Shields bespoke a performance at the new theatre there, the 31st regiment of Colonel Cotton sent its regimental band to accompany a torch-lit procession from the Freemasons' Lodge to the theatre and back again, and to play 'a great variety of marches and martial tunes'; the *Newcastle Chronicle* commented that they played 'in a stile that would have done credit to more veteran musicians'.[50] The band certainly impressed the Freemasons who invited it back six months later on the occasion of their next benefit. The play requested on this latter occasion – only six months before the outbreak of war with France – was *The Surrender of Calais*.[51]

By 1794, a year into the war with France, military bands were appearing almost as a matter of course in Newcastle concerts and probably elsewhere in the region too. The most active of these bands was that of the West York Militia who in 1794 appeared in Wright's Newcastle benefit in April, at the opening of the new organ in Tynemouth Church at the end of the same month, at the Newcastle Assize Concert in August, and at Thomas Thompson's benefit in Newcastle in October; they may also have taken part in a subscription series organized by Wright in the early months of the year.[52] Both Wright and Thompson composed new pieces for the band; Thompson advertised 'several NEW MILITARY PIECES' between the Acts' [of the concert] and Wright two 'Grand MILITARY PIECES of various Movements'.[53] The latter pieces give some idea of the composition of the West Yorks Band as they were performed by five clarinets, four horns, three bassoons, a serpent, a double-bass, and two kettle drums.[54]

Early in 1795, fears of a French invasion from the coast of Holland led to the foundation of Volunteer Corps along the coast of Britain. In the north-east, Volunteer regiments were set up at Durham, South Shields, North Shields and Tynemouth, Sunderland, Stockton and York, and possibly other places as well; a Newcastle Corps was embodied in January 1795. As was the case with all military regiments, the Volunteer corps were entitled to a band, providing the Corps' Commander and Officers were prepared to pay for it.[55] For the most part volunteer bands in the north-east seem to have consisted purely of a drummer and a fife player or two, although some seem to have been slightly larger or to have been subject to augmentation from time to time in order to play in the concert room. The North Shields and Tynemouth Volunteers, the Stockton Volunteers and the Sunderland Volunteers all took part in concerts or balls on an occasional basis, and the band of the York Loyal Volunteer Corps played at the theatre there in February 1795.[56] Pieces written for these bands by local composers suggest their resources: Thomas Wright's *Grand Troop* for the Newburn band (north of Newcastle) was written for three clarinets, horns, octave-flute and bassoon; William Shield's *March for the South Shields Loyal Volunteers* survives only in short score but has cues for drum, clarinets and a horn solo; John Friend's *March and Quick Step* for the Durham Loyal Volunteers is scored for clarinets, flutes, horns, bassoon, serpent and trumpet.[57]

The band of the Newcastle Volunteer Corps, however, was clearly of a different order and it was the only local band to give regular concerts – twice-yearly – for a period of at least seven years between 1795 and 1802. The band was probably embodied very shortly after the formation of the Corps – it was clearly in existence by July 1795 when one of its members was murdered by drunken thieves; the surviving Volunteer muster rolls do not list members of the band separately but advertisements suggest that the band included all the principal professional musicians of the town as well as some amateurs.[58] Thomas Wright was its leader; other members included Wright's younger brother, William, John Peacock the small-pipes player, William Grey, a cellist, John Thompson the breeches maker, and Alexander Munro Kinloch, a dancing master. The murdered member, Thomas Purves, was a carver and gilder. Music composed for the band indicates that its instrumentation was very similar to that of the Newburn and Durham bands, and included clarinets, horns and bassoons and an octave-flute. Some of the professional musicians were also string players (Wright played the violin, Kinloch and Grey the cello), and it is likely that the band was augmented in concerts by other military bands quartered locally, and by the Gentlemen Amateurs who generally took part in subscription and other concerts.

The band made its first known appearance at a field day for the Corps on 25 August 1795. The Volunteer Corps paraded on the Forth – the large area of open ground to the west of the town – dressed in full uniform of scarlet, green and white with gold loops, buttons and feathers, and with round hats sporting bear-skin crests. The band (described by the *Newcastle Courant* as 'excellent') played while the Corps paraded, were inspected and presented with their colours, after which Corps and band processed to the Commander's home in the town, where the colours were to be lodged.[59] Less than a month later, the commander and officers presided over a concert put on and directed by Thomas Wright. For the concert, the culmination of a day of celebration to mark the anniversary of the King's Coronation, the Volunteer band was augmented by the band of the West Yorks Militia and 'a great number' of Gentlemen Amateurs; the *Newcastle Courant* was delighted by the result. 'The music,' it said, 'was well adapted to celebrate the return of that happy day which gave to England her present beloved Monarch; the company was remarkably brilliant, and more numerous than we remember to have seen on any former occasion.' The women in the audience decked themselves out in the Volunteer Corps colours of scarlet and green, and the *Courant* commented 'we cannot help thinking it would be highly gratifying to the Volunteers, to have this compliment paid to them by the fair sex'.[60] The profits from the concert went to Wright's benefit.[61]

A month later, a second concert was held, on this occasion for the benefit of the band members themselves.[62] Each of the concerts was followed by a ball for which a separate band was engaged; for the band members' benefits, two dance bands were promised, one each for the large and small rooms in the Assembly Buildings on Westgate Road, suggesting that a very large audience was expected. (For the 1801 Volunteer band benefit, Bewick printed 400 tickets, an extremely large number for a benefit concert; Assize Concerts at this time generally warranted the printing of about 50-100 tickets.)[63] These two concerts, one for Wright's benefit and one for the benefit of the band, were given in September and October every year until 1798 when the band decided that their benefit suffered financially from following so closely on Wright's and therefore switched it to the spring. Wright's concert, however, remained firmly anchored at the time of the anniversary of the coronation.[64]

For these concerts, and for Thomas Thompson's Assize Week benefits in the last years of the century, a great deal of new music with a patriotic or nationalistic flavour was written. Much of this was of a general nature; both Wright and Thompson wrote a number of 'Military Sonatas' and 'Martial Songs', several local men wrote verses for songs which were set to music by men such as Wright, and a singing man from Durham Cathedral, George Ashton, published in 1799 a song. 'While danger encircles our land', dedicated to the Duke of Northumberland.[65] Few of the texts for these songs survive; Wright's 'Invocation to Peace', 'adapted to the Music of the favourite Portuguese hymn' (that is, *Adeste Fideles*) is likewise lost.[66] But the programme for a concert on 14 October 1801, preserves the words of an 'Address to Peace' written by Wright when the Peace of Amiens threatened. Wright's prose was of the same quality as Hawdon's in his Ode of 1783, but his preoccupations, and those of his audiences, were clear.

Hail, hail! O Peace divine!
Whose countenance benign
At length appears;
Thou com'st, with cheering smiles,
To bless the British Isles,
Reward the warrior's toils,
And end our cares.

Commerce will spread her sails,
Again will court the gales,
And plough the main;
While WEALTH, her sister fair,
With locks of golden hair,
Will still, sweet Peace, repair,
Where thou dost reign.[67]

A number of pieces were written to commemorate specific occasions, as was the song written by Wright for a concert in May 1800 'in Honour of the Queen'.[68] Wright also composed *General Suwarrow's March* to celebrate the exploits of a now obscure Swiss general and produced the military sonata in October 1797 that incorporated a Swiss tune 'Ranz des Vaches'.[69] A song produced by Wright in November 1798 was composed 'in Honour of our late Naval Victories, with a Chorus'.[70]

Although Thomas Thompson wrote some instrumental pieces for military band, he chiefly concentrated on writing songs; he is known to have composed around 46 songs of which at least 36 survive. The majority of these did not have a political connection – Thompson had a fondness for songs about fairies – but some refer to contemporary events if only in passing: a girl bids her lover farewell as he sails off to war, for instance. Most explicit of the songs is Thompson's response to the Battle of the Nile; this is no exhortation to patriotic fervour however – Thompson's song brings the war much closer to home, looking at the realities of war and at a consequence that must have been all too familiar. 'The Orphan Boy' sees the Battle of the Nile through the eyes of a young boy, in a town that might be Newcastle, celebrating the news of an English victory:

> How pleased was I when the glad sound
> Of Nelson's vict'ry came
> Along the lighted streets to bound,
> And see the windows flame!

But the victory has been bought at a high price on a personal level, as the boy finds out:

> To force me home my mother fought,
> She shuddered at my joy;
> For with my father's life 'twas bought,
> Unhappy Orphan Boy.[71]

Nevertheless, for the most part, Thompson's songs are comfortable songs, emphasizing the distant nature of the war and the remoteness of the actual fighting, showing how the war was experienced chiefly second-hand through its remote effects – bereavement, loss of trade, inflation and taxation.

The unexpected and enduring success of these Volunteer Band concerts ensured that Newcastle ran counter to the national trend, musically speaking. Elsewhere, a 'rage for music' that had been so noticeable in London in the 1770s and 1780s was fading under the pressures of inflation and a feeling that it was inappropriate to enjoy oneself when the country was under threat. Hawdon's 1783 Ode indicates that this was no new phenomenon, but it was not, perhaps, inevitable – entertainments had continued during other wars. Nevertheless, the loss of interest in organized entertainments in the region during the 1790s was widespread and rapid. At the theatre, Stephen Kemble found houses generally very thin from 1794 onwards; in Durham and Sunderland, Thomas Ebdon pulled out of concert promotion around 1793, and for the rest of the century only occasional benefits for the singing men were held in the city, apart from an unsuccessful attempt at a winter series in 1796.[72] Efforts by the local organist in Sunderland to revive the series there had collapsed by 1796.[73] In York, the subscription series limped on throughout the last decade of the century with scant support, prompting its ageing organizer to retire in 1800; his successor had little better success and a proposed Musical Festival in 1803 was cancelled at the last minute, after soloists had been hired and programmes advertised because of a general feeling amongst local music-lovers that the event was inappropriate.[74]

But in Newcastle, audiences flocked to the Volunteer Band concerts and to Thomas Thompson's Assize Concerts as a gesture of patriotic support, and the popularity of these concerts may have had a knock-on effect on the subscription series, prompting the Musical Society to organize a new winter series. The series had been moribund since the mid-1780s; spasmodic attempts to revive it between 1791 and 1792 and in 1794 seem to have roused no real enthusiasm although the series may have limped on with three concerts per year in the early years of the decade and seven in Thomas Wright's 1794 season. But it seems to have gained new life from around 1797 and was restored to the level of Charles Avison's series with 12 concerts at fortnightly intervals from October onwards, with additional benefits for its leader, Thomas Wright, and for the vocal soloists.[75] Taking into account the two Volunteer Band concerts and Thompson's Assize Concerts, Newcastle was probably better provided for musically than at any time since Avison's death.

The winter series cannot be said even at this time to have been hugely popular; it was always, in comparison with the Volunteer Band concerts, a minority interest – its meetings, in the Old Assembly Rooms in the Groat Market, suggest that even the smaller of the two rooms on Westgate Road was too large and expensive for its organizers. (Bewick's accounts do not record the printing of tickets for the end of century seasons but Thomas Wright's 1794 season only required 60 tickets.)[76] Nevertheless it seems to have been loyally supported for at least six or seven years and remained at the level of 12 concerts until 1803 when increasing expenses enforced its contraction to eight concerts. Its programmes were not overtly patriotic in character; the series was plainly designed for the serious music-lover who was prepared to invest time and energy in listening to music that was not necessarily immediately accessible. 'Antient' music was not well represented, only the occasional piece by Avison, Corelli or Geminiani being played, although Handel's overtures – though rarely his vocal works – were popular. (This may reflect the printed music available to the concert band.) Haydn's Military Symphony was occasionally played as was Kotzwara's *Battle of Prague*, a popular item in benefit concerts of the time. However, the habit of being less than specific on handbills – referring to instrumental and vocal music only by genre rather than by title or composer – may hide the performance of a substantial amount of patriotic music.[77] The real significance of the series, however, is principally in its stability at a time when other series were finding it difficult or impossible to survive.

Peace

Ironically, this flowering of musical activity seems to have been brought to an end by the pressures not of war but of peace. The Peace of Amiens, temporary though it was, was disastrous for musical life in Newcastle. Reactions in the north-east to the signing of the treaty were ambiguous. Local newspapers had been reporting the negotiations for several months but without a great deal of detail or enthusiasm; nevertheless, the immediate reaction to the signing of the treaty was one of thankfulness. 'We congratulate our readers on the arrival of the DEFINITIVE TREATY OF PEACE,' wrote the *Newcastle Courant's* editor and proceeded to detail the crowds that had greeted the arrival of the mail-coach that brought the news, the firing of celebratory volleys by the Volunteers on the Sandhill, the general rejoicing. But there was unease too. Magistrates in Sunderland protested against a proposal to illuminate the streets of the town, on the grounds that the money would better be given to the poor; the inhabitants of the town ignored the comments and illuminated the streets anyway, as did the residents of Durham and Darlington.[78]

The *Courant* was firmly on the side of the Sunderland magistrates, quoting with approval the action taken by the Lord Mayor and magistrates of York in forbidding the illumination of the streets there and ordering that the money should instead be donated to the local hospital and charity schools. Amongst all the celebrations, certain sections of the community were still nervous of the power of the mob and fearful that the unrest that had overthrown governments in the American colonies and in France might yet spread to England; the *Courant* was 'sensible that illuminations are often attended by tumult, riot, and danger' and suggested that a donation to charity might amply demonstrate patriotism but avoid the dangers of public demonstrations. The paper suggested that in Newcastle the Infirmary was a suitable object for donations: 'the revenues of the infirmary are far from equal to its expenditure, independent of the sum still wanting to complete the new buildings'. 'The smallest donation thrown into the fund destined to alleviate human misery,' said the *Courant*, 'must be a far more acceptable offering to the God of Peace, than the idle blaze of millions of tapers.'[79]

The *Courant*'s appeal clearly struck a chord particularly with the middle and upper classes; the vicar of Bishopwearmouth supported the call to give to the poor rather than illuminating streets; a number of local gentlemen at once made donations to the Newcastle Infirmary.[80] And the subscribers to the winter subscription series proposed to hold a concert that would be a mixture of celebration and charity, with the proceeds going to the Infirmary – a proposal of which the *Courant* immediately approved. 'By the advertisement in the first page our readers will observe, that a grand selection of Vocal and Instrumental Music, will be performed at the Theatre on Easter-Tuesday, in celebration of Peace, and for the Benefit of the Infirmary. That the Produce of this concert will be very considerable we have no doubt, especially as the idea of an illumination seems now to be abandoned.' The Courant said it had no doubt that the concert itself offered 'a most inviting bill of fare' but that even if it did not, it must 'appeal … forcibly to the feelings of patriotism and humanity'.[81]

The concert took place on 20 April 1802 in the Theatre Royal on Moseley Street; it was a large-scale concert – the first three-act concert held in the town for over twenty years. The outer acts were arranged in the conventional manner, with alternating vocal and instrumental items, and orchestral pieces beginning and ending each act; the central act was a mirror image of the others, beginning and ending with vocal items. The concert had an unmistakable military air; instrumental music included the overture to Henry IV by [Sam]Martini, two Handel overtures with grand marches, the overture to *Lodoiska* by Kreutzer and Haydn's Grand Military Symphony. Where the vocal items were concerned, however, the ambiguous tone evident in the *Courant* was echoed and the mood was far from celebratory. The words of the six songs printed on the handbill strike an ambiguous note. The first, 'Tom Starboard' by Mazzinghi, tells of 'as brave a tar as ever sail'd' who survived a hatful of mischances on his journey home to be reunited with his prospective bride; Tom was first shipwrecked, then impressed into the army, lost an arm in battle and finally reached home only to find his love newly dead of grief having been incorrectly told he was dead. A pastoral ditty by Thompson, 'Learn to relish', sings the praises of 'tranquil pleasures' and 'calm delight' as if Thompson feared the returning warriors would miss the cosmopolitan bustle of war. Arne's well-known song, 'The Soldier Tir'd of War's Alarms' warns that the soldier may 'forswear the clang of hostile arms' but, should occasion arise, he is ready to 'dare again the field' – indeed that he 'burns' to do so. In Kelly's 'Ah, no! my love, no', a girl begs her lover to remember her while he is abroad. Even the two songs with no apparent reference to contemporary events were sombre in tone: 'The Sapling Oak' by Storace tells of an oak dying for lack of nourishment until the forester clears surrounding vegetation; the last song, a hunting song by Reeve, tells of the death of a deer. These are not the celebratory accents to be expected in a concert of this type; the concert raised over £82 for the Infirmary but there was clearly a feeling of weariness and unease.[82]

The Peace of Amiens provoked the disbandment of the Volunteer Corps and its companion, the Armed Association which had catered for gentlemen a little higher up the social scale; this too had had a band with Thomas Wright as its leader, although it had held only an occasional benefit.[83] The disembodiment of the two corps and their bands reduced income for many of the professional musicians of the town, and the constriction of the winter subscription series in 1803 for financial reasons further increased their difficulties. Although the Volunteer Corps at least was re-embodied when war broke out in 1804, the Volunteer band never again reached such popularity; no trace of concerts given by the band after that date can be found and local newspapers cease to record even the small number of social events that took place. The subscription series too may have ceased or run at a very low level until around 1809. Ironically, war had brought prosperity to Newcastle's musicians but peace reduced it, reversing Matthias Hawdon's hopes, expressed in his 1783 Ode, that in peace the 'Scattered Arts need not fear decay'.[84]

Notes

[1] Burchell, *Polite or Commercial*, 63-4; Hutchings, *Baroque Concerto*, 252–68.
[2] *NC* 10 November 1733.
[3] Ibid., 18–25 April, 15–22 August 1741.
[4] *YC* 19 August 1749. For details of the York Concerts' disastrous flirtation with the Italians, see Southey, *Commercial Music-Making*, 46–8, 55–60.
[5] *YC* 3 June 1746, 16 February 1748, 17 January 1749.
[6] Burchell, *Polite or Commercial*, 107.
[7] Cowper, *Letters*, passim.
[8] Southey, *Commercial Music-Making*, 265.
[9] Boyd, *Songs*, passim.
[10] *NA* 21 April 1798.
[11] *NC* 5 September 1761.
[12] *YC* 4 October 1748, 17 October 1749.

[13] *NC* 9 November 1765.
[14] Ibid., 18 November 1797.
[15] Ibid., 8 November 1755 et al.
[16] Ibid., 7 June 1765.
[17] *NCh* 25 January, 7 June, 26 July, 16 August 1766; *NJ* 22–9 March 1766; *NC* 3 May 1766.
[18] *NCh* 24 May 1794.
[19] *NC* 14 September 1765.
[20] Ibid., 23 November 1754.
[21] Ibid., 20 February 1796.
[22] The chorus was usually advertised in Newcastle as extracted from its original source, *Joshua.*
[23] *A Collection of Anthems*, passim.
[24] *YC* 21 January 1793.
[25] *NCh* 29 December 1792.
[26] *NC* 7 November 1795.
[27] *YC* 16 December 1788, 10 March 1789.
[28] *NC* 22 November 1788.
[29] *NCh* 22 December 1793.
[30] *NC* 21 March, 4, 25 April 1789.
[31] Ibid., 2 May 1789.
[32] Ibid., 25 April 1789.
[33] Idem. Unlike at Framlington, Newcastle's inhabitants were specifically forbidden to illuminate their houses as 'inconsistent' (according to local magistrates) 'with the purpose for which the day is appointed'.
[34] *NA* 22 December 1792.
[35] Ibid., 5 January 1793.
[36] *NC* 22 December 1792; *NA* 5 January 1793.
[37] *NA* 5 January 1793.
[38] Boyd, *Songs*, 14 December 1792.
[39] *NC* 9 September 1758.
[40] Ibid., 8 February 1783.
[41] Idem.
[42] *NC* 19 March 1791, 21 January 1792; Boyd, *Songs*, 22 March 1791, 2 May 1792.
[43] *NCh* 29 December 1792.
[44] *NC* 20 April 1793.
[45] Ibid., 24 May 1760.
[46] Lubbock, *Herschel*, 13.
[47] Ibid., 25 March 1780.
[48] Ibid., 12 August 1780, 21 October 1780.
[49] *NJ* 7-14 May 1763.
[50] *NCh* 24 December 1791.
[51] *NA* 2 June 1792.
[52] *NC* 29 March, 19 April, 16 August, 27 September 1794.

[53] Ibid., 27 September 1796.
[54] Ibid., 29 March 1794.
[55] *NA* 31 January 1795.
[56] *YC* 29 February 1796.
[57] Thomas Wright, *Grand Troop for ... the Use of the Newbourn Band* (Newcastle: William Wright, n.d.); William Shield, *The South Shields Loyal Volunteers March, Troop, and Quick Step arranged for the Piano Forte or Harp* (London: Preston, n.d.); John Friend, *The Durham City Loyal Volunteers, March and Quick Step, for a Military Band, also Arranged for the Piano Forte* (London: Preston, n.d.).
[58] *NCh* 4 July 1795. The *Newcastle Chronicle* insisted that the murder would not have taken place if the parties involved had been morally courageous enough to avoid drinking on a Sunday. The composition of the Volunteer Band can be partially reconstructed from advertisements for its benefits which list musicians from whom tickets could be purchased.
[59] *NCh* 29 August 1795.
[60] *NC* 26 September 1795.
[61] Ibid., 12 September 1795.
[62] Ibid., 10 October 1795.
[63] Accounts of Thomas Bewick, passim.
[64] For a more detailed discussion of the Newcastle Volunteer Band and its activities, see Southey, R., 'The Volunteer Band', Section 2 of 'Music and Politics' in *Resisting Napoleon: The British response to the threat of invasion, 1797–1815*, ed. Mark Philp (London: Ashgate, 2006).
[65] *NC* 2 March 1799.
[66] Ibid., 2 March 1799; *NCh* 23 March 1799.
[67] Boyd, *Songs*, 14 October 1801.
[68] *NC* 17 May 1800.
[69] Thomas Wright, *Genl. Suwarrow's March for Clarinets, Horns, Bassoons, and Octave-Flute, Adapted for the Piano-Forte* (Edinburgh: John Hamilton, n.d.).
[70] *NA* 3 November 1798.
[71] Thomas Thompson. 'The Orphan Boy', (London: Goulding, Phipps and D'Allmain, n.d.).
[72] *NC* 12 November 1796.
[73] The last recorded subscription concert in Sunderland was on 17 December 1796 when the local organist, Mr Weyllandt, hired Thomas Wright of Newcastle and John Friend of Durham Cathedral as soloists [*NC* 12 December 1795]. Thereafter, only military band and charitable concerts were held in Sunderland and no concerts are recorded after 1797.
[74] *YC* 22 August 1803.
[75] Boyd, *Songs*, passim.
[76] Accounts of Thomas Bewick, 11 January 1794.
[77] Boyd, *Songs*, passim.
[78] *NC* 3 April 1802.

[79] Idem. Newcastle's magistrates had also objected to illumination of the town on the occasion of Thanksgiving for the King's recovery in 1789, considering that it was inappropriate to the occasion (see fn 33).
[80] *NC* 10 April 1802.
[81] Idem.
[82] Boyd, *Songs*, 20 April 1802; *NC* 24 April 1802.
[83] Ibid., 2 December 1800.
[84] *NC* 8 February 1783.

PART FIVE

MUSIC AS A MEANS OF MAKING A LIVING

Chapter 9

Commercial Opportunities

Early training and finding a job

Music was frequently a family affair – sons followed fathers into the profession. Charles Avison followed his father Richard and was in turn followed by his two surviving sons, Edward and Charles; the Martins, Kells and Rosses were all families of waits in Newcastle, the Picks, Shaws and Bulkeleys in York. In Durham, the choristers at the cathedral came from the same families year after year, younger brothers following elder brothers into the choir stalls and sometimes into the ranks of the singing men too – the Parkinsons and the Paxtons. For these men much of their early training must have taken place within the family context; Charles Avison almost certainly received his earliest instruction from his father as did Thomas Hawdon from his father, Matthias. It is possible, however, that Richard Avison was not necessarily thinking in terms of a musical career for his sons; it has been suggested that Charles was apprenticed to a local merchant, Ralph Jenison, who was the dedicatee of Avison's Opus 1 – this idea, based on a passing comment in the dedication of that work, though at first consideration apparently unlikely, may be supported by the fact that Charles's elder brother, Edward, also musical, was apprenticed outside the profession, to a local stay-maker.[1] No definitive evidence survives to either support or refute the suggested apprenticeship with Jenison.

For talented children from non-musical families, an apprenticeship was the usual way into the profession. Musicians frequently placed advertisements for apprentices, with apparently mixed success – both Robert Barber, in 1783, and Matthias Hawdon, in 1784, seem to have anticipated receiving unsuitable applications. Barber stressed that 'None need apply but such as have a musical genius' (using the word in the original sense of a talent rather than in the inflated Romantic sense); Hawdon was more concerned with financial considerations, remarking tartly that 'none need apply that will not allow for Board, Lodging, &c'.[2] The master benefited from a good apprentice twice, not only taking in the premium paid by the apprentice's family for living expenses, but also appropriating any money the apprentice earned. Apprentices frequently played in concert and dancing assembly bands but were not necessarily always trouble-free; Avison listed the maintaining of such apprentices as a necessary part of the expenses of a subscription series, and a burdensome one, although he did not state precisely why; he may have been thinking, as he wrote, of the difficulties he had had with one of his apprentices, George Williams, who had run away in 1739, prompting Avison to advertise for him in local papers.[3] (Williams probably returned and completed his training – a Mr Williams is known to have given a concert in Durham in 1754.)[4] The only other apprentice known by name in the north-east is John Ross, apprentice to Matthias Hawdon, who found a permanent and lucrative post in Aberdeen and settled there for life but Ross was from a musical family whose other members included waits in Newcastle. Towards the end of the century, the more frequent use of the word 'pupil' – usually reserved for those who studied music as a hobby, for young women seeking accomplishments, or for boys with a dilettante interest in music – confuses the issue of apprenticeships; Thomas Thompson, for instance, intended for a musical career from an early age, was described as the 'pupil' of Hawdon's youngest son, Thomas, but so was a blind boy, David Shafto Hawks, who was the son of a local gentry family and not expected to earn his living.[5] It is possible that the system of apprenticeships may have begun to give way to a less formal relationship; no certain references to apprentices are known after Hawdon's advertisements of the early 1780s.

Young boys with good singing voices could find employment as choristers in Durham Cathedral; the boys in the choir came from country areas and from local towns such as Sunderland as well as from the city itself. The Dean and Chapter took care to arrange apprenticeships for these boys, contributing 40 shillings towards their premiums; these apprenticeships were rarely musical in nature – boys were apprenticed to shoemakers, breeches makers and even the cathedral cook. Many returned to the choir a few years later as adult singing men but most never earned their living from music alone, maintaining their trades as their principal source of income.[6] Cornforth Gelson, a County Durham boy, was one of the rare choristers who became a full-time professional musician; he left the choir to become a wait in Newcastle then returned to the choir for several years as a singing man before eventually establishing himself in Edinburgh as a music teacher and performer.[7] Another choir member, chorister Stephen Paxton, the youngest of three brothers in the choir, left for London after an argument with the Dean and established himself as a highly successful musician there.

Paxton's trip to London was not unusual. Once out of apprenticeship, it was common for any young musician with pretensions to excellence to travel for 'improvement'. The Dean and Chapter's willingness to allow singing men to visit London has already been noted; they were not alone. Charles Avison undertook a visit to London, probably in the early 1730s, and became there a pupil of the Italian composer and violinist, Geminiani. (He is also rumoured to have travelled abroad on the basis of remarks that he made about psalm-singing on the continent; again, however, no evidence survives to corroborate this.)[8] The money to permit travelling was often provided by the musician's employer, who agreed to continue playing the musician's salary while he was absent. George Barron, the young organist of St Andrew's Church in Newcastle from 1783, was given permission for six months' paid leave in London by his employers, the Newcastle Corporation; the Corporation also continued to pay Charles Avison junior's salary while he visited St Petersburg in the late 1770s.[9] Both Barron and Avison had to pay deputies to perform their duties while they were away and it is not clear whether they had also to find their own travelling expenses. (The Dean and Chapter of Durham Cathedral generally paid singing men's travelling expenses.)[10] Most of these trips occurred within the first months or years of a musician's first post – Barron, for example, petitioned the Corporation for permission to travel immediately upon appointment to the post. Some musicians may have funded their own visits to London; Thomas Wright of Newcastle probably financed his own stay in London in the late 1770s by playing at the Opera House.[11] Some musicians were tempted to stay, with varying degrees of success: Paxton died in 1787 worth, according to the *Newcastle Chronicle*, more than £10,000; Richard Elford failed to establish himself as an actor in London but eventually made a living singing at St Paul's Cathedral and at Westminster Abbey; William Shield – one of the north-east's best known exports and a pupil of Charles Avison – established himself as a composer of comic operas.[12] But surviving as a musician in a capital where Italian musicians were adored and home-bred musicians more often ignored was difficult and some musicians returned north voluntarily, possibly considering it better to be a big fish in the small pond of their home towns; it is likely that for most, a visit to London merely offered an opportunity to acquire more advanced instruction in their art and to gain knowledge of the latest fashions and developments in music rather than a permanent job. Such visits to London were considered prestigious and an indication of quality; Matthias Hawdon wrote of his son, Thomas, in 1788, that '[he] will give every satisfaction to his employers, and merit the favour of the Public, as he went through a regular and scientific Education in the Science of Music under one of the first Professors in London'.[13]

Finding that first job, or at least that first profitable job, might not be easy and musicians frequently travelled considerable distances to obtain the best post. Thomas Hawdon's extensive travels from Newcastle to Dundee, then to Hull and finally back to Newcastle (although the last removal was designed to help his ailing father) were not unique.[14] When Hawdon resigned the post at St Andrew's in Newcastle to travel north, one of the men who applied to replace him was the equally-well travelled Robert Barber, son of the Newcastle bookseller, Joseph Barber. Robert had studied in London and, after attempting unsuccessfully to establish himself in his home town in 1773, had travelled north to Aberdeen where he stayed for a decade.[15] Despite marrying a local girl, Barber was so eager to return south that he gave up his post in Aberdeen and moved back to Newcastle before being sure of the St Andrew's post.[16] He lost out to George Barron and was forced to move on again, to Manchester, where he finally settled.[17] Avison too had offers of jobs far from his native town – in Edinburgh (where he was evidently offered £200 a year), and in Dublin – but chose not to take them.[18] Nor did the travelling stop even after a job was secured; musicians like Thomas Wright of Newcastle travelled on a regular basis throughout the year from their bases to the smaller towns of the region such as Sunderland, Tynemouth and Morpeth, to promote and perform in concerts. Some singing men from Durham Cathedral travelled extensive distances to sing in concert series in Carlisle, Aberdeen, Edinburgh, Leeds and Ripon, and, at the end of the 1780s, established such a dominance in musical life in the region that almost every concert and charity sermon, and the entertainment at many private dinners, included one or more of them. Others, like Charles Avison, John Garth and Thomas Ebdon of Durham, travelled considerable distances to teach – Garth was frequently to be found in

Yorkshire, and Ebdon sometimes accompanied prebendaries of Durham Cathedral to their estates in the south of England. And all this in addition to the extensive travelling normally undertaken by peripatetic musicians such as theatre musicians, dancing masters, fiddlers and psalm teachers.

Salaried posts

Most professional musicians seem sooner or later to have sought a salaried job, no matter how badly paid, to ensure at least a small amount of regular income. In many places, the worst-paid post available was that of wait. In Durham, the Dean and Chapter – in their determination to prevent singing men Abraham Taylor and Peter Blenkinsop from holding wait's posts which clashed with their cathedral duties – offered them an extra £5 on their salaries, suggesting that that was the wait's salary locally as it was in Newcastle. In York, the retainer system, whereby waits were paid only a nominal sum (£5 per annum divided between five waits) and were paid extra for individual performances, made the post more desirable and ensured that an industrious and reliable musician could make a considerable amount of money. This led to a better quality of musicians taking up the post; from the beginning of the century, York waits were professional full-time musicians in distinction to the situation elsewhere in the region where the wait's post was usually seen as extra income for men of another profession. As the century progressed, the professionalization of the waits' posts also became more pronounced in Newcastle and the five posts were all held by professional musicians when the position was abolished in 1793.[19]

The singing men, by contrast, were among the most highly paid musicians in the area, particularly with increases in their salaries throughout the century, from an average of £20 per annum in the first half of the century (with £50 occasionally paid to an exceptional singer such as Jasper Clark who came to the Cathedral from Winchester in 1753), to an average of £50 by the end of the century.[20] The organist at the Cathedral was the highest paid salaried musician in the north-east; the salary varied according to the Dean and Chapter's assessment of the quality of the incumbent and ranged from £40 per annum for William Greggs, the organist in 1700, to £100 per annum for his successors, James Hesletine and Thomas Ebdon. Hesletine started in 1711 on a salary of £70 which was augmented three times by £10 per annum; Ebdon started on £80 per annum, augmented twice.[21] All three men derived extra income from carrying out minor tuning work on the organ and teaching the choristers. Compared to these figures, other organists around the region did less well; the average salary in most churches in Newcastle and elsewhere in the region was £20 or £25. The situation of the organist at St Nicholas in Newcastle was a little better – he was paid £25 in 1700, rising to £40 in the 1720s and £50 by mid-century.[22] But these salaries were always at the mercy of external factors; the cutback in Corporation spending that saw the waits abolished also led to a cut in salary for the St Nicholas organist from £50 to £30 – probably a disastrous loss of income for the incumbent, Charles Avison junior, who was already in financial difficulties.[23]

The scarcity of such salaried posts was exacerbated by the fact that several musicians held more than one. In Newcastle, Solomon Strolger was appointed organist of All Saints and a wait at the same time in 1725; Charles Avison senior held two organist's jobs – those of St John's and St Nicholas – for the last 27 years of his life.[24] Avison turned this to family advantage by appointing his two surviving sons, Edward and Charles, as deputies, paying them a portion of his salary and keeping the remainder; at Avison's death, Edward and Charles were so well established in the roles that the Corporation did not think it worthwhile officially confirming them in-post.

Other salaried posts for local musicians were extremely few and far between. Local Musical Societies generally hired professional violinists to lead them, and an occasional cellist to provide a solid bass line; in the 1790s, Mr Brown of the North Shields Theatre company acted as leader for the Sunderland Musical Society, and Thomas Wright for the Newcastle Musical Society.[25] Winter subscription series generally had a resident paid leader (in Newcastle, this was again Thomas Wright) and the Newcastle series also hired a Master of Ceremonies for the seasons between 1798 and 1803.[26] Wright was also leader of Stephen Kemble's theatre band from at least 1800 and probably earlier. Few details of payment for these posts survive; in the 1780s, Tate Wilkinson paid the leader of his band a guinea per week (for three performances) and rates were probably comparable in other theatre companies across the region.[27]

Additional activities

After the securing of a salaried post, the mainstay of a musician was teaching. All musicians probably undertook teaching, although not all advertised, recruiting no doubt by word of mouth. The most eminent of local musicians –men like Avison, Garth, Hesletine and Ebdon – taught the children of aristocratic or gentry parents; Garth enjoyed the patronage of men like Lord Barnard and the Noels and Milbankes of County Durham, Avison of the wealthy Northumbrian families, the Jenisons and Ords, Hesletine and Ebdon of the families of the well-connected Cathedral prebendaries. Avison also taught three days a week at his home in the 1750s, probably to the children of the wealthier tradesmen, charging a guinea entrance for new pupils, and half a guinea per month thereafter; this covered eight lessons – the length of each lesson is not specified.[28] Visits to the houses of pupils were usually charged at a higher rate. At the other end of the scale, musicians like John Simpson, organist of St John's in the 1770s, charged half a guinea entrance and one guinea per quarter thereafter, probably catering for less wealthy families.[29] Towards the end of the century, charges seem to have been fairly uniform for all teachers – advertisements often simply state that the 'usual rates' will be charged – but there was still room for an eminent teacher to charge higher rates. Matthias Hawdon attempted to take advantage of this when he returned to Newcastle from Beverley in 1776, advertising his teaching rates as one guinea entrance and two guineas a quarter thereafter.[30] He had miscalculated, however; these may have been the rates he was accustomed to charge in Yorkshire, but they were too high for Newcastle tastes. He was given 'hints' that the charges were too high and reduced them to one guinea entrance and one and a half guineas per quarter.[31] In addition to these resident teachers, visiting musicians from time to time would offer themselves as teachers, often using a concert as an advertisement for their musical abilities, as did the anonymous lute-master who visited Newcastle in 1725.[32] Walter Claget, younger brother of Charles, not only taught cello and flute during the three or four months he stayed in the town but also offered to draw up for his pupils a plan of study for them to follow after he had left the area.[33]

After teaching, performance was probably the most lucrative activity available to musicians, and the area where less prominent and able musicians were most likely to earn a substantial amount of money. In Newcastle, a large number of different bands played in different venues for different purposes: the theatre band, the Spring Gardens' band, the subscription concerts' band and the Musical Society band, the Dancing Assembly band, the Country Dance Band and at least two military bands associated with volunteer organizations during the French Revolutionary Wars. Owing to the small number of professional musicians in the town – rarely into double figures at any one time – the personnel in these bands was probably identical; on several occasions concerts or other events had to be postponed because the members of the band were playing elsewhere.

Payments for performers in these bands was variable but worthwhile. The leader of the theatre band might expect a guinea a week (seven shillings a night); the leader of the subscription concerts in the 1735–6 season received 10s a concert.[34] The rate for rank and file members of the concert band in 1802 was 3s. 6d. for one rehearsal and a concert – the cost of a ticket to the concert they played in – and Tate Wilkinson paid the rank and file members of his theatre band between 2s. 6d. and 3s. for each performance (probably varying according to the amount of music to be played); trumpeters and drummers, if required, were paid 1s. per night.[35] Rates paid by other theatre companies were probably about the same. Wilkinson was a prompt payer, having once been a musician himself in Bath; Austin and Whitlock, managers of the Newcastle Theatre Company, were more dilatory and in 1778 provoked a strike by the Newcastle band. Faced with the impossibility of putting on the night's performance without the band – they had planned a comic opera – Austin and Whitlock capitulated, ungraciously, sending a note to the *Newcastle Courant* insisting that 'the musicians … took the advantage of the Managers putting up an Opera for that night, and sent them Word, in a very hostile manner, that if they would not advance their salaries they would not attend'. This, Austin and Whitlock said, they were 'compelled' to comply with, allegedly to avoid disappointing the public.[36] A similar attempt by the band to use strike action to increase wages came to grief; Charles Dibdin, visiting the town to give a concert, was horrified by the demands of the theatre band but followed the advice of local engraver Thomas Bewick to do without them and sing to the sole accompaniment of a piper instead. According to Bewick, the novelty was much appreciated by the audience.[37]

Compared to theatre rates, dancing assemblies offered much better payments; the organizers of the dancing assemblies at the stylish New Assembly Rooms on Westgate Road (built in 1776) paid half a guinea per musician for a night's performance.[38] Race Week could be particularly lucrative as dancing assemblies were held every night of the week (as well as an additional concert). But the small size of the band (generally four musicians except on special occasions when eight were employed) and the lesser frequency of dancing assemblies in winter (only one night per week compared to the theatre's three) limited the income from this source. Nevertheless, a good and reliable player might hope, during the theatre season in the winter, to play almost every night of the week – at three theatre performances, one concert (every other week) and one dancing assembly, earning around £1 3s. for his week's work. In York, payment was 15 shillings per night in Race Week for the waits; between half a guinea and 7s. 6d. a night (with the higher sum being paid more frequently) for musicians brought in from elsewhere to augment the band – the band here was usually ten strong.[39]

These payments all apply to instrumentalists; singers were usually much better paid, although opportunities were fewer – most concerts for most of the century got by with only one vocal soloist. Concert organizers frequently suffered the dilemma of having to choose between the quality of a London singer, who could prove expensive, and of a local singer who might be of lesser ability but was almost certainly cheaper. Opting for the first choice bankrupted the York subscription series in 1742 and caused severe difficulties for the Newcastle subscription series in 1802 and 1803. Rates charged by these nationally and internationally known soloists are not recorded but even soloists of a lesser stature could prove expensive. William Evance, one of the singing men at Durham Cathedral, was paid thirty guineas in 1789 for a three-month stay in Aberdeen, singing at the subscription series there, thus earning more than half his yearly salary at the Cathedral.[40] In 1792, the Lancashire singer Miss Worrall was offered £16 for three nights' singing at the Durham Musical Festival; she so enchanted the organizer that he offered her a further ten guineas and organized an impromptu collection for her at the last performance.[41] Many people regarded these payments as much too high. An anonymous writer to the *Cumberland Pacquet* in December 1786 castigated the high wages paid to musicians, quoting the 2000 guineas Haydn was reputed to have been offered to visit England – the writer was particularly incensed by the fact that the parish clerk at St Nicholas, Whitehaven, had received only £20 for singing an estimated 12,960 psalm tunes while Madame Gertrude Mara had had 1000 guineas for 'singing half a dozen song-tunes'. Even more pointedly, he remarked: 'He [the parish clerk] has *walked* eight thousand, six hundred and forty miles, to do his duty; and she was too proud even to *stand up* while she did hers. Oh, ye *Dilettanti*! there is neither *time* nor *modulation* in such *movements*!'[42]

Singing was almost the only area in which opportunities existed for women in the musical profession, apart from the rare records of women as parish organists, although occasionally an exceptional woman might make a career as an instrumentalist, as did Madame Louisa Gautherot, who appeared in York in 1792.[43] But such was the association of female performers and the voice, that Madame Gautherot, although she led the band and played a violin solo, was forced also to offer a vocal item as if to legitimize her appearance. Elsewhere, female names occur only as singers: Miss Alphey, whose sudden marriage threw Edward

Avison's concert plans into confusion in 1772; Miss Harwood, who came to Newcastle with her teacher, Robert Jobson of Leeds and went on to greater things in London; Signora Passerini who passed through Newcastle with her husband in 1752 and Signor Cremonini, who sang for Avison in 1762 (both ladies were fleeing uncongenial engagements in Edinburgh in the hope of greater profits in London); Miss Dennet and Miss Dall, whose engagements in successive years at the beginning of the 19th century put much strain on the precarious finances of the subscription series in Newcastle.[44] Newcastle did not have resident singers until the late 1790s when the Miss Cliffords – Miss J. Clifford and Miss Diana Clifford – sang in subscription concerts; almost no information is known about the sisters other than that they lived with their mother in Northumberland Street.[45] The only true home-grown talent amongst female singers was Frances Hudson of York. Born Frances Hawkeswell, she was a mantua-maker until her marriage in 1763 to the local wait and French horn player, William Hudson. She probably spent the early years of her marriage learning her trade; she first appeared in the York subscription series from 1769 and then rapidly expanded her reputation, singing in concerts in York, Hull, Wakefield and Leeds, and specializing in oratorios. She was invited to sing in Thomas Arne's oratorios in London and became the north's only female concert promoter in 1776, albeit in conjunction with a male colleague, when she took on the York subscription series; she later ran the series in collaboration with her husband.[46]

Concert promotion

Many musicians, both prominent and otherwise, attempted to promote at least one benefit concert, that is, a concert whose profits went entirely to the promoter (or, occasionally, to a charity), which argues that such concerts, if successful, could bring in a substantial amount of money. The fact that a large number of these musicians only made one attempt suggests that it was a hard trick to pull off. In the four years immediately following Charles Avison's death in 1770, benefits were held in Newcastle by two music teachers (John Simpson and Robert Barber), two dancing masters, one actress, one singing man from Durham Cathedral, and Charles Avison junior – only Avison repeated the experience. Regular benefits were rare although Charles Avison senior generally held a benefit in Assize Week and established a precedent by which the concert was considered a benefit for the organist of St Nicholas's Church throughout the rest of the century. Matthias Hawdon's Assize Week concerts were always large-scale events designed to bring in as large an audience as possible and were probably used to offset some of the losses incurred by the failing winter subscription series. In York, a regular benefit in March was used by the organizers of the subscription series to similar effect.

The costs of organizing any concert, be it an individual benefit or a winter subscription series, were high. In Newcastle in the last quarter of the century, the best venue available was the New Assembly Rooms on Westgate Road; here, a large room and a smaller side room were available, both lit by chandeliers – the large room cost two guineas to hire, the smaller room one guinea.[47] Benefit concerts, particularly those in Race and Assize Weeks where big audiences could be hoped for, were held in the large room; the winter subscription series, less well-attended, caused a dilemma for its organizers. In the cold winter of 1782, Matthias Hawdon hired the large room, found the number of subscribers too few to fill it and changed to the smaller room to lessen expenses; complaints from his audience forced him to return to the large room despite Hawdon pointing out that the smaller room, if less elegant, would be warmer.[48] Toward the end of the century, the series returned to the smaller and less expensive rooms in the Groat Market where the series had been held earlier in the century.[49] The Assembly Rooms in York charged by the series rather than by the individual concert – 20 guineas in the 1780s, rising to 30 guineas despite clear evidence that the concerts were struggling, with the result that the organizers defaulted on payment.[50] In Durham, probably in the 1770s, Thomas Ebdon had a room in his own house in the North Bailey fitted out for concerts, presumably considering that the expense of the work would be outweighed by the savings made in hiring the usual venue, the long room of the Red Lion Tavern. (The only description of Ebdon's room is in a newspaper advertisement of 1790 which describes it as 'the large Assembly Room … with three Glass Chandeliers'.)[51] Coals for heating the concert room, and candles for the chandeliers, were an extra expense particularly as the Directors of the Assembly Rooms in both York and Newcastle insisted upon the use of the high-quality and expensive Spermacetti candles, which caused less damage to the decoration of the rooms. Matthias Hawdon tried to economize in this area too, by lighting only a limited number of candles – he was again forced to back down on the issue.[52]

To these expenses had to be added the cost of advertising the concert. The *Newcastle Courant*'s rates in the 1750s were 2s. 6d. for an advertisement not exceeding 140 words; an extra 100 words (or part of it), or alterations to the advertisement cost an extra 6d. A second placing of the advertisement could be obtained at a lower rate. With such costs in mind, it was commonplace for only the first concert of a series to be advertised, perhaps twice, to remind subscribers to pay for their tickets; Durham organizers often advertised the first and last concerts of a series, which were generally more ambitious in scope than the others. A notification of when the series stopped for Christmas or started again in the New Year could usually be 'smuggled' into the newspaper's local column free by writing a letter to the editor. Occasionally, promoters went to greater lengths. When Matthias Hawdon first held subscription series in Newcastle in the early 1780s, he advertised every concert with a full programme – an expensive undertaking presumably justified by the supposition that prospective concert-goers would not know what to expect from a promoter new to the area; he ceased the practice halfway through his second series, possibly because the audience now knew what to expect, possibly because he was already falling into the financial difficulties which were to bankrupt him in mid–1781. In York, advertisements for the subscription series became progressively more frequent as the series struggled to continue and became more reliant on ticket sales to 'strangers', that is, non-subscription tickets sold on the night. Ironically, this tendency means that more information is available about failing series than about those that thrived and did not need to advertise extensively, such as Avison's series in Newcastle and Ebdon's in Durham.

Almost all the tickets for concerts in the north-east were printed by the Newcastle engraver, Thomas Bewick; Bewick's customers included musicians from York, Beverley and Hull as well as those nearer home.[53] He generally charged between ten and 15 shillings for engraving a plate, and two or three shillings per 100 cards printed in black and white from the plate. (Extra colours were more expensive.) His records hint at the size of the audiences expected for these concerts. Hawdon, for instance, regularly ordered 50–100 tickets for his Assize Concerts and 200 for the subscription series – this latter number seems wildly optimistic in view of the fact that Charles Avison estimated the usual number of subscribers in his time at around 110.[54] In April 1781, Bewick printed 900 tickets for Hawdon's performance of oratorios; this was almost certainly an overestimation of the potential audience as only three months later Hawdon was forced into bankruptcy.[55]

Individual ticket prices rose from 2s. 6d., charged by Charles Avison and others in the first half of the century, to 3s. 6d. at the end of the century; subscription prices for series varied but were around half a guinea in the 1730s, rising to around 15 shillings in the 1760s. (Later advertisements are reticent about prices.) If Hawdon sold all his customary 50 tickets for an Assize Week concert, he could count on an income of £8 15s. only, roughly a quarter of which would be swallowed up by the hire of the large Assembly Room and the provision of coals and candles. Hire of instrumental players might eat up a further £2 with vocal soloists extra. Savings could be made by using as band players Gentlemen Amateurs, who would not require to be paid, but this in turn could decrease the number of people buying tickets. Thomas Wright, in the early 1790s, lessened the cost of hiring soloists by performing all the solo roles himself, including that of leader, clarinet soloist and vocal soloist.[56] However, Wright's more usual practice was to go to the opposite extreme, staging large-scale concerts – some including a double orchestra and up to 50 performers (both vocal and instrumental) – in the hope of attracting large audiences.[57] His repetition of this formula suggests that it was a successful one.

The income from concerts could be extremely variable. Avison's concerts held in the 1750s for the benefit of the newly-built Infirmary which might have been expected to reap an extra income because of their charitable purpose, met with mixed fortunes; over the four years of the concerts' life, income decreased from £36 10s. (1751) to only £13 4s. 6d. (1753).[58] No figures survive for Avison's subscription concerts. Other surviving figures tend to be for large-scale musical festivals in the Yorkshire/Lancashire area: local newspapers record incomes of £380 (Leicester, 1785), £600 (Sheffield, 1787) and £1033 1s. 11d. (Sheffield, 1797). But, even here, expenses could eat up huge parts of the profits. No less than £748 was laid out in expenses in Sheffield in 1797 and only a little over £300 reached the benefiting charities. An earlier festival in the town paid £40 to charities from an income of £450; a concert at Driffield in 1795 produced only £8 11s. for the poor it was intended to benefit.[59] The total raised from the Durham

Musical Festival for the City's Infirmary may have been relatively slight – £50 8s. 4d. – because of the organist's generosity towards Miss Worrall.[60]

If the organizers of concerts for charity found it difficult to make a substantial profit, the problems faced by private beneficiaries were more difficult still. Of the eight concert promoters who held benefits in Newcastle in the four years after the death of Charles Avison in 1770, only one, Charles junior, held more than one concert suggesting that the effort had been worthwhile. The tide could turn quickly however; Charles's benefit of 21 April 1774 was followed by another only a month later indicating that the first had been disastrously unprofitable.[61] (He left the area shortly afterwards for Russia.) Audiences could also be brutally indifferent. In York in 1789, Mrs Iliff (one of the actresses in Tate Wilkinson's company) took over the role of vocal soloist in the local subscription series during the illness of the usual soloist; she was, as she herself said 'an entire Stranger in York'. Nevertheless, she held a benefit concert which she had 'Vanity enough to suppose would be fully attended'.[62] She was mistaken; she made such a disastrous loss that Tate Wilkinson, ever sympathetic to the financial difficulties of the profession, immediately gave her an extra benefit night at the Theatre.[63]

A letter to the *York Chronicle* in December 1776 vividly illustrates some of the difficulties concert promoters could face through no fault of their own. Robert Jobson had been organist of Wakefield before moving to Leeds; as well as taking on the Leeds subscription series, he maintained control of the Wakefield series. But the Leeds series ran into serious difficulties in the autumn of 1776 and, after a series of trials, Jobson wrote to the *Chronicle* 'under a disagreeable necessity of troubling the public with an appeal in vindication of his censured conduct respecting the concerts'. According to Jobson, he had decided that it was impossible to run a winter subscription series in Leeds that year for lack of performers. He had been told that his regular vocal soloist, Frances Hudson of York, was unable to sing in the concerts that year and that four regular instrumentalists in the band were also unable to attend. He had hunted around for substitutes, found only one and then been told that that one was also not available. Jobson had therefore decided that 'the band would be unequal to the task of amusing an audience for two or three hours together'. The lack of a singer was most serious but in addition there would not even be sufficient players to make up a string quartet, or to accompany a concerto. Moreover, he claimed 'there would not be one person in it that would attempt anything principal, except himself'. The shortage of players had evidently been acute for some time as Jobson had previously indicated that he would not be willing to continue without a singer 'as the exertion of strength and spirits that must from these circumstances fall to his share, was more than could be expected from any single player'. (It seems likely from this comment that Jobson was able, though not willing, to take on the vocal role himself.) Jobson therefore informed the subscribers that the concerts could not continue. To protests that he continued to run the Wakefield series despite a similar lack of personnel, he said categorically that the situations were not at all similar. The Wakefield series had a reliable singer and the band, though small, boasted a number of other players willing to take solo parts.

Jobson was then surprised and shocked to see the series advertised in the papers and was informed that some individual subscribers had placed the advertisement, being determined the series should continue ('though it had but barely the resemblance of one'). Jobson protested that the concerts would not only be of poor quality but would reflect badly on him as their director; he was then told that the subscribers had in fact written to Frances Hudson and the organizers of the York concerts asking them to run the Leeds series. Surprisingly, in view of Hudson's original refusal to sing in the series, they had agreed. The series went ahead, under the direction of Hudson and her collaborators in York and with, presumably, extra performers brought in from York, but Jobson seems in the long term to have carried his point; he took up the organization of the series again the following year, continuing until his retirement 20 years later.[64]

Nevertheless, for those who were prepared to test the waters carefully, and to move by carefully calculated steps, concerts could be extremely profitable. Thomas Ebdon, organist of Durham Cathedral, was invited to perform in Sunderland in 1769 to mark the opening of St John's Chapel there; he quickly perceived an opportunity, put on an oratorio in the town the following year and within two years had set up a subscription series in the town.[65] By the second half of the 1770s, he was running a concert on the King's birthday (4 June) which was in effect a benefit for himself; he continued these until he gave up concert promotion at the beginning of the 1790s.[66]

In Newcastle, Thomas Wright was the man who exploited the possibilities of the benefit to its full. Having cut his teeth in the late 1780s holding benefits in Sunderland and Morpeth, he held his first benefit in Newcastle in March 1791, making a splash by holding a large-scale concert of the type rarely seen in the town – each half of the concert began with an overture for double orchestra and ended with a chorus from Handel, and Wright promised a band (of both instrumental and vocal performers) of 50 performers. He must have saved on some expenses by persuading Gentlemen Amateurs to make up a large portion of the band, but hired the large Assembly Room on Westgate Road despite the greater expense.[67] A brief review in the *Newcastle Courant* indicates a 'numerous' audience and Wright must have made sufficient profit to consider holding a similar concert the following year, advertising that 'the stage will be considerably enlarged as Mr. Wright hopes to have a Band equal, if not superior to that of last year'. (This is the only certain indication that temporary staging was brought in to the New Assembly Rooms to raise the band above the level of the audience.)[68] At this second benefit, Wright offered two of Haydn's symphonies, allegedly some of those composed since Haydn's arrival in London and performed at Salomon's concerts in the capital. Again he used amateur players in his band but splashed out on two vocal soloists – William Evance and John Friend from Durham Cathedral – making a third himself for glees performed between the acts.[69]

Although no further benefits of this type appear to have been held by Wright in Newcastle, he took the same kind of concert to Sunderland when he took over the King's birthday concerts from Ebdon, involving the 'Gentlemen Performers' of both Newcastle and Sunderland.[70] Performers in Sunderland were clearly at a premium as Wright took with him a small band of professional musicians from

Newcastle to play at the ball that followed the concert – possibly the Country Dance Band whose members included his younger brother. Although Wright seems after this to have given up mounting his own benefits, this may have been because various organizations bespoke them for him; by mid-decade, he was the recipient of benefits from at least two military bodies whose bands he led, and enjoyed benefits from the subscription series for most of the 1790s. From at least 1795, therefore, he could count on at least two benefits, and in 1800 he had no less than four, two from the Volunteer Band, one from the Subscription Concerts and one from the Armed Association.

Composition and publication

Wright worked hard for these benefits, composing a very large amount of music. As a solo clarinettist, he, like most instrumentalists of the period, wrote his own works, turning out concertos concert after concert. Very few of these can be precisely identified; advertisements most commonly refer simply to a 'new' concerto but many ended with a rondo based on a popular folk tune, such as the concerto composed for a concert in November 1798 which used the tune 'The Highland Laddie'.[71] Towards the end of the century, many of these concertos may have recycled material from earlier works. Apart from these concertos, Wright's earliest known works were written for the theatre, chiefly songs to be sung between the acts of the play, and he continued to write for the theatre throughout his life, producing a comic opera and two pantomimes in addition to many smaller scale works. During the French Revolutionary Wars, he produced an abundance of military pieces for benefits, as well as miscellaneous pieces for the subscription series, including symphonies, canzonets and an *Address to Peace*, and also provided symphonies and canzonets for the subscription series.[72] Some of these pieces were turned out at high speed. In 1793, Wright was called in to play at a concert put on by the visiting clarinettist, John Mahon; Mahon's partner, the cellist Alexander Reinagle, with whom he had originally organized the concert, had been unexpectedly called away. At no more than two weeks' notice (possibly less), Wright produced a work for the idiosyncratic combination of Voce Claria (a new instrument pioneered by Mahon) clarinet and cello; this was most likely an adaptation of works he had previously composed, possibly from the ubiquitous clarinet concertos.[73]

Wright's pragmatic approach to composition was shared by other musicians in the town. In the last two decades of the century, there was practically no musician in Newcastle who did not turn out at least one composition. Thomas Thompson, the young organist of St. Nicholas, turned out military pieces for his own and other musicians' benefits, and huge quantities of songs for the subscription concerts. Dancing masters such as Abraham Mackintosh, Alexander Munro Kinloch and Ivie Gregg published their books of tunes, often naming the tunes after eminent pupils to encourage purchases; during the French Revolutionary Wars, patriotic songs and marches were widely composed and published, undoubtedly partly in a spirit of nationalism but equally undoubtedly intended to provide a little extra income.[74]

This pragmatic view of composition must be extended even to Charles Avison. Despite his strong opinions about the form and significance of music as expressed in the *Essay*, and his forthright comments about the deleterious effect of market forces on the quality of works by composer such as Handel, Avison was still forced to take practical considerations into account when composing. His concerti were composed initially for his Newcastle concert band to play and bear the marks of this in their relatively simple accompanying parts, suitable for amateur players, and their more complex solo parts, for the professional members of the band. Some of Avison's compositional preferences – his dislike of double-stopping for instance – are clearly attributable, at least in part, to his experiences with the amateur portion of that band, and this practicality made the works enormously popular with Musical Societies throughout the country, as attested by the subscription lists to these works – Opus 4 for instance, lists amongst the subscribers Musical Societies at Aberdeen, Edinburgh, Fakenham (Norfolk), Hull, Lichfield, Norwich, Oxford and York.[75] The extensive sale to these Musical Societies indicates how admirably Avison succeeded in producing music that was pleasing both to the ear and to the less than nimble fingers of many amateur players, and it is difficult to believe that such commercial considerations were not in Avison's mind when he composed; he was not immune from such practical considerations but he appears to have succeeded better than most in marrying commercial appeal with his musical principles.

The usual method of publication of this music – in the case of longer pieces at least – was by the subscription method: proposals for publishing were advertised in local papers, interested purchasers paid in advance, and the money raised was used to defray the expenses of printing. Ebdon's *Sacred Music* was advertised in this way in April 1788 at a guinea per copy; Ebdon asked for the money only on delivery of the printed music but needed a list of subscribers in advance to be certain he could cover his costs.[76] John Garth's edition of Benedetto Marcello's psalms came out by this method between 1757 and 1765, as did Wright's *Six Songs* in c1788; a prominent list of subscribers was provided at the beginning of the volumes as a gentle form of flattery to the subscribers. Some shorter pieces were published without subscribers, usually at the composer's expenses, the money being then recovered from sales. Thus Robert Barber in 1783 advertised four of his compositions: six sonatas for the harpsichord (10s. 6d.), six trios for the harpsichord (10s. 6d.), songs, catches, and glees (10s. 6d.) and a single harpsichord lesson (1s. 6d.).[77]

Publication was generally by such London companies such as Goulding, Preston or Longman and Broderip, or occasionally an Edinburgh publisher such as Hamilton, but the area was not without its own publishers. A flourishing trade in chapbooks was long established in Newcastle, possibly the largest centre of such publishing outside London; these chapbooks offered the words of popular songs, mainly traditional but also including some from popular comic operas. The books, usually of poor quality, were frequently illustrated but never included music, presumably on the assumption that the tunes of such popular ditties were already well-known and were generally published by local stationers.

In mid-century, the bookseller Joseph Barber of Newcastle advertised himself as a copper-plate engraver of music and included music on some of the broadsides he published, most notably on an extravagant tribute to the local families of Blackett and Fenwick, published in 1741; this squeezed the tune 'on an easy Key' onto the bottom of the sheet, below a large and detailed allegorical drawing and a considerable number of verses.[78] Barber's music-publishing activities, however, seem always to have been limited and he soon dropped the service from his advertisements. Not until the final years of the century was music publishing re-established in the town when William Wright, younger brother of Thomas, started to print and publish music from his music shop on High Bridge.[79] Over the next five years or so, he published a number of short pieces by his brother (mainly military marches), a variety of short piano pieces of poor quality, probably written by himself, the books of dancing tunes by Peacock, Mackintosh, Kinloch and Gregg, and songs and a music dictionary by Thompson. It is not known when he ceased publishing. William was taking advantage of the burgeoning domestic music-market; his own short piano pieces are aimed at the uncertain talents of the amateur player, and the military brass-band pieces written by his brother were all published with either a piano reduction or a piano accompaniment that could be played on its own. In addition, many of the pieces maximized selling appeal by advertising themselves as suitable for playing on a number of different instruments.

Instrument sale and manufacture

Throughout the century, music teachers advertised musical instruments for sale on an ad-hoc basis, either importing new instruments from London or selling second-hand instruments on behalf of pupils; thus Thomas Thompson in February 1794 advertised that he 'has got from London several fine-toned PIANO FORTES, to be sold'.[80] Although wealthier families, like the Delavels of Seaton Delaval Hall, imported their instruments directly from London, shipping them north regardless of expense, such local sales, probably to the better-off tradesmen, formed a significant part of the income of many professional musicians. Nevertheless, for much of the century the chief source of musical goods – instruments, music and accessories – was the stationer's shop, run by men like James Fleming, whose shop was on the Tyne Bridge itself, or John Hawthorne, 'at the Dial in the Head of the Side', the narrow lane winding up from the Quayside towards St Nicholas's Church.[81] Hawthorne's advertisement of 1757 indicates the range of goods available; Hawthorn was principally a clock and watch-maker and, after listing his wares in that respect, he added that he also sold 'Music and Musical Instruments, with Violins, Cases and Bowes for D^{o}. Hautboys, German Flutes of all Sorts, Fifes, Flageolets, Tabor and Pipes, Aeolian Harps, Mock Trumpets, Pitch-pipes, French Horns, Reeds for Hautboys and Bassoons, Wire for Harpsichords, Hammers for D^{o}. Mutes for Violins and Basses, Bridges, Pins, and Nuts for D^{o}. Music Stands, Reed Cases, rul'd Books, rul'd Paper, Mouth-Pieces for French-Horns, &c.' plus instruction books, pieces of music, fiddle strings and spurs for cocks.[82]

In the 1760s, Joseph Barber set up a music section in his bookshop in Amen Corner behind St Nicholas's Church; his son, Robert, returning to Newcastle in 1773 after a period of study in London, took over this stock, setting it up as a separate shop not far away in the Wool Market.[83] But Robert's failure to obtain a salaried post or to establish himself as a teacher caused him to abandon the town for an organist's job in Aberdeen and the sale of musical goods was subsumed back into his father's shop. Stationers thereafter remained the sole source of supply of musical goods until the 1790s, augmented at infrequent intervals by the arrival of travelling wholesalers such as John Pillemont; Pillemont, who described himself as a 'foreign merchant', travelled in the north in the late 1760s, selling violins, flutes, oboes and other instruments together with necessary accessories such as strings (which he claimed to wind himself), and offering cheap prices to music-teachers who wanted to buy in bulk to sell on.[84]

In 1792, with domestic music-making apparently on the increase, Robert Sutherland, organist of Gateshead, set up a music shop or 'warehouse' in Gateshead churchyard (that is, in the buildings surrounding the church).[85] Sutherland was on the lookout for activities that would add to his income – he had already come to an agreement with Newcastle's two main organists of the period, Thomas Wright and Charles Avison junior, that he would act as principal musical instrument tuner for the area.[86] In his warehouse, he offered new and second-hand instruments (including some from the most fashionable London makers), for sale or exchange, and also restored old instruments, particularly violins and basses. The shop was only open on demand; Sutherland requested that enquiries about instruments should be directed to the auctioneer next door, or to a bookseller in Newcastle.[87] His venture was without competitor until 1795 when two music shops opened in quick succession, suggesting that the domestic market was still expanding. William Wright opened his shop in December 1795 on the High Bridge (from which he later operated his music publishing business) and John Thompson, Thomas's father, followed suit only six months later, selling music from a shop next to his breeches shop on the Side.[88] Their competition prompted Sutherland to move into Newcastle itself from Gateshead in 1798; his advertisements at this time show that he was employing local craftsmen to repair and restore instruments.[89] Thompson closed his music shop in 1800, selling the stock to William Wright, but Wright and Sutherland both seem to have thrived and were joined, in the early years of the new century, by Thomas Wright, setting up a shop at a time when other sources of income were drying up.[90] For a short period there were two Wright's music shops on Pilgrim Street, causing public confusion and, no doubt, family dissension. In all these shops, a full range of goods was available; Thompson offered special rates to gentlemen of the army and navy and William Wright advertised that he could procure any new music within a few days of publication in London.[91] Would-be purchasers elsewhere in the region continued to rely on stationers and local teachers, or to send to the Newcastle shops; residents of towns on the North Shields theatre company circuit could also, in the early 1790s, expect to buy instruments of the company's leader, Mr Brown.[92]

Although some of the instruments sold in these shops were imported from London, it is likely that the bulk of the stock was of local manufacture.

Information on instrument manufacturers in the area, however, is fragmentary. The earliest-known manufacturer in Newcastle is William Prior who advertised in local papers in the 1720s and 1730s; he was active from at least 1700 when he repaired a drum for the Corporation.[93] Prior combined instrument making with the making of false teeth, just as his descendant (probably a grandson), Matthew Prior, later in the century combined instrument-making with assaying.[94] A violin maker, Ralph Agutter, who claimed to be related to the local gentry family of the Jenisons, advertised extensively in 1712 but died at the end of the summer; he had just returned to Newcastle from a prolonged stay in London.[95] Fiddle-makers were certainly active in Newcastle throughout the century but are generally known only from brief references in local papers: the fiddle maker who fought a 'duel' with a plumber; William Christie of High Bridge whose entire stock was destroyed in a fire of 1799.[96]

Rather more is known of two organ-builders, William Bristowe and John Donaldson. Donaldson's career has already been discussed; Bristowe worked in Newcastle in the 1720s and 1730s, building chamber organs and exhibiting them for sale, mending the 'little organ' in Durham (possibly the organ in the Song School) and arguing with almost everybody, including the organist of All Saints, and two mapmakers whom (on the basis of an advertisement in the *Courant*) he accused of incompetence and challenged to a competition, only to pull out on some imagined slight when his challenge was taken up. The latter argument was the result of an ill-conceived attempt, together with a local painter, to set himself up as a surveyor; it is possible that organ building brought in insufficient income.[97] Bristowe was paid two guineas for his work on the Durham organ; no price is mentioned for the organs he exhibited, although he seems to have followed the common practice of raffling the instruments.[98]

Collaboration and competition

Given the difficulties of making an adequate living, it is hardly surprising that some musicians came into conflict. Avison and Garth's argument with Durham Cathedral musicians in the 1750s was directly attributed, by Spencer Cowper, Dean of the Cathedral, to the jealousy and insecurity of James Hesletine, the Cathedral organist; Charles Claget attributed the same fear of competition to Charles Avison and his supporters in 1758, and a letter from an unknown music-lover to the *Newcastle Courant* in 1741 suggested that similar feelings had led to the disparagement of the visiting harp player, Mr Parry, who suffered small audiences 'owing to the Opposition of some Persons, who can't bear that a Stranger should meet with any Encouragement in Newcastle'.[99] Avison's power struggle with the Swiss leader of the Newcastle concert band in 1736 may have also been owing to the insecurity of the two sides and their need to run a significant competitor out of town. The quarrel may have been in part manufactured by partisan supporters but it played upon the insecurity inherent in the profession of musician.

Despite these conflicts, the principal emphasis in the north-east throughout the century was on collaboration rather than competition, not only in a formal sense, as in the Avison/Garth relationship but also in more informal ways. This collaboration existed from the beginning of the century when musicians from York, Durham and Newcastle worked together to promote concerts and was manifested again in mid-century when Thomas Ebdon and John Garth promoted mid-year concerts together in Durham for a decade during the 1760s. Much of Thomas Wright's progress in the early part of his career was owing to the informal patronage of a singing man from Durham Cathedral. In the 1790s, all musicians appeared in all concerts, no matter the beneficiary or the promoter; given the small number of local musicians, this was perhaps inevitable, but the result was that all locally promoted concerts were almost identical in style and content, and almost indistinguishable from each other. This did not prevent quarrels. Henry Monro, who took over as organist of St Andrews in 1796 replacing Thomas Wright, was quick to condemn his predecessor for the poor state of the organ; Wright and the churchwardens of St Andrew's had parted on the worst of terms and Monro perhaps thought it politic to sympathize with his new employers' point of view.[100] But ultimately musicians always rallied round their colleagues in time of need. When Cornforth Gelson was dismissed from Durham Cathedral in 1755, following his flirtation with the Avison/Garth series, his fellow singing men immediately put on a benefit concert for his wife and family; in 1797, musicians in Newcastle acted similarly to help the widow and children of Walter Claget, the cellist at the theatre and, two years later, to help the family of Adam Kinloch, a dancing master killed in a fall from his horse, whose children included the cellist, Alexander Munro Kinloch.[101] Musicians always played free of charge at these concerts, perhaps aware that the next concert might be to their own benefit.[102]

Notes

[1] Stephens, *Charles Avison*, 2–3.
[2] *NC* 21 June, 16 August 1783, 29 May 1784.
[3] *NC* 17 February 1739; *NJ* 4–11 November 1758.
[4] *NJ* 16-23 February 1754. Williams's escapade led Avison to advertise for his return in the *Newcastle Courant*; the advertisement included a description of Williams which, although brief, is the most detailed account of the appearance of any musician in the north-east during this period. Avison wrote: 'He is about 16 Years old, but little of his Age, has sore Eyes, a fair Complexion, wears a Wig, and plays very well upon the Fiddle'. It is probable that Williams was the apprentice that Avison used to lead the Newcastle Concert Band during the dispute with the Swiss violinist at the end of the first subscription series in 1736, and who was supposed to 'fight' a musical duel with the Swiss.
[5] *NC* 8 February 1794.
[6] DCAB, passim.
[7] DCAB and DCTA 1736/7–1746/7; DCAB 20 November 1751; CCN 19 January 1749.

[8] Stephens, *Charles Avison*, 4.
[9] CCN 15 April 1776, 7 December 1783.
[10] DCAB and DCTA, passim.
[11] The subscription list for Wright's *Six Songs* published in c1788 lists six musicians from the Opera House in London.
[12] *NCh* 20 October 1787; Burney, *A General History*, 481, 482, 488; Linda Troost, 'Shield, William', *The New Grove Dictionary of Music and Musicians* (London: Macmillan, 2001), 23, 262–5.
[13] *NC* 9 November 1788.
[14] Ibid., 25 January 1783, 22 December 1787, 19 September 1789; *NA* 30 November 1793.
[15] *NC* 1 November 1783.
[16] Barber also suffered a murder attempt in Aberdeen only a fortnight before his wedding when a man with a sword broke into his room in the middle of the night. No motive is known for the attack [*NCh* 3 May 1777].
[17] *NC* 19 June 1773, 30 April 1774, 17 May 1777, 21 June 1783; *NCh* 3 May 1777; *YC* 5 July 1785.
[18] *NJ* 10-17 March 1759.
[19] CCN 23 December 1793.
[20] DCTA, passim.
[21] DCAB 20 January 1710/11, 3 July 1721, 20 July 1734, 19 November 1750, 20 November 1758, 28 September 1764.
[22] CAN, passim.
[23] Idem.
[24] CCN 30 September 1725, 20 October 1736, 10 October 1748.
[25] *NC* 19 March 1791, 7 January 1797.
[26] Boyd, *Songs*, passim.
[27] Tate Wilkinson, *Nett Receipts*, passim.
[28] *NC* 10-17 November 1750.
[29] *NG* 5 November 1796.
[30] *NC* 8 February 1777.
[31] Ibid., 8 February 1777, 27 November 1779, 25 January 1780.
[32] Ibid., 22 May 1725.
[33] *NJ* 2-9 June 1759.
[34] *NC* 24 April 1736.
[35] Wilkinson, *Nett Receipts*, passim.
[36] *NC* 21 February 1778.
[37] Bewick, *Memoir*, 96.
[38] NARA 16 April 1798.
[39] ARA 23 August 1733.
[40] Farmer, *Olden Days*, 71.
[41] *NC* 27 October 1792.
[42] *CP* 13 December 1786. Madame Mara's refusal to stand up and sing in oratorio choruses (a refusal by no means unique) had angered some audience members. In addition, her behaviour at the Handel Commemoration of 1785, during the

rehearsal and performance of *Messiah*, had triggered a vicious campaign against her in the press, which was only halted by a public apology and, very probably, payments to certain newspapers. For details see McVeigh, *Concert Life*, 76, 213.
[43] *YCh* 23 August 1792.
[44] *NC* 23 May 1752, 2 October 1762, 3 October 1772, 21 October 1780, 14 September 1782; Boyd, *Songs*, 1801–3, passim.
[45] Boyd, *Songs*, 1799–1803, passim.
[46] For details of Frances Hudson's career, see Southey, *Commercial Music-Making*, 134-9, 224–34, 259–73.
[47] NARA, 26 February 1782.
[48] *NC* 12 January 1782.
[49] Boyd, *Songs*, passim.
[50] ARM 20 October 1798.
[51] *NC* 20 November 1790.
[52] Ibid., 12 January 1782.
[53] Accounts of Thomas Bewick, passim.
[54] Ibid., 13 October 1779, 14 October 1780; NJ 4–11 November 1758.
[55] Accounts of Thomas Bewick, 28 July 1781.
[56] *NC* 21 January 1792.
[57] Ibid., 19 March 1791.
[58] Ibid., 31 August–7 September 1751, 16 September 1752, 8 September 1753, 13 August 1754.
[59] *YC* 28 August 1787, 26 August 1788; *YCh* 19 October 1797, 15 January 1795.
[60] *NC* 3 November 1792.
[61] *NCh* 16 April, 14 May 1774.
[62] *YC* 10,17 February 1789.
[63] Ibid., 17 February 1789.
[64] *YCh* 20 December 1776.
[65] *NC* 15 April 1769, 9 June 1770, 8 February 1772.
[66] *NCh* 29 May 1779.
[67] *NC* 19 March 1791.
[68] Ibid., 21 January 1792.
[69] Idem.
[70] *NC* 26 May 1792.
[71] *NA* 3 November 1798.
[72] Boyd, *Songs*, 14 October 1801.
[73] *NC* 12 January 1793.
[74] Ibid., 8 February 1783, 2 March 1799.
[75] Charles Avison, *Eight Concertos*, Op. 4.
[76] *NCh* 12 April 1788.
[77] *NC* 7 June 1783. The process of publication is considered in more detail in Burchell, J., '"The first talents of Europe"; British Music Printers and Publishers and Imported Instrumental Music in the Eighteenth Century', in Wollenberg and McVeigh, *Concert Life*, 93–113.
[78] Ibid., 25 April–2 May 1741.

[79] Ibid., 5 December 1795.
[80] Ibid., 8 February 1794.
[81] *NJ* 20-27 November 1756.
[82] Ibid., 1–8 January 1757.
[83] *NC* 19 June 1773.
[84] *NJ* 8-15 October 1768.
[85] *NC* 22 September 1792.
[86] Ibid., 31 March 1792.
[87] Ibid., 22 September 1792.
[88] Ibid., 5 December 1795.
[89] Ibid., 4 August 1798.
[90] Ibid., 3 May 1800, 12 May 1803.
[91] Ibid., 4 February 1797.
[92] *NA* 20 March 1790.
[93] CAN 1699/1700.
[94] Thomas Bewick, *Memoir*, 92–3.
[95] *NC* 28–30 April 1712; Parish registers of St Nicholas, Newcastle, 5 September 1712.
[96] *NA* 9 February 1799.
[97] *NC* 26 September, 3, 10 October 1730.
[98] DCAB 22 June 1728; *NC* 25 April 1730.
[99] Cowper, *Letters*, 159, 26 November 1752; *NJ* 9–16 December 1758; *NC* 10–17 October 1741.
[100] Vestry minutes of St Andrew, Newcastle, 10, 27 October, 3 November 1796.
[101] *NC* 11 January 1755, 28 January 1797, 6 July 1799.
[102] For a more detailed account of collaboration and competition between musicians, see Southey, R., 'Collaboration and Competition: Concert promotion in Newcastle and Durham', in *Concert Life*, eds. Wollenberg and McVeigh, 55–70.

Chapter 10

Success and Failure

To avoid the need for charity, some musicians took on an astonishing variety of jobs. Charles Avison combined teaching, composition, writing and concert promotion with his income from the organists' jobs at St Nicholas and St John; Thomas Wright accumulated sources of income even more assiduously. Like Avison, he taught and promoted concerts; he began his performance career as a clarinet soloist, then expanded his activities as leader of local bands, and finally took on the role of vocal soloist at many concerts, usually in a supporting role which suggests that his voice was good but not first-rate. He acted as guest soloist in concerts within the north-east (in Newcastle, Sunderland, Durham, Tynemouth, Hexham and Morpeth) and outside the area too (he appeared at the Hull Musical Festival of 1791).[1] He acted as leader of at least five local bands during the 1790s and was hired as leader by visitors to the area, including John Mahon, Madame Gertrude Mara and a host of lesser lights. He composed and published large amounts of music for theatre, concert hall and military band. In the early 1800s, at a time when income from other sources was drying up, he opened a music shop. But there was an inevitable price to be paid. Wright's alleged neglect of his duties as organist at St Andrew's and his frequent use of a deputy in 1795 was directly owing to his diverse workload. He sent in his resignation in October 1796, in a letter which the churchwardens had no hesitation in calling 'disrespectful'. 'Gentlemen,' Wright wrote, 'I here send you the Keys of your organ, together with my resignation of the place of Organist. – I have been so chagrined and teaz'd by the many ridiculous blunders which have so lately happened that I most sincerely lament I ever took the place.' Wright briefly defended his use of a deputy but ended: 'I shall not take up your time with a long vindication of my conduct, as I have some reason to think it would be as useless as tedious. – Permit me, however, to observe to you that I flatter myself the Malevolence of my enemies will ultimately tend as much to my advantage as the good wishes of my Friends'. He signed with the customary, but in this case, ironic, salutation: 'I am, Gentlemen, Your Ob^{t} and Humble Servant', and the association was at an end.[2] The loss of the £20 salary was no doubt serious but the next eight years marked the busiest point of Wright's career in the town and the numerous benefits he received in that period from a number of organizations probably more than compensated for the loss of the St Andrew's salary.

Other musicians were equally busy. Alexander Munro Kinloch was principal cellist at most concerts in Newcastle in the 1790s, Master of Ceremonies at the subscription series at the turn of the century, composed a little and for a short time was organist at All Saints, as well as being a wait and playing in most local bands;

by far the greater proportion of his income, however, came from his activities as a dancing master. John Thompson, father of Thomas, organist of St Nicholas, was one of the few full-time musicians in the area who relied substantially on income from another profession. He had been a chorister at Durham in the 1750s and had learnt his music there from James Hesletine; on leaving the choir, he had been apprenticed to a breeches maker in his native town of Sunderland, before moving to Newcastle shortly after his marriage. By August 1777, he was advertising himself as a breeches maker and glover, with a shop in the Groat Market.[3] He was using music teaching as a side-line at this time but over the next decade dedicated himself more and more to musical activities, perhaps leaving the breeches business to employees. In 1779, he advertised the opening of a singing Academy, which seems to have been short-lived or stillborn; he sang in concerts, probably played principal second violin in most concerts, and occasionally promoted his own benefits.[4] He was a wait until the abolition of the post in 1793 and in the early 1790s also took on the post of parish clerk at St Nicholas's church.[5] Late in the decade, his music shop briefly provided extra income.[6] He also took in lodgers, remarried late in life and in the early 19th century, was still singing, joining his son in founding the Harmonic Society, a group of six professional singers which promoted at least one winter subscription concert series, in 1815–16.[7]

Wright, Kinloch and John Thompson all thrived; others were not so lucky. Several early 18th century organists – Samuel Nichols and Thomas Powell at St Nicholas, and François de Prendcourt at All Saints – died in penury, their funeral expenses paid from the charity of their employers, the Corporation. Many a famous name ended in such difficulties; Signor Rossignol, who in the 1770s entranced audiences with his vocal imitations of birds and of violins, died in what the *Newcastle Chronicle* described as 'extreme penury and distress' at Staithes near Whitby in 1805.[8] Few, however, died in such obscurity as John Snaith, whose decline was accompanied by doubts as to his very existence. In 1773, a brief notice of Snaith's death in the Newcastle Chronicle described him as an 'eminent musician' of Stockton 'whose numerous and elegant compositions … will ever make his memory greatly esteemed'; the following week, the *Chronicle*'s competitor, the *Journal*, published an acid rejoinder claiming that although a man of that name had existed and had just died, he was neither a musician nor composer.[9] The *Chronicle* responded with a long letter from a Stockton man which, amongst jibes at the ignorance of the *Journal*'s correspondent, claimed that 'Mr. Snaith was a person so well known at Stockton and its neighbourhood, to the lovers of music at every capital place, and to the greatest composers in London, (particularly Dr. and Mr. Arne, from each of whom he had letters of recommendation …) that it is the highest degree of impudence in this paragraph writer to deny a fact so well known'.[10] Snaith had, he claimed, been a composer and a violinist, allegedly the 'best player in England'. He alleged that Snaith's songs had been sung at Vauxhall and published in various magazines, and that even as he wrote, a collection of his tunes was being prepared for the press, the proceeds of which were to go to his widow and children who were living in poverty. The *Journal*'s correspondent did not write again to dispute the facts but it is only fair to say that there are no further references to Snaith in the north-east, that the date and place of his death and burial cannot be found, and that the book of tunes, if it was ever published, has long since disappeared. Snaith, if he was the musician he was claimed to be, not only died in obscurity, but has since vanished almost completely from sight.[11]

Some musicians who came to grief managed to recover their position. Thomas Perkins, an oboist from York, spent at least a year in a debtor's prison in the city in 1754; his debts, however, were probably a result of his over-ambitious plans in his second profession as landlord of a local coffee house.[12] After being released following a benefit concert held for him by his fellow musicians, he recouped his position by travelling around Yorkshire, and as far north as Durham, playing in concerts.[13] Matthias Hawdon was even luckier. His bankruptcy in 1781 was partly a result of his own financial mismanagement, partly the result of a decline in interest in public music-making after Charles Avison's death; Hawdon came to an accommodation with his creditors, agreeing that his entire salary from St Nicholas (£50) and a further £10 from his other income, should be set aside each year for five years to pay his debts.[14] When he died only eight years after his bankruptcy, he had recovered sufficiently to leave an estate valued at around £300.[15]

Charles Avison junior was amongst those musicians who lived on the edge of financial security, always in danger of slipping over into crisis. Aged 19 at his father's death in 1770, he was probably already organist at St. John's at a salary of £20 per annum – he was also performing harpsichord solos in concerts, teaching pupils on violin and harpsichord and he was also almost certainly playing in the theatre band.[16] Between 1770 and 1774, he held a benefit every year, the only musician – apart from his elder brother who ran the regular mid-year and subscription concerts – to make a success of concert promotion in Newcastle at this time. But after an apparently disastrous benefit in April 1774, he gave up the practice and relied on his other sources of income for the next two years. In 1776 his employers, the Corporation, gave him permission to travel provided he arranged for a deputy to take the services at St John's. Charles travelled as far as St Petersburg and must have had strong hopes of succeeding there for he remained far beyond the time allowed by the Corporation and in September 1777 sent in his resignation.[17] But his hopes cannot have been fulfilled; by the end of 1779, he had returned to Newcastle and taken up the post of organist of All Saints.[18]

The early 1780s did not improve Avison's financial position. He was plainly in difficulties when, in January 1780, a well-wisher signing himself only *Clerimont* wrote to the *Newcastle Courant*: 'Give me leave, through the channel of your paper, to point out to the parishioners of All-Saints, one deserving the greatest encouragement, I mean, their Organist'. *Clerimont* described Avison as an individual 'who has had the courage to deviate from the licentious customs of the times' and who had given 'uncommon attention … in introducing Divine Harmony into their solemn Meetings'.[19] He advocated opening a book of subscription for contributions towards increasing Avison's salary; such a book was opened but it is not clear whether Avison ever benefited from it.[20] Work at the theatre and a number of benefit concerts held under the auspices of the Freemasons may have improved his position, certainly enough to allow him to marry in 1783, but he was clearly always living on the edge of solvency as his inability to pay his debts to

Thomas Bewick for the printing of tickets indicates; Bewick eventually got his money but only ten years after most of the debt was incurred, and only at the cost of taking out a summons against Avison.[21] In the early 1790s, Avison and his friend Thomas Hawdon attempted to revive the subscription series and may have lost money by the venture; worse, in 1794, the Corporation reduced Avison's salary at St. Nicholas from £50 per annum to £30.[22] By the time of his death the following year, at the age of 44, he was clearly deeply in debt, a situation that led to years of bitter wrangling between his widow and his creditors.[23]

Nevertheless, it was possible to make a success of the profession. At the time of his wife's death in 1766, Charles Avison senior described himself as a gentleman, a term usually used to indicate that the individual was living on income from invested money (although Avison continued to work until his death); his will, made on 24 June 1767, is alleged to show that he had gifted a total of £1000 to his three surviving children, with household goods, musical instruments, books and three harpsichords in addition.[24] He was not unique. In the administration order obtained by the heirs of Thomas Wright after his death in 1819, Wright was also described as a gentleman.[25] John Garth in old age married an heiress and died in 1810 a very wealthy man.[26] Solomon Strolger, organist of All Saints for 53 years, amassed around £4000, principally from teaching activities, despite having nine children; he invested the money with the Corporation providing his unmarried daughters with an income of around £180 per annum for many years after his death.[27] William Herschel had no difficulty in making a good living although he was not happy, telling his brother that he was tired of having no settled home and hated the manner in which he had to work.[28]

But the most spectacular, and public, success was that of Edward Meredith. For several years after his installation as a singing man at Durham Cathedral, Meredith's career proceeded quietly; he sang at the Cathedral (earning £50 per annum), took on the position of parish clerk at St Nicholas's church in Durham (for which he earned 30s a year) and performed at the subscription series in Durham, Newcastle and Sunderland.[29] But the success of the 1784 Handel Commemoration in London was the springboard for greater things; Meredith took part in an imitative festival in Leeds in November of that year and was thereafter rapidly in demand throughout Yorkshire and Lancashire as a singer in oratorio.[30] His popularity in the north-east also increased rapidly and he became the indispensable soloist in all concerts, to the extent that Matthias Hawdon had once to apologise for his absence from a concert in Newcastle owing to an engagement elsewhere.[31] His membership of the Freemasons and a reputation for good-humoured rendering of glees and catches and even bird medleys, contributed to his popularity; he received frequent benefits from such bodies as the Stewards of the Races (in both Newcastle and Sunderland) and the Gentlemen of the Forest Hunt (in Newcastle).[32] In December 1785, he collaborated with Thomas Ebdon to mount a subscription series in Newcastle, following Matthias Hawdon's withdrawal from concert promotion but the series was not sufficiently successful to be repeated – not even Meredith's popularity was able to tempt Newcastle music-lovers out on winter nights.[33] His benefits continued to be popular, however – the only concerts in Newcastle to draw the crowds at this period. Meredith extended patronage to

Thomas Wright, who had come to the town at the beginning of the decade, using Wright as leader in his concerts in preference to a fellow singing man who usually filled that role at this period, enabling Wright to establish his reputation in that role and to expand his performing career into Durham, Sunderland and elsewhere in the region.

By 1786, Meredith was vocal soloist at subscription series in Durham, Newcastle, Morpeth and Leeds, and was spending large amounts of time travelling between various centres in the north. His schedule at the beginning of 1787 is typical of this period. On 1 January 1787, he witnessed a wedding at St Nicholas, Durham; on 10 January he was singing in Wakefield and two days later in Leeds.[34] On 16 January, he sang in the subscription concert in Newcastle, returning to Wakefield and Leeds for two more concerts at the beginning of February.[35] On 2 February, he was in York, fitting in another concert at Wakefield before returning for a second York concert a week later and travelling back to Newcastle for a concert on 13 February.[36] On 15 February, he was performing at a benefit held by Thomas Wright in Sunderland.[37] At the end of the month (28 February) he was performing in a private concert in York.[38] The Act Books of the Dean and Chapter of Durham Cathedral are full of requests from Meredith for leaves of absence; these seem never to have been refused even though, taking Meredith's duties at St Nicholas into account, he can rarely have been at the Cathedral to earn his £50 salary. Moreover, he could earn from his singing in concerts more than enough to make that £50 seem paltry; in March 1782, the Edinburgh Musical Society paid him £31 10s. for two nights' singing and in January 1786, a further £15 15s. 2d. for singing in oratorios.[39] While these amounts almost certainly had to cover travelling expenses, the mathematics was clear – Meredith's secular singing career was far more profitable than his membership of Durham Cathedral choir. In mid-1788, he performed at a benefit for Thomas Wright in Morpeth, attended the King's birthday concert in Sunderland, then resigned from St Nicholas and the Cathedral.[40] His later career is not so well documented, but it is clear that he settled in Liverpool and continued to sing in oratorios and concerts throughout Yorkshire and Lancashire until well into the next century. Two attempts to revive his career in London were unsuccessful but he seems otherwise to have thrived; on three occasions, in 1791, 1792, and 1796, he returned briefly to his old stamping grounds, singing at musical festivals in Newcastle and Durham, even deigning on the first of these occasions to pay Thomas Bewick money owed for tickets printed four or five years earlier.[41] North-eastern newspapers lamented the loss of his 'majestic ability' for several years after his departure.

Social status

Despite the adulation and admiration lavished on exceptional musicians such as Edward Meredith, the social status of musicians in the north-east was never high. The position of a professional musician such as Thomas Wright, expected to manage and lead a band comprised largely of his employers, cannot have been easy. Musicians such as the waits were clearly considered in the same light as any other Corporation employee, such as the mace-bearer and bell-ringers, and, at the beginning of the century at least, were generally believed to be of dubious morals. The expected courtesy of a personal visit by musicians to patrons to sell tickets for benefits inevitably placed the musicians on a subordinate level. Matthias Hawdon's advertisements repeatedly show his swift reactions to criticism: he received hints that his teaching prices were too high and immediately reduced them; he received complaints about the room used for the concerts and immediately changed to a room perceived to be better. He could not afford to ignore such complaints; his living depended on the good will of his patrons. Even Charles Avison, faced with a dispute over subscription ticket conditions, thought it prudent to write a long letter to the *Newcastle Journal*, explaining his position and complaints about a rise in subscription prices in 1765 led him immediately to modify his plans.[42] Avison was clearly in a better position than most, being on good social terms with many of the gentlemen who ultimately provided his livelihood, dining at the houses of prebendaries in Durham and playing on social occasions with local notables such as Dr John Brown, Rector of Newcastle and the bluestocking, Mrs Ord, but an edge of patronage must inevitably still have existed. John Garth, whose pupils came from many of the local gentry and noble families, was invited to dine with one of those families in Richmond and was apparently happily accepted by his fellow guests, but a pupil who found him there still remarked on his presence with a note of surprise.[43]

The clearest expression of the general opinion of musicians in the area is stated in *Clerimont*'s letter to the *Newcastle Courant* on behalf of Charles Avison junior. *Clerimont* suggested that Avison deserved the parishioners' patronage 'if industry and knowledge in his profession be any recommendation' but made amply clear that he considered Avison's position, and that of all musicians, to be a subordinate one, whose role was to please and ape their social betters. 'Let them not [the parishioners] therefore, check that spirit of industry which is conspicuous enough to merit their attention, but rather endeavour to encourage so meritorious a performance, by which means those branches of Society, whose dependence rest solely upon their favour, will be inspired with that spirit of emulation which will, I hope, be as pleasing to their benefactors as to CLERIMONT.'[44]

Notes

1 *YC* 12 April 1791.
2 Vestry minutes of St Andrew, Newcastle, 10 October 1796.
3 *NC* 30 January 1777.
4 *NC* 9 August 1779.
5 Vestry minutes of St Nicholas, Newcastle, 1774–95, 1795–1812.
6 *NC* 3 May 1800.
7 Concert programmes, Harmonic Society Subscription Series, 1815–16, passim.
8 *NCh* 20 April 1805.
9 Ibid., 30 October 1773; *NJ* 30 October–6 November 1773.
10 *NCh* 20 November 1773.

[11] Ibid., 30 October, 20 November 1773; *NJ* 30 October–6 November 1773.
[12] *YC* 24 December 1754, 5 February, 10 July 1753.
[13] *NI* 5 May 1756; Emily Hargrave, 'Musical Leeds in the Eighteenth Century', *Thoresby Society Publications*, xxviii (Leeds, 1928), 355.
[14] Accounts of Thomas Bewick, 28 July 1781.
[15] Durham Probate Records: will of Matthias Hawdon, 14 October 1788.
[16] *NC* 6 May 1769, 25 April 1772.
[17] CCN 15 April 1776, 7 April, 25 September 1777; *NC* 27 September 1777.
[18] *NC* 24 December 1779.
[19] Ibid., 13 January 1780.
[20] Ibid., 13, 20 January 1780.
[21] Marriage registers of Newburn, 17 April 1783; accounts of Thomas Bewick, 17 April 1783.
[22] *NA* 16 January, 27 February, 27 March 1790: CAN, passim.
[23] *NCh* 4 April 1795; *NC* 8 July 1797.
[24] Burial registers of St Andrew, Newcastle, 17 October 1766; P. M. Horsley, 'Charles Avison: The Man and his Milieu', *ML,* iv (1974), 5–23, 23. Horsley was apparently writing from an original document; the present whereabouts of this will are not known.
[25] Durham Probate Records: administration of estate of Thomas Wright, 1819.
[26] CA, Auckland Receiver general's accounts, financial and audit 1659–1856, Box 36: will of John Garth, 1810.
[27] CAN, 1773–1794, passim.
[28] Lubbock, *Herschel*, passim.
[29] DCAB 20 November 1778; baptismal registers of St Nicholas, Durham, 18 May 1781.
[30] *YC* 9 November 1784.
[31] *NC* 23 July 1785.
[32] e.g. *NC* 2 November 1782 (Sunderland), 18 June 1785 (Newcastle), 10 December 1785 (Forest Hunt).
[33] Ibid., 24 September 1785.
[34] Registers of St Nicholas, Durham; *LI* 19, 26 December 1786, 9 January 1787.
[35] *NCh* 13 January 1787; *LI* 16, 23 January 1787.
[36] *YC* 23 January, 5 February 1787; *NC* 3 February 1787.
[37] *NC* 10 February 1778.
[38] *LI* 6 March 1787.
[39] Minutes and accounts of the Edinburgh Musical Society, 1781–2, 1786–7.
[40] DCTA, passim; baptismal registers of St Nicholas, Durham, 5 July 1788.
[41] *NC* 18 June 1891, 13 October 1792; accounts of Thomas Bewick, 20 April 1791.
[42] *NC* 21 September 1765.
[43] A. M. Elwin, *The Noels and the Milbankes: Their Letters for Twenty-Five Years, 1767–1792* (London: Macdonald, 1967), 146, 240.
[44] *NC* 13 January 1780.

Afterword

Music-making was not a socially or politically neutral act. John Brown's view of music as a moral instrument was echoed elsewhere; the *Cumberland Pacquet* considered that psalm singing gave children an occupation that prevented them indulging in other activities 'disgraceful to a christian country'.[1] When misused, this powerful instrument for good could wreak havoc; the tradesmen's assembly set up in York in 1749 was depicted as a frivolous waste of time that gave its participants ideas above their station, encouraging them to be idle instead of industrious – idleness was something reserved for their social betters, the aristocracy. Worse, music could sometimes even be subversive – ballad singers, peddling their sometime irreverent songs, were condemned by Bewick and others. And double standards were often evident. While the catch clubs of the gentlemen flourished and the eating and drinking associated with the glees was considered wholesome entertainment, the singing clubs of the poorer sections of society were a different matter – during the American and French Revolutions, for instance, when popular meetings were automatically suspect, singing clubs could only be regarded as subversive and sinister. They could only be 'managed and conducted by evil-minded, dissolute, and disorderly pretences' that had 'seduced and drawn into their infamous associations numbers of Apprentices, Journeymen, Shop-Servants, Gentlemen's Servants, and other unwary Young Men, to their great loss and discredit'.[2] The 'whimsical' songs with which the actor James Cawdell entertained the freemasons of Sunderland in the late 1780s and the temperate comments of Dr. Brown's address to the same gentlemen were unquestionably legitimate activities worthy of a short and humorous article in local newspapers; the activities of the 'unwary Young Men' were, on the contrary, 'Bawdy toasts, Lewd Songs, Obscene and Prophane Discourses … branding things good with ridicule and marks of Contempt, to the great Shame and reproach of Rational Beings'. Worse, these things led inevitably to the 'inconceivable mischief and injury of the Public'.[3]

There was a clear acceptance that music was an occupation best reserved for the upper strata of society. Both Charles Avison and Thomas Thompson believed that music could only be appreciated by those with good taste, good judgement and a good ear, and Avison's opinion was that such good taste could only be obtained through careful study of good music – not an activity which the men and women of the lower strata of society had time or leisure to pursue. Avison said unequivocally that the patrons of music were people of 'the genteeler Sort' and condemned music in gardens such as the Spring Gardens in Newcastle as inferior, implying that it catered for people of little or no taste with its low ticket prices. William Hayes went further and insisted that music could only be appreciated by the true gentleman, the musical dilettante, with time, money and learning enough to carry out an objective study of the subject. For those involved in the Academy of

Ancient Music in the early part of the century, and the Concert of Ancient Music and the Handel Commemorations in the later decades, even Hayes' views were too restrained; not only could such gentlemen judge the true quality of music, but they had a positive obligation to do so, to encourage patriotism and national pride, to stand up against the frightening mobs rampant in the American colonies and in France, to strengthen the standing of the threatened aristocracy and monarchy, as the rightful leaders of the nation, if only in matters of musical taste.[4]

But even such serious matters as these were all too prone to trivialization; high political acts could easily degenerate into mere fashion and amusement. Handel's music, and ancient music, thrived in London because it became part of the fashionable round, and the many provincial imitations of the Handel Commemorations were treated as the latest novelty in places such as Newcastle, a chance to see the latest stars of the musical world, and to be seen in turn. Condemnation of such trivialization did exist – Brown condemned mere 'amusement' and the *Cumberland Pacquet*'s anonymous correspondent was indignant at the huge sums paid to such luminaries as Madame Mara – but these criticisms did not seem to have any effect. Fashion was not capable of rational objectivity and frequently was self-contradictory; despite the widespread belief in British superiority and a general xenophobia, audiences still lauded foreign musicians – the Italians, the Germans – to the detriment and hardship of British performers and composers.

Yet even fashion could become a political statement. North-eastern audiences were eager for the latest London sensations as if asserting their right to be seen not as an out-of-touch backwater, but as fully up-to-date and fashionable as the capital. The adulation of the Italians in York, of Signora Cremonini at Avison's concerts, of Salomon and Giardini in the latter part of the century, and even of Signor Rossignol's novelties in mid-century, the speed with which the latest ballad operas came north, the playing of Haydn's latest symphonies, the boasting of music sellers that they could obtain the latest music within days of publication in London – these were evidence not only of a certain snobbishness but of a determination to assert the right of the north-east to an equal share of eminence as the capital, as far as entertainment was concerned. The performance of *Alexander's Feast* in Durham in 1749, for example, was considered by the *Newcastle Courant* to 'equal, if not exceed, the continual performance of it in London, especially in some of the grand Chorus'.[5] This was not however a slavish adherence, an uncritical acceptance of the capital as mentor and fount of all good things to be carefully copied; audiences and musicians in the north-east were capable of making their own decisions, of rejecting what did not suit them, and altering and amending those things that did appeal. So, the passion for Handel lost much of its patriotic emphasis (although this was never entirely absent, particularly in Durham), and was regarded much more as fashion; even the philanthropy associated with such performances in concerts as far north as Lancashire and Yorkshire, was much less obvious in the north-east. Moreover, a certain practicality was also evident – the huge expense of Handel performances was beyond the resources of many local promoters. Likewise, ancient music, as performed in concerts in London and Bath – the music, largely speaking, of *dead* composers – came very late to the north-east and disappeared immediately; even in London and Bath it had been the preoccupation of an aristocratic elite, and their presence in the north-east was small and seasonal.

The temptation to treat the north-east as a homogeneous region with uniform tastes should be rejected; real differences existed between the musical characters of Durham, Newcastle and the smaller towns. In essence, Durham and Newcastle – the two large centres in the region – may be taken as largely representative of two strands in the musical life of the century. Durham stood for the old values: the strengths of the old church music, the baroque virtues of Corelli and Geminiani, the nationalistic worth of Handel, and the just and proper place of the aristocracy as arbiters of good taste and governors of the country. Newcastle was eager for fashionable things: for new instruments, new music, garden concerts, new ballad operas, the latest singers, for Madame Mara and Signora Cremonini, for Haydn's music and Pleyel's. And if some of these novelties – Mr Bryson's prodigious children, Signor Rossignol's 'sung' violin concertos, Mr Lambourn's musical glasses – were less music and more entertainment, then, as John Jortin commented, where was the harm?

Ironically, both fashion and serious musical values came to the same thing in the end; when the Peace of Amiens faltered and war broke out again between England and France, both fashion and taste agreed that music must be considered too frivolous in such a situation. Music retreated into the private home, as it had during the Commonwealth a century and a half earlier, and became a quiet, private pleasure whose propriety could not be doubted. Many of the professional musicians of the area turned increasingly away from public music-making, dedicating themselves, like Thomas Thompson, to teaching or, like the Wright brothers, to music and musical-instrument selling. Public music-making became almost invisible, certainly as far as local newspapers are concerned, although the survival of a few handbills indicate it did not die out altogether; when it reappeared, around 1809; a definite change in character is discernible with an increase in the amateur character of the concerts, and the emergence of the choral and other societies so familiar from Victorian and later days. The professional musicians still plied their trade but were much less prominent, no longer – like Charles Avison – the dominant organizers of the musical life of the town, but rather the employees of the local societies, the tradesmen William Hayes had implied they really were.

But none of these factors should detract from an appreciation of how widespread music-making was in the region during the 18th century, nor the extent to which it infused every aspect of life, reaching, in one form or another, almost every strata of society. Whether in concert, church, theatre or tavern, music was a part of everyday life, and – despite the inevitable hardships of the profession – considerable rewards awaited the musician who was prepared to work hard, to take the initiative, and to keep in touch with the changing tastes of his audience.

Notes

[1] *CP* 9 August 1786.
[2] *NC* 8 December 1781.
[3] *NC* 8 December 1781.
[4] See Weber, W., *The Rise of Musical Classics in Eighteenth-Century England: a study in canon, ritual and ideology* (Oxford: Clarendon Press, 1972) for a more detailed consideration of the political implications of ancient music and the Handel Commemorations, particularly Chapter 8: 'The 1784 Handel Commemorations as Political Ritual', 223–42.
[5] *NC* 18-25 November 1749.

Biographical Index of Musicians Resident in the North-East during the Eighteenth Century

This index includes all professional musicians known to have been resident in the north-east during the 18th century. Gentlemen Amateurs are therefore excluded as are actors and actresses who earnt their living principally from acting activities. Dancing masters are, however, included as many played in local concerts and other events. Bold type indicates a separate entry.

ACTON, Thomas singing man at Durham Cathedral. He came to Durham from Lichfield Cathedral in March 1782 and was paid £50 per annum. He is known to have sung in concerts in Newcastle, Sunderland and Durham.

AGUTTER, Ralph (?–1712) violin maker. Agutter, who was related to the Jenison family of Northumberland, had spent some time working in London before returning to Newcastle in April 1712. He advertised extensively in local newspapers during the summer of 1712, claiming both to make new instruments and to restore old ones, but died in September of the same year.

ALDRIDGE, John (fl. 1780–1790s) wait in Newcastle from 1786. Aldridge is known to have been a member of several local bands, including the Volunteer Band and to have played in a numbers of concerts in the region. He may have been organist of the Catholic Chapel in Newcastle (or to have been the father of the organist).

ALLAN, James (fl. 1770s) piper. Allan was the best-known of local pipers, being employed locally by notables such as the Duke and Duchess of Northumberland; he travelling widely throughout the border country and as far as Dublin and London. He was extensively involved in criminal activities, including horse-stealing and eventually died in Durham gaol.

ALLINSON see **ELLISON.**

ANDERSON, George chorister at Durham Cathedral between 1789 and 1799. He is known to have sung at a number of concerts in Tynemouth, Newcastle and Durham.

ASH, John singing man at Durham Cathedral, 1721–31. He was sworn in in 1721 at a salary of around 40 guineas and was one of the highest paid singing men of the period.

ASHTON, George (d. ?1830) singing man at Durham Cathedral. A local man, Ashton worked his way through the choir from chorister, (1758–70), to probationer singing man (1771) and to full singing man (1775). He was also well-known as a cellist and during the 1780s and 1790s was the principal cellist in almost all north-eastern concerts. He published a patriotic song, 'When Danger encircles our land', in 1799.

ATKINSON, George A chorister at Durham Cathedral between c1698 and 1704, Atkinson briefly became a singing man (probably supernumerary) but was dismissed in 1707 and given £5 to set up in trade.

AVISON, Ann (?–1749) wife of **Richard** and mother of 11 children, including **Edward** and **Charles senior**. Ann is believed to have taken on the post of organist at St Mary's Church, Gateshead after the death of her husband in 1721.

AVISON, Charles, senior (c1709–70) Son of **Richard** and **Ann Avison**, Charles probably received his early training from his father but travelled to London in his late teens or early 20s, where he became a pupil of Geminiani. Returning to Newcastle in mid–1735, Charles became organist, first of St John's Church then of St Nicholas's, and was involved in the setting up and running of a subscription series. He assumed full control of the series in 1738 and organized it until his death. For 35 years he was the dominant personality in Newcastle music-making; he taught extensively, was involved in private music-making with his patrons (the so-called Gentleman Amateurs), and composed much music for the use of his concert band and others. He collaborated with **John Garth** in the running of concerts in Durham, in competition with the Cathedral series there, and produced the first book in English on the aesthetics of music – *An Essay on Musical Expression* (published in 1752). By the time of his wife's death in 1766, he was probably living off invested income, describing himself as a 'gentleman', but continued working until his death.

AVISON, Charles, junior (1751–95) The younger surviving son of **Charles Avison senior**, Charles probably acted in his teens as his father's deputy as organist of St John's Church, Newcastle. After his father's death, he continued in post, promoting concerts in the town and playing at the theatre. In 1776, he obtained permission from his employers, the Corporation, to travel to St Petersburg where he remained for three years before returning to take up the post of organist at All Saints, moving on to St Nicholas's Church in 1789. He was active in teaching children to sing psalms and anthems, and in 1784 published a book of these works. He collaborated with **Thomas Hawdon** in the early 1790s to try and revive Newcastle's subscription series but died in mid–1795. He was constantly in financial difficulties, a fact which resulted in acrimonious disputes between his creditors and his widow in the late 1790s.

AVISON, Edward (1702–83) eldest son of **Richard** and **Ann Avison**, and only surviving brother of **Charles senior**. Born in Normanton, Yorkshire, Edward was apprenticed to a staymaker but continued interested and active in music-making throughout his life.

AVISON, Edward (1747–76) The elder surviving son of **Charles senior**, Edward acted as his father's deputy as organist of St Nicholas's Church in Newcastle and continued in post after his father's death. He impressed Geminiani with his harpsichord playing on the latter's visit to Newcastle in 1760. After his father's death, he also ran the regular concerts in Newcastle, but was probably consumptive and died, after a long illness, late in 1776 at the age of 29.

AVISON, Richard (?–1721) wait in Newcastle. Richard and his wife **Ann** came to Newcastle late in 1702 when Richard was appointed wait; they were possibly from Yorkshire and had previously spent some time in London. Richard remained wait until his death in Durham in 1721.

AVISON, William (d. 1751) organist at Holy Trinity Hull from 1720. William may have been a cousin of **Charles Avison senior**; he subscribed to Charles' Opus 3.

AYRTON, Edward Edmund (1765–1811) organist of Gateshead from 1789 to 1791. Ayrton was the son of the master of the Choir of the Chapel Royal and appears to have been found the Gateshead post after getting into trouble in Cambridge (possibly involving a clandestine marriage). During his stay in Gateshead, he undertook teaching in the area. He moved on to Swansea at the end of 1791 and, eventually, to Bolton in Lancashire where he died shortly after his arrival, of an illness possibly exacerbated by drinking.

BAKER, Thomas music engraver of Newcastle. The only known reference to him is in All Saints' parish registers in July 1760.

BANKS a musician who held a benefit concert at South Shields in December 1789. Banks described himself as 'late of the Cathedral, Durham'. He may have been Ralph Banks, a chorister who had left the choir the previous year after eight years in the choir. Ralph had acted as assistant master at the song-school in Durham; he continued doing so after leaving the choir. He may possibly also have been organist at St Hild's Chapel, South Shields.

BANKS, John chorister at Durham Cathedral, 1770–83.

BANKS, Ralph chorister at Durham Cathedral, 1739–52; singing man, 1751–76.

BANKS, Thomas chorister at Durham Cathedral, 1732–9.

BARBER, Robert (c1750–?) The eldest son of Joseph Barber, stationer and bookseller in Newcastle, Robert studied in London for some time before returning to Newcastle in 1733. After a failed attempt to establish himself as a teacher, concert-promoter and music-seller, he was appointed organist of the Episcopal Chapel of St Paul's in Aberdeen where he stayed for ten years during which he married and survived a murder attempt. He returned to Newcastle in 1783 to compete for post of organist at St Andrew's Church but failed to secure the position and moved to Manchester in 1784. Here he seems to have thrived and is known to have played in many musical festivals and other concerts throughout Lancashire and Yorkshire.

BARRON, George (?–1787) Appointed organist of St Andrew's Church, Newcastle in preference to **Robert Barber**, Barron travelled to London immediately afterwards to study for six months. He wrote and published some piano works before his death in 1787 at the age of 19.

BATEY, George piper, Hexham 1719–20.

BEILBY, Thomas organist at Scarborough. He published a number of sonatas for harpsichord and played in concerts (particularly at oratorios) through Lancashire and Yorkshire in the 1770s and 1780s.

BELL, Chester (d. 1750) musician in Newcastle.

BELL, David chorister at Durham Cathedral from 1797.

BELL, Rowland (fl. 1794–7) musician in Hexham.

BELL, William chorister at Durham Cathedral, c1698–c1702.

BELL, William chorister at Durham Cathedral, 1751–5.

BLACKETT, Francis chorister, Durham Cathedral, 1706–10.

BLAND, Joseph chorister at Durham Cathedral, 1794–1800.

BLENKINSOP, Peter (d. 1778) wait, innkeeper and singing man at Durham Cathedral. He entered the choir as a chorister in 1712, becoming a singing man in 1728 at a salary of £40 per annum. The Dean and Chapter gave him an extra £5 salary p.a. in 1733 as an inducement to give up his post as wait. He took part in Durham concerts but was alleged by the Dean to sing through the nose 'like a penny trumpet'. The subscribers to the rival Gentlemen's Subscription Series held their annual meetings in the inn he managed, the Star and Rummer.

BLENKINSOP, Robert (fl. 1705-25) wait in Newcastle. In 1705, Corporation minutes record that he was considered too infirm to continue in office and ordered that he should be given a pension to be paid out of other waits' salaries. In 1725, however, he complained that he did not receive the pension.

BLUNDEVIL/BLUNDEVILLE, John (d. 1721) Originally a singing man at York Minster, Blundeville was approached by the Dean and Chapter of Durham Cathedral to name his terms for coming to Durham. He did not arrive in the city until 1707 at which time he may have been past his best. He was excused his duties in the choir on account of old age and infirmity in 1718.

BONE, Peter chorister at Durham Cathedral, 1765–72 and wait in Durham from 1788.

BONE, Stephen chorister at Durham Cathedral, 1765–71.

BORUWLASKI, Count Jozef Polish dwarf and player on the Spanish guitar. He performed at concerts in York in 1785 and 1789, and at Leeds and Beverley in the early 1790s. Towards the beginning of the 19th century, he was 'adopted' by **Thomas Ebdon,** organist of Durham Cathedral, living in Durham until his death.

BOSTON, Robert (fl. 1780s–1790s) organ-builder. Boston was assistant to **John Donaldson** and moved to York with him in 1790.

BOYD, William (d. 1748/9) musician in Newcastle.

BRASS, Cuthbert (d. c1782) A chorister at Durham Cathedral from 1717 until 1727, Brass was apprenticed in the latter year, probably to a shoemaker, but moved immediately into a role as singing man, in which post he remained until his death. He looked after the choristers in the organist's absence and copied a substantial amount of music for use in the Cathedral.

BRASS, John chorister at Durham Cathedral, 1722–9.

BRASS, William chorister at Durham Cathedral, 1748–58.

BRIDGEWATER, Thomas (fl. from 1671: d. 1706/7) musician in Newcastle.

BRIGNALL, Thomas (d. 1712) chorister at Durham Cathedral, 1704–9 and singing man from 1711.

BRIGNELL, Anthony chorister at Durham Cathedral 1697–c1702.

BRISTOWE, William (fl. 1728–35) organ-builder based in Newcastle. Bristowe worked on the organ of the Song School at Durham Cathedral and produced at least one chamber organ for sale in Newcastle. A venture into surveying, in collaboration with a local artist, was short-lived. He appears to have had an argumentative nature quarrelling with, amongst others, **Solomon Strolger**, organist of All Saints.

BROCKETT, Ralph chorister at Durham Cathedral, 1709–15.

BROWN Leader of the North Shields theatre company, he described himself in an advertisement as 'from London'. He traded in music and instruments in the towns in which the company played and also acted as leader of the Sunderland Musical Society in the early 1790s. (He is known to have suffered a hand injury at about this time but recovered from it.)

BROWN, Nathaniel Originally from the Cathedral at Peterborough, he became a singing man at Durham in 1795.

BROWN, Robert (fl. 1768) musician in Newcastle.

BUGLASS, Caleb (fl. 1798) musician in Berwick.

BURLETSON, Thomas chorister at Durham Cathedral, c1725.

BURLINGSON, William wait in Durham, 1778.

BURLISON, John chorister at Durham Cathedral 1710–18; singing man, 1720–33.

BURLYSON, Thomas chorister at Durham 1723–33.

CALLENDER, E. R. (d. 1802) Possibly a member of the Newcastle gardening family, Callender was appointed organist at All Saints, Newcastle in 1798; he undertook a considerable amount of teaching but died leaving a young family.

CAMPBELL The organist of North Shields, Campbell was also a violinist and concert promoter, holding concerts in North and South Shields, and in Tynemouth in the early 1780s.

CANT, William (fl. 1780s) piper, pupil to **William Lamshaw**.

CARR, George (?-1790) Carr, who was blind, was appointed organist at St Andrew's Church, Newcastle, in 1787 but died at his uncle's home near Berwick only three years later.

CHAMERS, Mark fiddler in Newcastle, 1710–11.

CHARLTON, John musician in Newcastle, 1797.

CHATTO, J., musician in Sunderland, 1723.

CHATTO, R., musician in Sunderland, 1703.

CHIPCHASE, Joseph chorister in Durham Cathedral, 1756/7.

CHRISSOP, George Chrissop was deputy organist at Durham Cathedral in the late 1790s and schoolmaster at the song school. He may have originated in Staindrop, County Durham, and was paid for tuning the organ there.

CHRISTIE, William A Newcastle musical instrument maker, Christie suffered a fire in his workshop on High Bridge in 1799, in which he lost most of his stock.

CLAGET, Charles (c1740–c1795) Born in Ireland, Claget came to England in his late teens and tried to establish himself in Newcastle in 1758–9 as a dancing master and music teacher. Following an argument with **Charles Avison senior**, he seems to have withdrawn from concert promotion, confining himself to appearances in the theatre. In late 1759, he moved on to Edinburgh, and thence, after some time, back to Dublin. By 1776, he was resident in London.

CLAGET, Walter (c1741–97) The younger brother of **Charles**, Walter seems to have followed much the same career path, coming to Newcastle in early 1759 and spending three months teaching there and holding a number of concerts with his brother before moving on, probably to Edinburgh. By 1784, he was playing in theatre orchestras in London; in 1790, he moved to Newcastle to play with Stephen Kemble's company. He appeared as a cellist in a number of local concerts and was probably principal cellist for the local Musical Society. He died after a long illness; the Musical Society held a benefit concert for his widow and young family.

CLARK, James (d. 1743) Organist of St John's Church, Newcastle from 1736–43, he is the only known amateur organist in the town during the century. He was a saddler by trade.

CLARK, Jasper (d. 1767) singing man at Durham Cathedral. He came to the Cathedral from Winchester in 1753 and was a regular singer at Durham concerts. He was also the first violin of the concert band and acted as barber to his fellow singing men.

CLARKE, John chorister at Durham Cathedral, 1766–73.

CLIFFORD, Miss J. and Miss Diana These two sisters, who were the regular vocal soloists at subscription and other concerts in Newcastle from 1797 until c1803, lived with their mother in Northumberland Street, Newcastle: nothing else is known of them.

COLLING, Stephen chorister at Durham Cathedral, 1717–23.

COMIN, Andrew chorister at Durham Cathedral, 1712–17.

COOPER, Walter He was appointed wait in Newcastle in 1755 but removed from office for 'misbehaviour' and lack of qualifications ten years later.

COOK, William (d. 1712/3) musician and wait in Newcastle.

COULSON psalm teacher who was active in Northumberland. His scholars from Bedlingham sang at Morpeth Chapel in mid-1791.

COWEN, John chorister at Durham Cathedral, 1724–33.

COWLEY (d. c1782) organist of Sedgefield from at least 1771, possibly in succession to John Garth.

CRAIG, George (d. 1789) organist at St Mary's, Gateshead.

CUMIN, Richard (d. 1722) chorister at Durham Cathedral from c1685–96; later musician in Newcastle.

CUTTY, Edward (d. 1700) musician at Sunderland.

DAVISON, George musician in Newcastle, 1733–5.

DEMSEY, Hugh (fl. 1720s) dancing master in Newcastle and Cumberland.

DICKENSON, John (d. 1765) fiddler in Newcastle.

DIXON, Joshua (fl. 1715/6) musician in Newcastle 1715/6.

DONALDSON, John organ-builder in Newcastle and York. Probably born in North Shields, Donaldson trained for some years in London as a watchmaker and on his return to Newcastle in 1780 opened two shops in the town – a watchmaker's and an organ-manufactory. The watchmaking business probably closed at an early date. Donaldson and his assistant **Robert Boston**, worked on all four of the town's organs and also carried out work on organs as far afield as Aberdeen, Whitehaven, Bradford and Dublin. In 1790, Donaldson moved to York where he opened a shop and manufactory. He became a freeman of York in 1797 and a common councilman of the city in 1800.

DRUMMOND (d. 1792) lame fiddler from South Biddick. He died in Chester-le-Street after a drinking bout.

DUNN, Martin chorister at Durham Cathedral, 1756/7.

EALE(S), John chorister at Durham Cathedral, 1753.

EALE(S), Richard chorister at Durham Cathedral, 1742–55.

EALLES A singer who came to offer himself as a singing man at Durham Cathedral in 1759 but was rejected. He may have been either **John** or **Richard Ealles**.

EBDON, Christopher chorister at Durham Cathedral, 1712–19.

EBDON, Thomas (1738–1811) organist of Durham Cathedral. The son of a Durham cordwainer, Ebdon entered the Cathedral choir in 1748 as a chorister and became a singing man in 1756. He was elected organist in succession to **James Hesletine** in disputed circumstances in 1763 and was confirmed in post the following year. As director of the Cathedral band, he also directed local concerts and promoted concerts in Sunderland, Newcastle and South Shields. He composed much music both for sacred and secular purposes, including a Second Service for the use of the choir. In 1793, he was elected alderman of Durham but paid the fine to be released from the post after pleading that his work forced him to be away from home on a frequent basis. In 1793, he gave up concert promotion to concentrate on teaching.

EDINGTON, Robert (fl. 1762–98) musician in Newcastle.

ELFORD, Richard (?1675–1714) Originally a chorister at Lincoln Cathedral, Elford came to Durham Cathedral as a singing man and was given leave to go to London to study. In the capital, however, he spent his time there singing in the theatre and was eventually dismissed from the Cathedral. He continued to live in London and became a singing man at Westminster Abbey and at St Paul's Cathedral.

ELLISON/ALLINSON, Edward musician in Berwick.

EVANCE, William singing man at Durham Cathedral. Evance came to Durham from Oxford in 1767 at a salary of £50 per annum and became a regular vocal soloist in north-eastern concerts, particularly after the arrival of **Edward Meredith** in 1779. He also appeared in some local concerts as an organist or harpsichordist and composed and published a number of works for keyboard instruments. He also performed as vocal soloist in concerts in York, Doncaster, Aberdeen and Ripon, and undertook some teaching at the Cathedral's song school.

FAIRLESSE, John (d. 1726) Having been a chorister at Durham Cathedral from 1695, Fairlesse was appointed a singing man from 1698 but was suspended for neglecting his duties in 1707. He was almost immediately reinstated and served as a singing man until his death.

FAIRWEATHER, John wait in Hexham, 1788.

FOREMAN, George chorister at Durham Cathedral, 1756/7.

FORSTER, George chorister at Durham Cathedral, 1709–13.

FRANKS wait in Newcastle. He left his post, and the town, without permission in 1739.

FRAZIER, John fiddler to **Ivie Gregg**, dancing master, in Newcastle during the 1780s and early 1790s.

FREEMAN, George chorister at Durham Cathedral, 1776–82.

FRIEND, John Admitted singing man at Durham Cathedral in 1782 at a salary of £40 per annum (and therefore considered not to be of the first rank of singers in the choir), Friend was nevertheless in demand throughout the north-east as a tenor soloist in concerts and oratorios. He fell into 'distressed circumstances' in late 1791; although he recovered, he was again in difficulties, probably financial, in 1797.

GALE, John (d. 1765) wait in Newcastle.

GALLEY, John (fl. 1775–80) musician from Westoe, Co Durham; married and lived thereafter in Newcastle.

GALOT leader of the Morpeth Gentlemen's Subscription Series. Galot advertised himself on a concert programme as being originally from Naples; he was leader of the concerts in Morpeth from 1785 to 1786 and may have taken up the post again at a later date. A Peter Galot was organist for the Freemasons in Sunderland in the early 19th century and may have been a relative.

GAMSTER, John (fl. 1765) fiddler in Hexham.

GARTH, John (1721–1810) cellist, composer, teacher and concert promoter. Garth established himself in Durham in the mid-1740s, teaching and holding occasional concerts. His aristocratic patrons financed a subscription series for him in Durham from 1752, which Garth organized in conjunction with **Charles Avison senior** and the band of the Newcastle concerts. This was held in competition with the Cathedral series in the city until the end of the decade when Garth collaborated with the Durham Cathedral organist, **Thomas Ebdon**, to mount joint concerts. He retired from concert-promotion in 1772. He was also organist at Sedgefield Parish Church until the beginning of the 1770s and of the Bishop of Durham's private organ at his residence in Bishop Auckland. From 1772, Garth concentrated chiefly on teaching; he retired from music upon his marriage in 1794, and managed his wife's estates. He died at Cockerton near Darlington and is buried at St Cuthbert's Church, Darlington.

GATES singing man at Durham Cathedral c1709: probably a supernumerary.

GELSON, Cornforth A County Durham man, Gelson was chorister at Durham Cathedral from 1736–47. After leaving the choir, he became a wait in Newcastle for four years but returned to the Cathedral as a singing man in 1751. He was the leader of the Cathedral band but was alleged not to be able to draw a good tone from his violin. **Avison** and **Garth** attempted to recruit him as vocal soloist for their Durham subscription series; Gelson thereby incurred the wrath of the Dean – shortly after an argument, he was dismissed from the choir in 1755 for fathering an illegitimate child. After a difficult year, he was appointed teacher of church music in Edinburgh and settled there with his family for the rest of his life, teaching and leading the band of the Edinburgh Musical Society.

GIBSON, William musician in Hexham, 1791.

GOODCHILD, George (d. c1792) organist of St John's Chapel, Sunderland. Goodchild, who was possibly of a local gentry family, held the post from the mid-1770s, promoting annual benefit concerts for himself. When **Thomas Ebdon** pulled out of concert promotion in Sunderland, Goodchild took over the promotion of the subscription series and other concerts in the town but ran them for only two years before his death. He was also organist for the local Freemason's Lodge.

GRAY, William chorister in Durham Cathedral, 1755/6.

GREGG, Ivie (d. 1798) dancing master and composer, Newcastle. Of Scottish origins, Gregg lived in Newcastle for many years and published his only known work – a book of dances – in the year before his death.

GREGGS, William senior (d. 1710) Originally from York Minster, Greggs became organist of Durham Cathedral and Master of the Choristers from 1662.

GREGGS, William junior (d. 1714) son of **William Greggs**, organist, Durham Cathedral. He was appointed organist of All Saints, Newcastle in 1713, six months before his death.

GREY, Anthony chorister at Durham Cathedral, 1788–95.

GREY, Thomas musician in Newcastle, 1720.

GREY, William wait in Newcastle. Grey was appointed in 1788; he played the cello and sang at some local concerts.

GRIEVESON, William chorister in Durham Cathedral, 1702–5.

GRIFFITHS (d. 1777) haircutter and teacher of the German flute in Newcastle.

GUILDING, Thomas Of unknown origins, Guilding arrived in the north-east as a travelling psalm- and song-teacher in 1727. He taught charity children in Newcastle and Sunderland, teaching them his own anthems, but in 1729 took a position as singing man in Durham Cathedral at a salary of £30 per annum, becoming the highest paid singing man of the time. In 1731, he moved on to Lincoln Cathedral.

GUNN, Thomas organist in Newcastle. The births of his children are recorded in the registers of All Saints in 1784 and 1785 but his post is not known.

HAMILTON, George chorister at Durham Cathedral, 1777–81.

HAMMOND, William singing man at Durham Cathedral, 1749.

HARCULES, Edward see **HERCULES**

HARKER, George singing master in Hexham, 1700.

HARLE, Ralph chorister at Durham Cathedral, 1780–89.

?HAROARD, John chorister at Durham Cathedral, 1701.

HART, David (fl. 1738–43) musician in Newcastle.

HART, Thomas (fl. 1727–31) musician in Newcastle.

HAWDON, Matthias (?–1789) A Newcastle-born man, Hawdon was a pupil of **Charles Avison senior** through whose influence he obtained post of organist at Holy Trinity, Hull in 1751. In 1769, he moved on to Beverley Minster. He was active in concert-promotion both in Hull and Beverley and promoted a festival of oratorios for the opening of the new organ in Beverley in 1769. He was appointed organist of St Nicholas, Newcastle, in late 1776, supplementing his income with teaching, composition and concert-promotion, bringing complete performances of oratorios to the town. His management of the concerts suffered from lack of support and his own financial mismanagement; he went bankrupt in 1781 but continued to promote concerts until 1785, when ill-health contributed to his withdrawal from active music-making.

HAWDON, Thomas (c1765–93) youngest son of **Matthias**. As a child, he sang in his father's concerts in Newcastle; he was appointed organist of St Andrew's Church, Newcastle, in 1783 at the age of 18 but moved on within six months to a post in Dundee. By 1787, he was organist at Holy Trinity, Hull. In 1788, he returned to Newcastle to assist his seriously-ill father, being appointed organist of All Saints in late 1789. In the early 1790s, he organized subscription concerts in Newcastle in collaboration with **Charles Avison junior** but died in 1783 at the age of 28.

HEIGHINGTON, Dr. Musgrave Originally from Durham, Heighington moved to Great Yarmouth where he became organist. He fell into financial difficulties however and was dismissed from the post, later putting on a number of concerts (with his wife) to recoup his situation; these included a concert in Newcastle in 1747. His later history is not known.

HENDERSON, Joseph (d. 1755) musician in Newcastle.

HENDERSON, Mark (d. 1702) fiddler in Newcastle.

HENDERSON, William chorister at Durham Cathedral, 1735–42.

HENRY/HENDRY, William chorister at Durham Cathedral, 1718–24: dismissed in 1725 for unknown reasons.

HERCULES, Edward chorister at Durham Cathedral, 1750–56. He sang a number of solos in church and was mentioned by the vicar of Egglescliffe in laudatory terms.

HERON, Claudius A cellist, Heron gave a benefit in Newcastle in 1734 but is known to have been living in London in the 1750s. He may have been a member of the Heron family of Northumberland.

HERON, John chorister at Durham Cathedral, c1699–c1706.

HERON, John chorister at Durham Cathedral, 1733–9.

HERSCHEL, William (1738–1822) violinist, composer and astronomer. Originally from Hanover, Herschel came to London with his brother but found competition too fierce and took a post as leader of the band of the Earl of Darlington's militia, stationed at Richmond in Yorkshire. He later settled at Sunderland, carrying out teaching, and playing in **Charles Avison senior**'s subscription concerts and at the Spring Gardens in Newcastle. He seems to have flourished but disliked the uncertainty of the profession and looked for a salaried post, eventually moving to Leeds, Halifax and finally Bath, where he increasingly concentrated his attention on his interests in astronomy.

HESLETINE, James (c1692–1763) Hesletine was a chorister at the Chapel Royal under John Blow until 1707, and was appointed organist of a London church in 1709 before going to Durham Cathedral in 1711 where he stayed until his death 53 years later. As director of the Durham concert band, he came into conflict with **John Garth** and **Charles Avison senior**; he was reputed to be on particularly bad terms with the latter. Of an argumentative nature, he several times clashed with prebendaries of the Cathedral and allegedly destroyed many of his music manuscripts after one such argument.

HESLOP, John musician in Newcastle, 1797.

HILL, John (d. 1743) piper in Hexham.

HILL, Robert wait and piper in Hexham, 1757.

HILL, William wait in Hexham, 1724.

HILTON, Abraham chorister at Durham Cathedral, 1714–23.

HILTON, Isaac chorister at Durham Cathedral, 1742–9.

HOBSON, Thomas chorister at Durham Cathedral, 1771–7.

HOGG (fl. c1773) dancing master probably based in North Shields. He held a concert in Newcastle in Race Week 1773.

HOGGETT, George chorister at Durham Cathedral, 1772–7.

HOPPER, John chorister at Durham Cathedral, 1792–4.

HOUSEMAN, James (d. 1746) Houseman, who was probably from London, was appointed a singing man at Durham Cathedral in 1732, and was described as having an 'extraordinary voice' – he was probably a counter-tenor. He was paid £40 per annum, the highest salary for a singing man at that period, but his salary was reduced to £30 in 1745 owing to his negligence in carrying out his duties.

HOWARD, John chorister at Durham Cathedral, c1697–1701.

HOWGILL, Ann (1775–?) The only daughter of William Howgill, organist of Whitehaven in Cumberland, Howgill took up the post of organist at Staindrop in County Durham at the age of 18. She moved on to Penrith Church in 1797. She was also a singer and had performed at her father's concerts in Whitehaven; she had apparently a high soprano voice; one review of her performance in 1791 (aged 16) records her singing a high C.

HOWGILL, Thomas (d. 1755) wait in Newcastle.

HUDSPETH, Joseph (d. 1785) organist in Gateshead.

HULL, David ballad singer in Newcastle, 1707/8.

HUMBLE, Edward (d. 1795) The son of a stationer and bookseller in Newcastle, Humble was active as a musical instrument maker in the last two decades of the 18th century.

HUSTAS, Arthur drummer in Newcastle, 1776.

HUTCHINSON chorister at Durham Cathedral until 1704.

HUTCHINSON, George chorister at Durham Cathedral, 1756/7.

HUTCHINSON, Nicholas singing man at Durham Cathedral from 1698–c1709.

HUTCHINSON, Richard singing man at Durham Cathedral, c1686–c1706.

HUTCHINSON, Richard chorister at Durham Cathedral, 1706–12.

HUTCHINSON, Robert singing man at Durham Cathedral, c1699–c1701.

HUTCHINSON, Thomas chorister at Durham Cathedral, 1756/7.

JACKSON, John chorister at Durham Cathedral from 1795/6.

JESMOND, Thomas fiddler in Hexham, 1704–6.

JOHNSON, James piper in Newcastle, 1709.

JOHNSON, William (d. 1702) piper in Newcastle.

JONES pupil of **Thomas Wright of Newcastle**. He played a violin concerto in a benefit concert in Newcastle in 1787.

JUBB, John (d. 1712) Jubb was appointed wait in Newcastle in 1705, with special instructions to improve the quality of the waits and to reform abuses of the office after a period of unsatisfactory performance; he seems however to have been ineffectual.

JUBB, William (d.1742) wait in Newcastle.

KELL, Henry (fl. c1702) Probably one of the waits in Newcastle, he was given money by the Corporation to buy musical instruments.

KELL, Jasper (fl. 1711–33) fiddler and wait in Hexham.

KELL, Matthew (fl. 1730–38) fiddler and cordwainer in Hexham.

KELL, Simpson (d. 1763) appointed wait in Newcastle 1746.

KELLY/KELLOE, Thomas chorister at Durham Cathedral, 1760–71.

KIDD, Thomas ballad singer in Newcastle, 1721–2.

KIDSON, Thomas chorister at Durham Cathedral, 1756/7.

KINLOCH/KINLOCK, Adam (d. 1799) dancing master. He came to Newcastle from London in 1780 although he seems to have been of Scottish ancestry, and established an extensive teaching practice. He died after a fall from his horse near Tanfield, while returning home to Newcastle.

KINLOCH/KINLOCK, Alexander Munro Son of **Adam Kinloch**, he performed in public from an early age, giving exhibition dances between the acts of play at the theatre. In the early 1790s he became principal cellist at most concerts in Newcastle and many outside the town; when the subscription series was revived in 1797, he became Master of Ceremonies for the concerts. He was a member of most local bands, including the Volunteer band. In 1799, he inherited his father's dancing school after the latter's death.

LAMSHAW, William (fl. end 18th century) piper to Duke of Northumberland.

LAX, John (d. 1737/8) dancing master in Newcastle; known to be a rival of **Hugh Demsey**.

LAYE/LEIGH, Thomas (Laye the elder) singing man at Durham Cathedral, 1709–29. He acted as master of the choristers after death of **William Greggs** in 1711. Probably father of **William Leigh/Laye**.

LAYE/LEIGH, William (Laye the younger) singing man at Durham Cathedral, c1717–27. Laye was admonished for 'Drunkenesse and Disorderly Liveing' and neglect of duties in 1717 and was expelled from the choir. He was however still, or again, in position in 1721 when he was accused of 'incest' and suspended. He was restored a year later in April 1722 but this probably did not take effect as he was not paid after the end of 1721.

LE SAC, Sebastien (d. 1739) dancing master in Newcastle. His name and date of death makes it tempting to identify Le Sac as the Swiss violinist who clashed with **Charles Avison senior** after the first season of the subscription series in Newcastle; there is, however, no suggestion in the documents of the period to suggest that the violinist was also a dancing master, although he was supported by dancing masters within the band; moreover, newspaper reports suggest that he left Newcastle after the dispute. Nevertheless, the possibility cannot be totally discounted.

LIGHTFOOT, John chorister at Durham Cathedral, 1782–90.

LIN[D]SLEY, Joseph chorister at Durham Cathedral, 1771–5.

LITTLEFARE, James chorister at Durham Cathedral, 1739–48.

McCLOUD, Halcomb musician in Newcastle, 1745. He may have been associated with the Scottish regiments in the Jacobite rebellion.

McCULLOCH, John musician in Newcastle, 1745. He may have been associated with the Scottish regiments in the Jacobite rebellion.

McDONALD, John fiddler to **Neil Stewart**, a Newcastle dancing master in the last quarter of the century.

McFARLANE, William (d. 1788) wait in Newcastle.

McGILL, David wait and dancing master in Berwick.

MACKCLAINE, James musician in Newcastle, 1701–2.

MACKENZEY, William chorister at Durham Cathedral, 1788–90.

MACKINHEM, Jane (d. 1761) ballad singer in Durham.

MACKINTOSH, Abraham (fl. 1798–1800) dancing master in Newcastle. Mackintosh came to Newcastle around 1798, probably from London. His book of tunes was published at the turn of the century. He also played the cello in some local concerts.

MADDISON, George chorister at Durham Cathedral, 1698–1709.

MADDISON, John chorister at Durham Cathedral, 1727–33.

MARLEY, Bailey chorister at Durham Cathedral, 1746–52. He was the stepson of **Thomas Mountier senior**.

MARLOR/MARLOW, Robert singing man at Durham Cathedral, 1776–95. Marlor was admonished on a number of occasions for drunken behaviour in church early in his career but seems to have recovered for a while and sang in a number of concerts throughout the North-East. However, he was dismissed from his post in 1795 for 'gross and disorderly behaviour in Church in a State of great Intoxication'.

MARLOR/MARLOW, Samuel son of **Robert Marlor/Marlow**: chorister at Durham Cathedral, 1790–96. At the end of his time in the choir, the Dean and Chapter allowed him five guineas to facilitate his apprenticeship to a hatter in Manchester.

MARSDEN, Thomas chorister at Durham Cathedral, 1799–1800.

MARSHALL, Henry (d. 1755) Marshall was a chorister at Durham Cathedral from 1723 until 1734 and moved immediately into the ranks of the singing men. He received £30 per annum but was constantly in financial difficulties. After his death in 1755, the other singing men held a benefit concert for his widow and 'many orphans'.

MARSHALL, John chorister at Durham Cathedral, 1745–54.

MARSHALL, John (d. 1782) singing man at Durham Cathedral from 1764. Marshall received a salary of £30 per annum and was a watchmaker by trade.

MARSHALL, Thomas chorister at Durham Cathedral, c1700–4.

MARTIN instrumentalist in South Shields benefit: described as 'of Newcastle'.

MARTIN, John (fl. 1717–20) wait in Newcastle.

MARTIN, Robert (d. 1740) wait in Newcastle. When the Corporation decided to reform the waits in the first decade of the century, Martin was one of those accused of irregular practices – precise details are not given.

MARTIN, William (d. before 1735) wait in Newcastle.

MATTHEWS, John singing man at Durham Cathedral 1764–76. Matthews came to the Cathedral from Salisbury and was one of the highest-paid singing men at a salary of £50 per annum. He sang in local concerts and at Spring Gardens in Newcastle, and was also employed as a music copyist by the Dean and Chapter. After he left the choir in 1776, he remained in the area; his later history is not known.

MEREDITH, Edward (1741–1809) Probably a Welshman by birth, Meredith was a protégé of Sir Watkin Williams Wynn and attempted to make his career as a singer in London between 1773 and 1779. In the latter year, however, he took up a post as singing man at Durham Cathedral. Over the next decade, he established himself as the leading vocal soloist in the north-east, singing in subscription series in Durham, Newcastle, Sunderland, Morpeth and Darlington, and receiving benefits from local bodies. The Handel Commemoration of 1784 opened up new opportunities for him and he was soon in great demand for the many oratorio performances that were held in the north in imitation of the London event. In 1788, he left Durham for Liverpool, probably because the latter was within easier geographical reach of most of his engagements. In the 1790s, he twice tried to re-establish himself in London but failed; he continued to be extremely popular in the north. He died in Wrexham late in 1809.

METCALF, Christopher chorister at Durham Cathedral, 1734–41.

METCALF, Jeoffrey musician in Newcastle, 1763.

MIDDISON chorister at Durham Cathedral until 1704.

MIDDLETON, Sherriff chorister in Durham Cathedral, 1783–92.

MIDDLETON, William chorister at Durham Cathedral, 1778–86.

MITCHELL, Joseph musician in Newcastle, 1723.

MITCHELL, William chorister at Durham Cathedral, 1740–48.

MONRO, Henry (d. 1819) Monro was appointed organist of St Andrew's Church, Newcastle in 1796 in succession to **Thomas Wright of Newcastle** whom he accused of neglecting the organ. The two men, however, appeared together in turn of the century subscription series in the town; Monro played piano-forte sonatas and concertos, some of which were advertised for publication by subscription.

MOODY, Thomas musician in Newcastle, 1720.

MOUNTAIN, Cuthbert chorister at Durham Cathedral, 1762–9.

MOUNTAIN, Thomas chorister at Durham Cathedral, 1701–6.

MOUNTIER, Thomas senior (d. c1754) singing man at Durham Cathedral from 1735: father of **Thomas junior** and stepfather of **Bailey Marley**.

MOUNTIER, Thomas junior Originally from Chichester, Mountier became a popular singer in London concerts in the early 1730s. He became a singing man at Durham Cathedral in 1735 and also acted as vocal soloist in **Charles Avison senior's** subscription series in Newcastle. He was in trouble with the Dean and Chapter from early 1740, and his salary was suspended although he was allowed ten shillings a week for subsistence and money was advanced to him later in the year during the illness of his wife. The cause of the problems seems to have been his neglect of his duties; late in 1741 he was threatened with dismissal. He was not paid after the middle of 1742, and probably left the choir at that date.

MURRAY, William fiddler in Newcastle, 1715.

NEWBY, Richard senior (d. 1772) wait in Newcastle from 1763.

NEWBY, Richard junior The only known reference to Newby is to a solo cello he played in a benefit for **Charles Avison junior** in 1771.

NICHOLLS, Samuel (d. 1719) organist, St Nicholas, Newcastle, at a salary of £25 per annum. He almost certainly supplemented his income with teaching.

NORTON, Humphrey (d. 1726) Norton was a chorister at Durham Cathedral from 1702 until 1713 and became organist at Sedgefield in c1724.

OATES, John (d. 1705) musician in Sunderland from c1700.

OLIVER, John (fl. 1740) musical instrument maker. Oliver advertised a chamber organ for sale in Newcastle in 1740; he may have been related to Thomas Oliver, a dancing master and musical instrument seller in York.

ORRICK, Bartholomew (d. 1786) musician in Newcastle from at least 1776; he was appointed wait in 1783.

OSWALD, John wait in Berwick from 1735.

OTTWAY, Thomas (d. 1777) musician in Newcastle.

PALMER, William chorister at Durham Cathedral from 1795.

PARKINSON chorister at Durham Cathedral, 1711.

PARKINSON, Henry singing man at Durham Cathedral. Parkinson was first appointed in 1686 but was admonished and had part of his salary suspended for irregularity in attending services in 1704. Four years later, he was expelled from the choir for 'his noxious crime of Adultery', but was reinstated 12 years later in 1720, continuing in office until late 1727 when he probably died.

PARKINSON, Thomas (d. 1720) singing man at Durham Cathedral from c1685; he was probably the brother of **Henry Parkinson.** He was admonished for irregularity at the same time as Henry in 1704 and had part of his salary suspended but this was reinstated later the same year. He continued in post without further problems until 1718 when he was excused attendance by reason of old age and infirmity.

PARKINSON, William (d. 1714) chorister at Durham Cathedral, 1702–22; singing man, 1711–14.

PATTERSON, John musician in Newcastle, 1724.

PATTINSON, William chorister at Durham Cathedral, 1756–7.

PAXTON, George chorister at Durham Cathedral, 1759–60: probably son of **Robert Paxton**.

PAXTON, Robert (d. 1751) Paxton was the eldest of three brothers who followed each other into the Durham choir. A chorister from 1731 until 1738, Robert became first a probationary singing man in 1738 at a salary of £10 per annum then, from the next year, a full singing man at a salary of £20 – a relatively low salary for the period. He was fined in 1748 for negligence and non-attendance and in 1750 his salary was suspended for three months and he was warned that a further offence would mean his expulsion from the choir. He died the following year.

PAXTON, Stephen (d. 1787) The youngest of the three Paxton brothers, Stephen was a chorister at Durham Cathedral from 1745 until 1754. Following an argument with the Dean, probably over the fact that Stephen was planning to sing in the Garth-Avison Durham subscription series, Stephen left for London where he made his career as a cellist and composer. At his death he was reputed to be worth more than £10,000.

PAXTON, William brother of **Robert** and **Stephen**. William entered Durham Cathedral choir in 1734 as a chorister and became a probationary singing man in 1742 at £10 per annum; this was augmented to £20 the following year when he became a full singing man. In 1749 he was allowed three months' stay in London for study; on his return his salary was increased to £30 per annum. He sang in local concerts in Newcastle and Durham, holding several benefits in Durham during the 1740s and was eventually given a salary of £50 per annum at the Cathedral in 1764. He was one of those musicians who promoted a benefit in Newcastle after the death of **Charles Avison senior,** a concert which is notable for the first known concert appearance of **Edward Meredith**. He was last paid in mid-1777 and probably died shortly afterwards.

PEACOCK, John (fl. 1786–1801) Peacock was well-known as a player of the Northumbrian pipes and was engaged by the engraver Thomas Bewick to teach his son; Peacock published a book of tunes for the pipes in 1801. He was also a member of a number of local bands and was appointed wait in 1783, losing the post when it was abolished ten years later.

PEARSON (fl. 1785–9) psalm teacher in North Shields.

PEILE, John musician in Newcastle, 1787.

PERKIN(S), John chorister at Durham Cathedral, 1729–35.

POTTER, George chorister at Durham Cathedral, 1752–5.

POTTS, Thomas (d. 1767) fiddler, drowned in Gateshead.

POWELL, Thomas (d. 1736) Powell was organist at St Nicholas's Church, Newcastle from 1719. He was paid £40 per annum (with additions for tuning the organ) but died 'in poor circumstances'.

PRENDCOURT, François de (d. 1725) Prendcourt, a Catholic, had spent a large part of his early career as a musician at the court of James II in London. After James's deposition in 1688, he seems to have travelled throughout the country, working his way north to Derby in 1705. He may then have briefly acted as organist in Kendal; he was appointed to the post of organist at All Saints, Newcastle, in 1714 at a salary of c£16. Between 1720 and his death in 1725, his employers, Newcastle Corporation, made a number of charitable payments to him, but he was recorded as dying in poor circumstances.

PRINGLE, Robert chorister at Durham Cathedral, 1725–33.

PRIOR, Matthew musical instrument maker. Possibly a grandson of **William Prior**. Prior was also a wood-turner and assay-master.

PRIOR, William (d. 1759) A musical instrument maker in Newcastle, Prior is known to have been established in the city as early as 1699. He also made false teeth and during the 1730s this seems gradually to have taken precedence.

PROCTOR, Matthew An itinerant psalm teacher, Proctor is known to have taught in Staindrop and Houghton-le-Spring. In 1778, he advertised the proposed publication of a three volume book of Psalms; it is not clear whether this ever saw the light of day.

RADCLIFF, Thomas (d. prior to 1746/7) musician in Newcastle.

RADCLIFFE, James singing man, Durham Cathedral. Radcliffe was admitted in 1795, in succession to **Robert Marlow** at a salary of £50 – at this time the recognized salary for all singing men. He sang in many local concerts and also played the bassoon. He was frequently in debt and in 1799 was threatened with dismissal unless he improved his attendance. He continued to be paid into the next century but was probably not active in the choir.

RAILTON, George chorister at Durham Cathedral, 1760–65.

READSHAW, James verger at Durham Cathedral. Readshaw stood in as organist at the Cathedral after the death of **William Greggs** in 1711.

REAY/REAH, Thomas chorister at Durham Cathedral, 1770–78.

REYNOLDS, Master a violinist who played at a concert in Newcastle in 1757 when he was described as eight years old.

REYNOLDS/RHEINHOLD, John Reynolds replaced **Edward Meredith** as a singing man at Durham Cathedral in 1789 and like Meredith was a bass. He sang in concerts in Durham and Newcastle and also sang at the Manchester Musical Festivals of 1777 and 1781. He resigned from the choir in 1791.

RICHARDSON, John musician in Newcastle, 1735.

RICHARDSON, Matthew chorister at Durham Cathedral, 1704.

RICHARDSON, Robert piper in Newcastle, 1719/20.

RICHARDSON, William chorister at Durham Cathedral, 1794.

RIDLEY, Cuthbert chorister at Durham Cathedral, 1719–29.

RIDLEY, Cuthbert chorister at Durham Cathedral, 1753–62.

RIDLEY, John chorister at Durham Cathedral, 1723–32.

RIDLEY, John chorister at Durham Cathedral, 1755–65.

RIDLEY, Matthew chorister at Durham Cathedral, 1706–18.

ROBERTS, John musician in Hexham, 1775.

ROBERTS, Robert piper in Hexham, 1722.

ROBINSON, George chorister at Durham Cathedral, 1749–54.

ROBINSON, George A chorister at Durham Cathedral from 1780 until 1793, Robinson sang at oratorios and other concerts in Newcastle. He became organist at North Shields from 1794 and held concerts in Tynemouth and North Shields in the latter half of the decade.

ROBINSON, John chorister at Durham Cathedral, 1757–60.

ROBINSON, Joseph chorister at Durham Cathedral, 1755/6.

ROBINSON, Peter chorister at Durham Cathedral, 1766–77.

ROBINSON, Robert (d. 1795) A chorister at Durham Cathedral from 1771 until 1780, Robinson became a singing man in 1793, two years before his death. He was an upholsterer.

ROBINSON, Thomas Robinson was a chorister at Durham Cathedral from 1767 until 1775, and a singing man from 1778. He was appointed a master in the song school in 1780 and Director and assistant instructor of the choristers in 1785. He was first violin of the Cathedral band and performed at many concerts in Durham, Sunderland, Newcastle and other places in the north-east throughout the 1780s and 1790s.

ROBINSON, William chorister at Durham Cathedral, 1777–88.

ROBSON, Michael chorister at Durham Cathedral, 1756-7.

ROBSON, Robert (d. 1746) wait in Newcastle.

ROSS, John (1763–1837) Ross was probably the son of a family of waits in Newcastle and was apprenticed to **Matthias Hawdon.** In 1783, he was appointed organist of the Episcopal Chapel of St Paul's, Aberdeen in succession to **Robert Barber** and remained there the rest of his life, composing, promoting concerts and playing for the Aberdeen Musical Society.

ROSS, Thomas senior (d. 1786) musician in Newcastle from at least 1763; appointed wait in Newcastle in 1765.

ROSS, Thomas junior wait, Newcastle: son of **Thomas Ross senior**. He moved from the town after his father's death in 1786 to an unknown destination.

SCOTT, Robert chorister at Durham Cathedral, 1757–63.

SCOTT, Thomas musician in Newcastle, 1751.

SEWELL, George chorister at Durham Cathedral, 1795–1801.

SHADFORTH wait in Newcastle. He played an oboe concerto at a benefit in 1772.

SHAW, Alexander (d. 1706) organist in Durham.

SHAW, Robert (fl. 1759–89) A cellist who was active in Leeds in the late 1750s, Shaw was appointed organist of St Mary's Church, Gateshead, in 1789 but stayed less than two months and may have died at that time. He may have been related to the Shaw family of York musicians.

SHERWIN singing man at Durham Cathedral, 1707–10.

SHIELD, William (1745–1829) A north-easterner by birth, Shield was probably apprenticed to **Charles Avison senior**. and played in concerts and at the theatre locally before being taken up by the Sharp family (prebendaries at Durham Cathedral). He had moved to London by 1773 where he became well-known for his ballad operas. He returned to the north-east on a number of occasions to play in such events as the Durham Musical Festival in 1792 and in his own benefit concerts. His songs were frequently performed in North-eastern concerts, and his operas regularly staged in local theatres.

SHOLTON, Robert (d. 1723) dancing master in Newcastle.

SIMPSON, John (fl. 1770s–1790s) Originally organist of Gateshead, Simpson was appointed to St John's Church, Newcastle, in 1777. He taught extensively, tuned and sold instruments, and held at least one benefit concert in the years immediately following the death of **Charles Avison senior**.

SINCLAIR, William (d. 1783) wait in Newcastle from 1742.

SLEIGH/SLYE, chorister at Durham Cathedral, 1779–87.

SMITH chorister at Durham Cathedral from 1734.

SMITH petitioner for supernumerary singing man's place at Durham Cathedral, 1796.

SMITH, Masters choristers at Durham Cathedral who sang at concerts in Newcastle 1788; possibly **John** and **William**.

SMITH, Christopher Leader of the band of Austin and Whitlock's theatre company, he travelled extensively with the company and eventually married a Whitehaven woman and settled there, teaching and playing in concerts but deriving much of his income from work as a dancing master.

SMITH, Elias chorister at Durham Cathedral, 1739–46.

SMITH, Holmes chorister at Durham Cathedral, 1794–1801.

SMITH, John (d. 1799) chorister at Durham Cathedral, 1786–1800; also recorded as a musician in Durham registers in 1799.

SMITH, Nathan (fl. 1750s) fiddler in Durham. Probably son of **Elias Smith**.

SMITH, Nathan(iel) chorister at Durham Cathedral, 1775–81.

SMITH, Thomas chorister at Durham Cathedral from 1797–8.

SMITH, William (d. 1733/4) A chorister at Durham Cathedral from 1713 until 1722 and singing man from 1722, Smith obtained leave of absence to study in London between 1723 and 1727, and to study organ-playing in Newcastle in 1727.

SMITH, William chorister at Durham Cathedral, 1781–94. Smith may be identical with **William Smith** mason and wait.

SMITH, William (d. 1794) Recorded as a mason and wait, Smith died as a pauper.

SMITH, William chorister at Durham Cathedral, 1793–7.

SNAITH, John (?d. 1773) Snaith's existence was disputed in letters to the *Newcastle Chronicle* and *Newcastle Journal*, in late 1773; one writer claimed that he had been a pupil of the Arnes, had performed as a violinist in London and had composed much music. He was alleged to have died in Stockton upon Tees.

SOFTLEY, Robert singing man at Durham Cathedral, 1697–1704 at a salary of c£12 per annum. In 1701, he was given leave to go to London to improve his singing and music-copying.

SOFTLEY, Thomas chorister at Durham Cathedral, 1697–c1703.

SPENCE singing man at Durham Cathedral from 1751. He was originally from Chester.

SPENCER, James musician in Newcastle, 1799.

SPENDELOE, William (d. 1701) fiddler in Newcastle.

STANLEY, F. singing man at Durham Cathedral from 1791. Stanley came to Durham from Rochester and sang in concerts in Durham and Newcastle. He seems to have been regularly in debt and in 1795 was suspended from the choir for unknown reasons; he was reinstated shortly afterwards and seems to have managed better thereafter although he continued on occasion to receive advances of his salary from the Dean and Chapter. In 1799, he was appointed to teach the choristers in the Song School how to read and write at an additional salary of £16 per annum.

STEPHENSON, George According to the Dean and Chapter's Act Books, Stephenson was appointed as singing man at Durham Cathedral in 1700 but no entries appear for him in the Treasurer's Accounts.

STEPHENSON, Joseph chorister at Durham Cathedral, 1729–38.

STEPHENSON, Rowland chorister at Durham Cathedral, 1756–7.

STEPHENSON, Thomas (d. 1745) fiddler in Newcastle.

STEWART An instrumentalist at a benefit in South Shields in 1792 – he was described as 'of Newcastle'.

STEWART, Andrew chorister at Durham Cathedral, 1775–82.

STEWART, Neil dancing master in Newcastle in last decades of the century.

STOKOE/STOKER, George chorister at Durham Cathedral, 1777–9.

STOUT, John chorister at Durham Cathedral, 1706–15; singing man from 1715 until 1740 at a salary augmented of £20 per annum.

STROLGER, Solomon (1703–79) Strolger was baptised in St. Botolph Without Aldgate in London; family names suggest that the family may originally have been Jewish. He was appointed to the post of organist at All Saints' Church, Newcastle in 1725 in succession to **François de Prendcourt**, and was appointed wait at the same time. He probably had an extensive teaching practice and had amassed a considerable fortune by his death despite having a large family.

SUDWICK, William chorister at Durham Cathedral, 1725–30.

SUTHERLAND, Robert Following his appointment as organist of Gateshead in 1792, Sutherland set himself set up as a tuner, then opened a shop in Gateshead for instruments and music, the first shop dedicated solely to music goods in the area since the early 1770s. In response to competition from other shops, Sutherland moved his business to Newcastle in 1798. He also employed workmen to repair and restore old instruments, and experimented with instrument design, inventing a swell pedal for the piano forte.

SWEETING, Thomas (d. 1700) musician in Newcastle.

SYKES, Robert chorister at Durham Cathedral, 1754–8.

TAIT, Henry wait in Newcastle, known only from the report of a robbery at his home in 1776.

TATE, Henry (d. 1784) innkeeper and wait, Berwick.

TAYLOR, Abraham (d. 1749) A singing man at Durham Cathedral from 1709, he was given permission in 1711 to travel to London to study. He briefly acted as a wait in Durham but was persuaded to give up the post by the Dean and Chapter by the offer of an extra £5 salary per year.

TAYLOR, Stephen chorister at Durham Cathedral, 1762–6.

THOMPSON, Henry chorister at Durham Cathedral, 1757–61.

THOMPSON, John (d. 1706/7) A chorister at Durham Cathedral from 1697, he became a singing man in 1704 and was a tailor by trade.

THOMPSON, John (?-1828) Son of a linen-draper in Sunderland, Thompson became a chorister at Durham Cathedral in 1754. He left the choir in 1760 after being apprenticed to a breeches maker and set up his own business, moving to Newcastle in 1777. The breeches business seems to have been delegated to assistants while Thompson developed his musical activities. At various times he set up an Academy of Vocal Music (probably short-lived), taught various instruments, sang at local concerts and played in a number of bands including the Volunteer Band. In the 1790s, he became parish clerk of St Nicholas's Church, Newcastle. He opened a music shop next to his breeches business in 1796 but closed it in 1800. In the early 19th century, he was, together with his son **Thomas Thompson**, a leading member of the Harmonic Society promoting a local subscription series.

THOMPSON, Thomas (1777–1830) son of **John Thompson**. Born in Sunderland, Thompson moved with his family to Newcastle in 1777 and was playing in local concerts from c1790. He was a pupil of **Thomas Hawdon** and also travelled to London in the early 1790s to study with Clementi. He was appointed organist of All Saints' Church, Newcastle, in 1793 and of St Nicholas's Church in 1795. He promoted a number of concerts locally and played piano solos in local subscription series. He composed military pieces and piano works but was chiefly known for his large number of songs. In the early 19th century, he was, together with his father, a leading member of the Harmonic Society promoting a local subscription series.

THRELKELD/THIRKELL, William chorister at Durham Cathedral, 1774–6.

THWAITES, John chorister at Durham Cathedral from 1797/8.

TODD, Richard chorister at Durham Cathedral, 1727–34.

TURNBULL, Robert (d. 1761) fiddler in North Shields.

TURNBULL, Thomas (d. 1723/4) fiddler in Newcastle.

WALKER (d. before 1775) watchmaker and organ-builder in Newcastle. He was possibly associated with **John Donaldson**.

WALKER, James (d. 1786) violinist and wait in Newcastle. He was appointed in 1772 but removed from office in 1783. He was blind and died in a fall at home.

WALKER, Michael chorister at Durham Cathedral, 1733–9.

WALLACE, James fiddler in Newcastle, 1760.

WATSON, Christopher chorister at Durham Cathedral, 1757–67.

WATSON, George (d. 1724) fiddler in Newcastle.

WATSON, John drummer in Hexham, 1710.

WATSON, John chorister at Durham Cathedral, 1762–8.

WATSON, William chorister at Durham Cathedral, 1756–7.

WELCH, George (fl. 1768–70) musician in Newcastle.

WEST, William (1759–98) musician in Newcastle. Formerly of Leeds, he was drum-major in the Newcastle Volunteer Band.

WESTON, Ralph chorister at Durham Cathedral, 1787–95.

WETHERELL, Anthony chorister at Durham Cathedral, 1787–98.

WETHERELL, George chorister at Durham Cathedral, 1795–7.

WEYLLANDT (fl. 1795–7) organist at Sunderland and promoter of concerts in the town.

WHEATLEY, Robert chorister at Durham Cathedral, 1718–35.

WHEATLEY, Thomas chorister at Durham Cathedral, 1713–25.

WHITE A singing man at Durham Cathedral from 1703, he was dismissed in 1706/7 and given money to set up in trade.

WHITEHEAD, William, junior (fl. 1790) musical instrument maker.

WIGHTMAN, John (fl. 1739–46) wait in Newcastle; resigned in 1746.

WILKINSON, Joseph (d. 1730/1) wait in Newcastle.

WILKINSON, Thomas fiddler in Newcastle, 1719.

WILKINSON, Thomas chorister at Durham Cathedral until 1741.

WILLIAMS, George (b. c1726) apprentice to **Charles Avison senior** in Newcastle. He was probably the apprentice whose appearance as leader of the concert band for the subscription series in 1736 was the immediate pretext for the dispute between the supporters of Charles Avison senior and a Swiss violinist. He ran away in 1739 but probably returned and gave a concert in Durham 1754.

WILSON, Cuthbert (1731–93) A chorister at Durham Cathedral from 1742 until 1751, he was admitted as a probationer singing man in 1751 and a full singing man in 1757. He sang at some local concerts.

WILSON, Edmund chorister at Durham Cathedral, 1768–76.

WILSON, James fiddler in Newcastle, 1710.

WILSON, John chorister at Durham Cathedral, 1756–66.

WILSON, Nicholas singing man at Durham Cathedral, c1685–1707.

WILSON, Richard chorister at Durham Cathedral, 1705–13.

WILSON, Richard chorister at Durham Cathedral, 1728–35.

WILSON, Richard chorister at Durham Cathedral, 1739–42.

WILSON, Richard probationer singing man at Durham Cathedral, 1755–8.

WILSON, (?William) Wilson was a chorister at Durham Cathedral from 1764 until 1774. He sang at concerts in Newcastle in 1781. He may be the William Wilson, teacher of vocal music in Aberdeen, who in 1784 described himself as 'late of the Cathedral, Durham'.

WRIGHT, Robert (fl. 1766–72) organist of Stockton Parish Church, father of **Thomas Wright of Stockton**.

WRIGHT, Thomas organist, Stockton Parish Church from 1759 until c.1766. Father of **Robert Wright** and grandfather of **Thomas Wright of Stockton**.

WRIGHT, Thomas of Stockton (1763–1829) organist of Stockton Parish Church in succession to his grandfather, **Thomas** and father, **Robert.** He studied with **John Garth** and **Thomas Ebdon** and promoted concerts in Stockton and Darlington; as a violinist he played at the Musical Festival in Durham in 1792 and at benefits elsewhere. He composed much music. He resigned as organist in 1818 after a dispute over his salary and spent the rest of his life teaching.

WRIGHT, Thomas of Newcastle (c1760–1819) violinist, clarinettist, singer, composer, theatre musician, concert promoter. Wright's first known appearances in public were in York and Newcastle in 1780-1 as a clarinet soloist; he had probably been studying in London before this and possibly played at Covent Garden Opera House. In the 1780s, he probably worked for the theatre company of Austin and Whitlock and married one of the actresses in the company. At the same time he was establishing himself as a concert soloist and promoter, holding concerts in Sunderland, Durham and Morpeth. By the early 1790s he was the accepted leader of all local bands, a situation which was continued into the 19th century, even after he retired from clarinet playing. He composed a great deal of music for a variety of purposes, including theatre, military bands and the subscription concerts. In 1790, he took on the post of organist of St Andrew's Church in Newcastle but resigned in 1796 after an acrimonious argument with the churchwardens. In the early 19th century, as musical life in Newcastle suffered during the French Revolutionary Wars, he opened a music shop in direct competition with his brother, **William Wright**.

WRIGHT, William (d. 1830) Younger brother of **Thomas Wright of Newcastle**, William was appointed wait in 1786 but lost the post on its abolition in 1793. He was a member of most local bands. In 1795, he opened a music shop which seemed to have thrived; he expanded into Sunderland in 1802. He also established a music-printing business and published a number of works by local composers including his brother, and may have composed some of the anonymous works himself.

WRIGHT, William (c1736–1804) musician in Newcastle; possibly father of **Thomas** and **William Wright**.

WRIGHTMAN, William wait in Newcastle, 1739.

YEALES, J. musician in Sunderland, 1704.

YOUNG, Christopher chorister at Durham Cathedral, 1717–19.

YOUNG, Philip (d. 1788) wait in Durham.

Musical Sources

This is not a comprehensive list but notes those works referred to in the text. Most of the music mentioned in this book is not available in modern editions. Where works do not survive, they are marked with an asterisk.

Aldridge, John, jnr., *Nanny of the Tyne* (J. Goulding and Co., n.d.).

Anon, *A Favorite Rondeau arranged for the Piano Forte* (Newcastle: William Wright, n.d.).

Anon, *Six Favorite Waltz's arranged for the Harp or Piano Forte* (Newcastle: William Wright, n.d.).

Armstrong, William, *Psalms and Hymns and their proper Times in the Tenor Part, Collated from various Authors* (Berwick: for the author, 1784).

Avison, Charles, Opus 1: *Six Sonatas* (1737).

Avison, Charles, Opus 2: Later revised as Opus 6 (1740).

Avison, Charles. Verse anthem: *Hast thou not forsaken us?* (1741).

Avison, Charles, *12 concertos in 8 parts* (1742).

Avison, Charles, Opus 3: *Six concertos in seven Parts* (1751).

Avison, Charles, *Select pieces from the works of Rameau (1751).

Avison, Charles, Opus 4: *Eight concertos for Violins* (1755).

Avison, Charles, Opus 5: *Six sonatas for the Harpsichord* (1756).

Avison, Charles, *The Psalms of David, Imitated in the Language of the New Testament, And Applied to the Christian State and Worship*, I Watts (18th edition) (Newcastle: William Charnley, c1757).

Avison, Charles, Opus 6: *10 Concertos for violins* (revision of Opus 2 (1758).

Avison, Charles, Opus 7: *Six sonatas for the Harpsichord* (1760).

Avison, Charles, *March composed for the Yorkshire Buffs (1761).

Avison, Charles, *Psalm for celebrations of coronation of George III in Newcastle, based on psalm by Marcello: *The King shall be joyful in thy Strength* (1761).

Avison, Charles, **Ruth*: oratorio composed with Felice Giardini for Lock Hospital (1763).

Avison, Charles, Opus 8: *six sonatas for the harpsichord* (1765).

Avison, Charles, Opus 9: *12 concertos in 4 parts* (1766).

Avison, Charles, Opus 10: *six concertos in seven parts* (1769).

Avison, Charles, Manuscript: 'Twelve canticles taken from the compositions of Carlo Clari and adapted to English words selected from the Psalms by Mr. Avison. Collection 1st.' (1769).

Avison, Charles, Two manuscript commonplace books (undated).

Barron, George, *The German Spa, A Favorite Country Dance Adapted as a Rondo for the Piano Forte or Harpsichord* (London: Preston, n.d.).

Evance, William, **Six Sonatas* (London: Welcher, n.d.); *Concerto for Harpsichord or Piano Forte* (London: Longman and Broderip, n.d.).

Ebdon, Thomas, *Sacred Music, Composed for the Use of the Choir of Durham* (London: Preston and Son for the author, c1790).

Friend, John, *The Durham City Loyal Volunteers, March and Quick Step, for a Military Band, also arranged for the Piano Forte* (London: Preston, n.d.)

Garth, John, *The first fifty Psalms Set to Music by Benedetto Marcello and adapted to the English Version* (London: John Johnson, 1757–65).

Garth, John, *Six Sonata's for the Harpsichord, Piano Forte and Organ ... composed by John Garth, Opera Secunda* (London: for the author, 1768).

Gregg, Ivie, *Six Minuets For Two Violins and Violincello Adapted for the Harpsichord and Piano Forte With three Allemands and Three Reels* (Newcastle: n.d.).

Hawks, David Shafto, *Marches for a Military Band, also adapted for the Piano Forte* (London: Clementi, Banger, Hyde, Collard and Davis, after 1795).

Mackintosh, Abraham, *A Collection of Strathspeys, Reels, Jigs, c.* (?after 1798).

Monro, G.H., *A Grand Sonata for the Piano Forte with or without the additional Keys* (London: Preston, n.d.).

Peacock, John, *A favourite Collection of tunes with variations adapted for the Northumbrian pipes, violin or flute* (Newcastle: William Wright, 1801).

Shield, William, *The South Shields Loyal Volunteers March, Troop and Quick Step arranged for the Piano Forte or Harp* (London: Preston, n.d.).

Thompson, Thomas, 'The Orphan Boy' (London: Guilding, Phipps and D'Allmain, n.d.).

Wright, Thomas (of Newcastle), *Six Songs with a Thorough Bass for the Harpsichord ... composed by Thomas Wright, Newcastle upon Tyne* (?Newcastle, c1788).

Wright, Thomas (of Newcastle), *Two Marches for Clarinets, Horns and Bassoons* (Goulding and Co.: London, n.d.).

Wright, Thomas (of Newcastle), *Genl. Suwarrow's March* (John Hamilton: Edinburgh, n.d.).

Wright, Thomas (of Newcastle), *Grand Troop for Clarinetts, Horns, Flute and Bassoons, composed for the Use of the Newbourn Band, adapted for the Piano Forte* (William Wright: Newcastle, n.d.).

Wright, Thomas (of Newcastle), *The New Tyne Bridge* (tune in Mackintosh).

Wright, Thomas (of Stockton), *Concerto for the Harpsichord or Piano Forte with accompaniments for two violins, two oboes, two horns, a tenore and bass* (no publisher: c1797).

Wright, William, *William Wright's Collection of Reels and Dances, No. 1* (William Wright: Newcastle, n.d.).

Select Bibliography

Manuscript sources

GB:Yi Borthwick Institute of Historical Research, York (BI)

PR Y/MB 35–7: Vestry minutes of St Michael le Belfrey.

GB:DRc Chapter Archives, Durham (CA)

Act Books of the Dean and Chapter of Durham Cathedral.
Treasurer's Accounts of Durham Cathedral.
Probate records: will of Matthias Hawdon, 14 October 1788.
DRA/17: Deanery Accounts.

Durham Record Office (DRO)

EP/Du.SO/119–21, 133–4, 156: registers of St Oswald's Church, Durham.
EP/Du.SM/2–5: registers of St Margaret's Church, Durham.
EP/Du.MB/1/3: registers of St Mary le Bow, Durham.
EP/Du.SN/1/4–5, 13: registers of St Nicholas's Church, Durham.
EP/Su.HT/1/1–4, 30–9, 93–97: registers of Holy Trinity, Sunderland.
EP/Sto/38–41: vestry book 1762–1926, Stockton Parish Church.
EP/Sto 201–1–41: invoices, receipts etc for organists' salary and maintenance of organs, 1813–82.
EP/Sto 167/1–50: invoices, receipts etc. for wages for Sexton, etc 1758–1885.
EP/Stain 4/1–2: churchwardens' accounts, 1791–1849, Staindrop Parish Church.
EP/Stain 5/1: vestry meeting minutes, 1791–1828, Staindrop Parish Church.
EP/Du.SN 4/2, 5/2, 4/17: churchwardens' account book, St Nicholas's Church, Durham.
EP/Du.SO/112: vestry minutes, St Oswald's Church, Durham.
Du/1/35/3: minutes of election of officers of Durham Corporation.
Du 1/42/1–3, 8–26: Mayors' accounts, 1720–1765.
Du 1/35/1–3: minute books, Durham Corporation 1686–1822.
Du 1/4/6–8: Corporation minutes, October 1758–January 1834.

***GB:Dru* Durham University: Archives and Special Collections**

Receiver-General Accounts 1684–1702: Church Commissions Bishopric Estates.
Box 113: will of Robert Turnbull, fiddler of North Shields, 23 September 1764.
Box 114: will of Henry Tate of Berwick, innkeeper and wait, 1 December 1778.
Box 114: receipt for payment of salary of organist at Bishop Auckland Castle, 2 November 1793.
Box 114: will of John Garth, 1810 (proved 30 May 1810).

Newcastle Central Library

L780.73: Boyd, William (collector), *Songs sung at the subscription, and other, concerts in Newcastle upon Tyne 1790–1883.*
L780.79: *Some Musical Festivals in Newcastle and Gateshead,* 1791–1860 (programmes).
L792: playbills for the Newcastle theatres.
L942.52: *Regulations of the Subscription Concerts*, 1809.
SL780.92 A958: Avison, Charles, *Twelve Canticles taken from the Compositions of Carlo Clari and adapted to English words Selected from the Psalms by Mr. Avison, Collection 1st.* (1769) (ms).
SL780.8: commonplace book thought to belong to Charles Avison (ms) c1745.
commonplace book thought to belong to Charles Avison (ms) n.d. [at present under restoration, Newcastle University].
concert programmes, Harmonic Society Subscription Series, 1815–16.

Northumberland Record Office (NRO)

EP 9/7–14, 40–48: registers of All Saints' Church, Newcastle.
EP 13/4–7: registers of St Andrew's Church, Newcastle.
EP 73/5–9, 20–22: vestry minutes of St Andrew's Church, Newcastle.
EP 86/3–6, 12–14, 38: registers of St John's Church, Newcastle.
EP 13/77: registers of St Nicholas's Church, Newcastle.
EP 13/80: vestry minute book, St. Nicholas's Church, Newcastle.
minute book of the 4 and 20, St Nicholas's Church, Newcastle.
EP 13/68–9: churchwardens' accounts 1663–1764, St Nicholas's Church, Newcastle.
EP 86/10–9: churchwardens'accounts 1764–1812, St Nicholas's Church, Newcastle.
EP 86/101–6: churchwardens' accounts 1684–1812, St Nicholas's Church, Newcastle.
EP86/120: minutes of restoration committee, St John's Church, Newcastle.

Tyne and Wear Archives (TAWS)

543/74–154: Chamberlain's Accounts of the Corporation of Newcastle upon Tyne.
Gu/Ty/15/1–14: Common Council minutes of Newcastle Corporation.
1269/1–237: accounts of Thomas Bewick.
160/1/29, 56-64, 203, 221 accounts, minutes and miscellaneous papers of the New Assembly Rooms, Westgate Road, Newcastle.
160/82: receipts and bills for the Assembly Rooms, Westgate Rd., Newcastle.
160/1/120: vestry minutes of St John's Church, Newcastle.
1074–85: vestry minute book, 1764–1833, St John's Church, Newcastle.

York Central Library

L792: Tate Wilkinson, *Nett Receipts of the Theatres Royal, York and of Leeds, Halifax, Wakefield, Doncaster and Hull.*
L792: Tate Wilkinson, *Statement of income and expenditure of the Theatre at Hull, York, Leeds, Wakefield, Doncaster, Sheffield from 1781 to 1784.*

GB:Y York Minster Library (YML)

Playbills for theatres in York, Newcastle and Beverley, 1766–1802.
Add. Ms 65/1: account book of D'Arcy Dawes.

York Record Office (YRO)

Acc 30: 1–4 York Musical Society minute book, 14 September 1767–28 December 1792.
B39–81: City of York House Book containing Minutes of the Proceedings of the Corporation, 1685–1800.
C37–67: Chamberlain's Accounts of the City Corporation.
M23/4 and 4a: account book of the Assembly Rooms, 1730–1883.
M23/1: minutes of the Assembly Rooms.
T2a: diary of Jonathan Gray during a tour of Scotland, 1796.

Primary printed sources prior to 1810

Newspapers

Cumberland Pacquet
Newcastle Courant
Newcastle Chronicle

Newcastle Journal
Newcastle Advertiser
Newcastle Gazette
Newcastle Intelligencer
York Courant
York Chronicle

Books printed before 1810

Anon., A Collection of Anthems As the same are now Perform'd in the *Cathedral Church of Durham* (Durham: Isaac Lane, 1749).

Avison, Charles, *An Essay on Musical Expression* (London: C. Davies, 1752); 2nd edition (London: C. Davies, 1753).

Baillie, John, *An Impartial History of Newcastle* (Newcastle, 1801).

Bennet, Benjamin, *Occasional Hymns: chiefly for the Lord's Day, and Lord's Table, being a Collection from others with an Addition of New Hymns* (Newcastle: J. Button, R. Akinhead, M. Brison, 1722).

Bewick, Thomas, *A Memoir of Thomas Bewick written by himself*, ed. Iain Bain (Oxford: Oxford University Press, 1979).

Brown, John, *A Dissertation on the Rise, Union, and Power, the Progressions, Separations and Corruptions of Poetry and Music, as they are found to exist in their several kinds and Gradations amongst Mankind* ... (London: L. Davis, C Reymers, 1763).

Burney, Charles, *A General History of Music* (London, 1776), ed. Frank Mercer (New York: Dover, 1957).

Cawdell, J., *The Miscellaneous Poems of J. Cawdell, Comedian* ... (Sunderland: for the author, 1785).

Cowper, Spencer, *Letters of Spencer Cowper, Dean of Durham, 1746–1774*, ed. Edward Hughes, Surtees Society 165 (Durham/London: Andrew and Co./Bernard Quaritch, 1950).

Defoe, Daniel, *A Tour thro' the Whole island of Great Britain* (1724–6) (London: Frank Cass, 1968).

Errington, Prideaux, *Copies in Verse, for the Use of Writing SCHOOLS, and HYMNS for Charity Schools* (Newcastle: for the author, 1723).

Fiennes, Celia, *The Journeys of Celia Fiennes* (1698), ed. Christopher Morris (London: Cresset Press, 1947).

Hawkins, Sir John, *A General History of the Science and Practice of Music* (London, 1776) (New York: Dover, 1963).

Kemble, Stephen, *Odes, Lyrical Ballads and Poems on Various Occasions* (Edinburgh, 1810).

Marsh, John, *The John Marsh Journals: The Life and Times of a Gentleman Composer (1752–1828)*, ed. Brian Robins (Stuyvesant, New York: Pendragon Press, 1998).

Noel, *The Noels and the Milbankes: Their Letters for Twenty-Five Years, 1767–1792*, ed. M. Elwin (London: Macdonald, 1967).

North, Roger, *Roger North on Music: Being a Selection from his Essays written during the Years, c1695–1728*, ed. J. Wilson, (London: Novello, 1959).

Ritson, Joseph, *The Bishoprick Garland, being a Choice Collection of Excellent Songs, relating to the above country, full of agreeable Variety and pleasant Mirth, A new Edition, corrected* (Newcastle: Hall and Elliot, 1792).

Ritson, Joseph, *The Northumberland Garland: or Newcastle Nightingale, A Matchless Collection of Famous Songs* (Newcastle: Hall and Elliot, 1793).

Scouton, Arthur H. (ed.), *The London Stage 1600–1800* (Carbondale, Illinois: Southern Illinois University Press, 1961), Part 3, 1729–1747.

Thompson, Thomas, *A Dictionary of Music, Containing an explanation of the French, Italian and other Words, &c. Made Use of in that Science* (Newcastle: William Wright, 1801).

Whitehead, William, *The First Newcastle Directory* (Newcastle: W. Whitehead, 1778).

Whitehead, William, *Newcastle and Gateshead Directory* (Newcastle; W. Whitehead: 1790).

Wilkinson, Tate, *The Wandering Patentee; or, a History of the Yorkshire Theatres from 1770 to the Present Time* (York; for the author, 1795).

Printed sources from 1810

Allan, James, The History of James Allan, the celebrated Northumberland piper *(Newcastle: John Ross, c1850).*

Anon, *A Short History of the Old Assembly Rooms, Westgate Rd., Newcastle upon Tyne* (Newcastle, 1929).

Baldwin, D., and Wilson, T., 'Elford, Richard', *The New Grove Dictionary of Music and Musicians* (London: Macmillan, 2001), 8, 114–5.

Bicknell, Stephen, 'The Donaldson Organ in the Holywell Music Room, Oxford', *The Journal of the British Institute of Organ Studies,* 11.

Borsay, Peter, 'Concert Topography and Provincial Towns in Eighteenth-Century England', in *Concert Life in Eighteenth-Century Britain* eds. Susan Wollenberg and Simon McVeigh (London: Ashgate, 2004), 19–33.

Boydell, Barra R. 'Clagget, Charles', *The New Grove Dictionary of Music and Musicians* (London: Macmillan, 2001), 5, 888–9.

Boydell, Brian, 'Clagget, Walter', *The New Grove Dictionary of Music and Musicians* (London: Macmillan, 2001), 5, 889.

Brewer, John, *The Pleasures of the Imagination: English Culture in the Eighteenth Century* (London: HarperCollins, 1997).

Brown, Geoffrey, 'John Garth, the *Galant* Organ Voluntary, and the Organs at Sedgefield and Auckland Castle in Country Durham', BIOS, *Journal*, 26, 2002, 138–9.

Burchell, Jenny, *Polite or Commercial Concerts? Concert management and Orchestral Repertoire in Edinburgh, Bath, Oxford, Manchester, and Newcastle, 1730–1799* (New York and London: Garland Publishing, 1996).

Burchell, Jenny, 'Musical Societies in subscription lists: an overlooked resource', *A Handbook for Studies in 18th-Century English Music IX* (Oxford: Burden and Cholij, 1998), 1–75.

Burchell, Jenny, '"The first talents of Europe": British Music Printers and Publishers and Imported Instrumental Music in the Eighteenth Century', in *Concert Life in Eighteenth-Century Britain* eds. Susan Wollenberg and Simon McVeigh (London: Ashgate, 2004), 93–113.

Burrows, D., 'Sir John Dolben, Musical Patron', *Musical Times*, cxx (1979), February, 65–7.

Burrows, D., 'Sir John Dolben's Music Collection', *Musical Times*, cxx (1979), March, 149–51.

Burrows, D., and Dunhill, R., *Music and Theatre in Handel's World: The Family Papers of James Harris, 1732-1780* (Oxford: Oxford University Press, 2002).

Burton, M. C., 'Mr. Prencourt and Roger North on Teaching Music', *Musical Quarterly*, xliv (1958), 32–9.

Charleton, R. J., *A History of Newcastle upon Tyne from the earliest records to its formation as a city* (Newcastle: Wm. H. Robinson, n.d.).

Chevill, E.J., *Music Societies and Musical Life in Old Foundation Cathedral Cities 1700-60*, PhD Thesis, University of London, 1993.

Corp, Edward T., 'Further Light on the Career of "Captain" François de Prendcourt', *Music and Letters*, lxxviii (1997), 15–23.

Corp, Edward T., [reply to letter], *Music and Letters*, lxxix (1998), 645–6.

Crosby, Brian, 'A Service Sheet from June 1680', *Musical Times*, 121 (1980), 399–401.

Crosby, Brian, *Durham Cathedral Choristers and their Masters* (Durham: Dean and Chapter, 1980).

Crosby, Brian, *Come on Choristers, A History of The Chorister School, Durham* (Durham: for the author, 1999).

Crosby, Brian, 'Stephen and Other Paxtons: An investigation into the identities and careers of a family of eighteenth-century musicians', *Music and Letters*, 81 (2000), 41–64.

Crosby, Brian, 'Private Concerts on Land and Water: The Musical Activities of the Sharp Family, c1750–c1790', *RMA Research Chronicle*, 34, 2001.

Crosby, Brian, 'Greggs, William', *The New Grove Dictionary of Music and Musicians* (London: Macmillan, 2001), 10, 369.

Cudworth, Charles, 'Avison of Newcastle, 1709–1770', *Musical Times*, cxi (1970), 480–3.

Dean, Winton, *Handel's Dramatic Oratorios and Masques* (London: Oxford University Press, 1959).

Dodds, Madeleine Hope, 'The Northern Stage', *Archaeologia Aeliana*, 3rd series, XI (1914), 31–64.

Dubois, Pierre (ed.), *Charles Avison's Essay on Musical Expression, with Related Writings by William Hayes and Charles Avison* (London: Ashgate, 2004).

Edwards, Owain, 'Charles Avison, English Concerto-Writer Extraordinary' *Musical Quarterly*, lv (1974), 5–23.

Ehrlich, Cyril, *The Music Profession in Britain since the Eighteenth Century: A Social History* (Oxford: Clarendon Press, 1985).

Ellis, Joyce, 'A dynamic society: social relations in Newcastle-upon-Tyne, 1660–1760', in *The Transformation of English Provincial Towns*, ed. Peter Clark (London: Hutchinson, 1984), 190–227.

Farmer, H. G., *A History of Music in Scotland* (London: Hinrichsen, n.d.).

Farmer, H. G., *Music Making in the Olden Days: The Story of the Aberdeen Concerts 1748–1801* (London: Hinrichsen, n.d.).

Fiske, Roger, *English Theatre Music in the Eighteenth Century* (London: Oxford University Press, 1973).

Green, Ian, *Print and Protestantism in Early Modern England* (Oxford: Oxford University Press, 2000).

Griffiths, David, *A Musical Place of the First Quality: A History of Institutional Music-Making in York, c1550–1990* (York: York Settlement Trust, n.d.).

Hargrave, Emily, 'Musical Leeds in the Eighteenth Century', *Thoresby Society Publications*, xxviii (Leeds, 1928), 320–55.

Hauger, George, 'William Shield', *Music and Letters*, xxxi (1950), 337–42.

Hinde, John Hodgson, 'Public Amusements in Newcastle', *Archeologia Aeliana*, IV (1860), 229–48.

Hope, W. H., *Notes on the History of the Phoenix Lodge, No. 94: An address delivered to the members of the Sunderland and District Lodges* (Sunderland: for the author, 1929).

Horsley, P. M., 'Charles Avison: The Man and his Milieu', *Music and Letters*, lv (1974), 5–23.

Husk, W. H. and Brian Crosby, 'Ebdon, Thomas', *The New Grove Dictionary of Music and Musicians* (London: Macmillan, 2001), 5, 809.

Hutchings, A. J. B., *The Baroque Concerto* (London: Faber and Faber, 1959).

Johnson, David, *Music and Society in Lowland Scotland in the Eighteenth Century* (London: Oxford University Press, 1972).

Kassler, Jamie Croy, 'Wright, Thomas', *The New Grove Dictionary of Music and Musicians* (London: Macmillan, 2001), 27, 579–80.

King, Robert, *North Shields Theatres* (Gateshead: Northumberland Press, 1948).

Kingdon-Ward, M., 'Charles Avison', *Musical Times*, xcii (1951), 398–401.

Lawrence, R. M., *John Ross, Composer, Aberdeen, His Circle and Work* (Aberdeen: D. Wyllie, 1927).

Leppart, Richard D., 'Music Teachers of Upper-Class Amateur Musicians in Eighteenth-Century England', in *Music in the Classic Period: Essays in Honor of Barry S. Brook*, ed. Allan W. Atlas (New York: Pendragon Press, 1985).

Lubbock, Constance A., *The Herschel Chronicle: The Life-Story of William Herschel and his Sister Caroline Herschel* (Cambridge: Cambridge University Press, 1933).

Mackenzie, E., *A Descriptive and Historical Account of the Town and County of Newcastle upon Tyne, including the Borough of Gateshead* (Newcastle: Mackenzie and Dent, 1827).

McVeigh, Simon, *Concert Life in London from Mozart to Haydn* (Cambridge: Cambridge University Press, 1993).

McVeigh, Simon, 'Felice Giardini: A Violinist in late eighteenth-century London', *Music and Letters*, lxiv (1983), 162–72.

McVeigh, Simon, 'Noferi, Giovanni Battista', *The New Grove Dictionary of Music and Musicians* (London: Macmillan 2001), 18, 15–16.

Merryweather, James, *The story of a City's Music from 1304–1896* (York: Sessions, 1988 and 1992).

Middlebrook, S., *Newcastle upon Tyne: Its Growth and Achievement* (Newcastle: Newcastle Journal and North Mail, 1950).

Middleton, Lydia Miller, 'Mountier, Thomas', *The Dictionary of National Biography*, ed. L. Stephen and S. Lee (Oxford: Oxford University Press, 1963–4).

Milner, Arthur, 'Charles Avison', *Musical Times*, xcv (1954), 16–18, 73–5.

Oswald, Harold, *The Theatres Royal in Newcastle upon Tyne: desultory notes relating to the drama and its homes in that place* (Newcastle: Northumberland Press, 1936).

Pickering, J. M., *Music in the British Isles, 1700 to 1800: A Bibliography of Literature* (Edinburgh: Burden and Cholij, 1990).

Pritchard, Brian W., *The musical festival and the choral society in England in the eighteenth and nineteenth centuries: a social history*, PhD thesis, University of Birmingham, 1968.

Pritchard, Brian W., 'Ashley', *The New Grove Dictionary of Music and Musicians* (London: Macmillan, 2001), 2, 107–8.

Purdue, A.W., *Merchants and Gentry in North-East England, 1650–1830* (Gateshead: University of Sunderland Press, 1999).

Rendall, F. G., Hogwood, Christopher, Boydell, Barra R., 'Charles', *The New Grove Dictionary of Music and Musicians* (London: Macmillan, 2001), 5, 497–8.

Richmond, Thomas, *The Local Records of Stockton and the Neighbourhood OR, A Register of Memorable Events, Chronologically arranged, which have occurred in and near Stockton Ward and the North-Eastern Parts of Cleveland* (Stockton: William Robinson, 1868).

Robinson, K.E., 'Stephen Kemble's management of the Theatre Royal, Newcastle upon Tyne', in *Essays on The Eighteenth-Century English Stage*, ed. Kenneth Richards and Peter Thomson, proceedings of a symposium sponsored by the Manchester University Department of Drama (London: Methuen, 1972), 137–48.

Rohr, D. A., *The Careers of British Musicians, 1750–1850: A Profession of Artisans* (Cambridge; New York: Cambridge University Press, 2001).

Sadie, Stanley, 'Garth, John', *The New Grove Dictionary of Music and Musicians* (London: Macmillan, 2001), 9, 552.

Salvetti, Guido and Osvaldo Gambassi, 'Piantanida, Giovanni', *The New Grove Dictionary of Music and Musicians* (London: Macmillan, 2001), 19, 698–9.

Scarr, R., 'Georgian Musician who lived at Cockerton', *Darlington and Stockton Times*, 25 June 1960.

Shaw, Watkins and Crosby, Brian, 'Hesletine, James', *The New Grove Dictionary of Music and Musicians* (London: Macmillan, 2001), 11, 459.

Smith, G. H., *Hull Organs and Organists* (London/Hull: A Brown, 1910).
Southey, R., '"Captain" Prendcourt revisited', *Music and Letters*, lxxix (1998), 645 [letter].
Southey, R., 'Biographical Data on Eighteenth-century Musicians from Northern Newspapers: 1700–1805', *A Handbook for Studies in 18th-Century English Music XI* (Oxford: Burden and Cholij, 2000), 1–69.
Southey, R., 'Compositional Activity in Newcastle upon Tyne at the end of the 18th Century', *The Consort* (Journal of the Dolmetsch Foundation), Summer 2000, 56, 17–32.
Southey, R., *Commercial Music-Making in 18th century north-east England: A pale reflection of London?* PhD dissertation, University of Newcastle, 2001.
Southey, R., 'Competition and Collaboration: Concert Promotion in Newcastle and Durham, 1752–1772', *Concert Life in Eighteenth-Century Britain*, eds. Susan Wollenberg and Simon McVeigh (London: Ashgate, 2004), 55–70.
Stephens, Norris Lynn, *Charles Avison: an Eighteenth-century English composer, musician and writer*, PhD dissertation, University of Pittsburgh, 1968.
Tams, Gordon, *Music and Newcastle Cathedral*, MLitt dissertation, University of Newcastle, 1980.
Temperley, Nicholas, 'John Playford and the Metrical Psalms', *Journal of the American Musicological Society*, xxv (1972), 331–78.
Temperley, Nicholas, *The Music of the English Parish Church* (Cambridge: Cambridge University Press, 1979).
Thomas, John Hugh, 'Edward Edmund Ayrton: The Swansea Ayrton', *Morgannwg*, The Journal of Glamorgan History, xxxix (1995), 30–49.
Tilmouth, Michael and Corp Edward, 'Prendcourt', *The New Grove Dictionary of Music and Musicians* (London: Macmillan, 2001), 20, 297.
Todd, Thomas Olman, *The History of the Phoenix Lodge No. 94 Sunderland 1753–1905* (Sunderland: for the Subscribers, 1906).
Troost, Linda, 'Shield, William', *The New Grove Dictionary of Music and Musicians* (London: Macmillan, 2001), 23, 262–5.
Weber, William, *The Rise of Musical Classics in Eighteenth-Century England: a study in canon, ritual and ideology* (Oxford: Clarendon Press, 1992).
Welford, Richard, 'Newcastle Assemblies', *Archaeologia Aeliana*, Series 3, ix (1912), 25–35.
Wilkes, Lyall, 'Charles Avison', *Journal of the British Music Society*, 9 (1987), 1–6.
Williams, Roger B., 'Ross, John', *The New Grove Dictionary of Music and Musicians* (London: Macmillan, 2001), 21, 712–13.
Wollenberg, S. and McVeigh, S., *Concert Life in Eighteenth-Century Britain* (London: Ashgate, 2004).
Zaslaw, Neal, 'The Compleat Orchestral Musician', *Early Music*, vii (1979), 46–57.
Zaslaw, Neal, 'The Orchestral Musician completed', *Early Music*, viii (1980), 71–2.

Index